How to boost your

A Study Guide _and_ a Revision Guide

You may be starting – or part of the way through – your GCSE Food Technology course. You may be thinking about your coursework, part way through it or getting close to mock or final exams. Wherever you are in your course, this book will help you. It will improve your understanding of Food Technology. It will help you to boost your coursework grade. It will show you the best way to answer exam questions. These three pages will show you how to get the most out of this book so that you can boost your grade!

An up-to-date book to match your course

This book has been written specifically to match the new GCSE Design and Technology: Food Technology syllabuses and covers the syllabus content that is common to all of the Examination Boards. Your teacher will tell you which syllabus you are following and which topics you need to cover. Use the contents list and the index to find quickly and easily the topics that you want to study or revise.

Short, manageable sections to study

This book is divided into two main sections:
Section I Coursework
Section II Knowledge and understanding

These sections are divided into short chapters that you should be able to cover in around 45 minutes. The headings tell you clearly what you are going to read about. Short chapters mean that you can concentrate on understanding a small area before moving on. This also makes it quick and easy to find what you want when you are revising or doing coursework or homework.

Coursework hints

- As you work through your coursework project, read through the chapters in Section I of this book.

- Check that, at each stage, your own coursework matches the quality standards set out clearly in the chapters.

The chapters in Section I contain numerous examples of work that students have produced at different stages in their coursework project.

There are Examiner's comments on all of them which highlight the good points and the areas for improvement. This tells you what examiners are looking for in order to award a high mark to a coursework project. You can assess your own coursework against the examples provided and find ways to improve it.

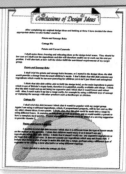

Checking your progress

Check yourself

QUESTIONS

Q1 What could a food manufacturer do within a quality assurance system to make sure that only the best and freshest raw materials and components are used?

Q2 How would a research and development team apply quality assurance procedures to the development and formulation of a new food product?

Q3 Why do some food companies use systems such as TQM (total quality management) or British Standard 5750?

Q4 What is meant by the terms quality assurance and quality control?

Check yourself sections let you check your progress quickly and easily. They tell you what examiners are expecting and how to boost your grade.

At the end of each short section, there is a *Check yourself* panel which consists of several short questions that will let you see if you have read and understood the section properly.

We have purposely placed the answers straight after the questions so that you can **either**:

● **Cover up the answers so that you can test yourself properly. When you have written down your answers, check whether you are right.**

or:

● **Read through a question, then read through the answer and tutorial. Here you're not using the *Check yourself* as a test; you're using it as an interactive way of revising.**

Tutorial help – upgrade your exam result

The examiners have written a *Tutorial* for every question. If you did not get the answer right, the *Tutorial* will tell you where you may have gone wrong and will guide you back to where you can find more help. Many of the *Tutorials* point out where candidates often make mistakes in the exam or in their coursework. They also show how you can improve an answer to boost your grade, e.g. from a D to a C or a B to an A.

Every answer is accompanied by helpful advice in a *Tutorial*.

ANSWERS

A1 The desired qualities of food products and ingredients must be preserved during transportation and storage.

A2 The main reason why sandwiches are wrapped is to prevent contamination, i.e. to keep the sandwich in hygienic conditions.

A3 The cardboard carton is rigid and will protect the pizza from being damaged or crushed. These cartons will also stack easily in the freezer. Information labels can be printed on the outside of the carton.

TUTORIAL

T1 *Many people think that the function of food packaging is only to make a food product look attractive. The important functions of the packaging are to protect or contain the product or to provide information about the contents.*

T2 *Sandwiches can be wrapped in flexible, stretch-wrap plastic or in rigid plastic containers. The rigid plastic containers will stop the sandwich from being crushed during transportation or while on display.*

T3 *Other pieces of packaging may be used but this would increase the cost, e.g. the pizza may be put on a plastic-coated board and it may be overwrapped in a clear thin plastic film. These both protect the pizza and help to keep ingredients such as grated cheese on top of the pizza.*

Practising real exam questions

Section II of the book contains a number of Exam Practice sections. Some of the exam questions have sample student's answers with examiner's comments underneath. The others are for you to try. The answers are at the back of the book so that you can treat the question just as you would in the exam.

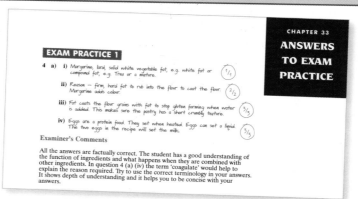

You can practise with real exam questions and then check the answers to see how you've done.

Examiner's comments – upgrade your exam result

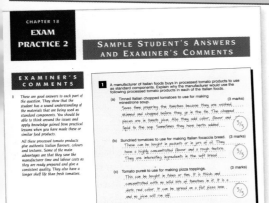

The sample student's answers and the answers at the back of the book have examiner's comments on them. These show you:

- how to tackle the questions
- common mistakes to avoid
- how marks are awarded
- how to improve your answer to boost your grade

Final revision – a sample examination paper

There is a completed examination paper at the end of the book. This lets you see sample student's answers to questions and how marks are awarded. The examiner's comments point out areas for improvement. In this way, you can see what you need to do to score high marks in your own written exam.

Feeling confident

Using this book will help you to enjoy your course because you'll understand what is going on. You'll feel confident and ready to take your exams. And remember –

for every topic and every question, there are Answers, Tutorials and Examiner's comments, so you're never left without help!

Food Technology

GCSE Syllabuses

All the Exam Board syllabuses have to meet the requirements of National Curriculum Design and Technology. This means that they are all quite similar. This book has been written to support all the GCSE Food Technology syllabuses and provides help and guidance for both the written examination and coursework.

What is assessed?

In GCSE Design and Technology: Food Technology, you have to develop your knowledge and understanding of materials and components, design techniques, systems and control, and industrial practices. All these areas are covered in this book.

You then have to apply this knowledge through the skills of designing and making.

Designing is about knowledge and understanding combined with the design and communication skills needed to design products for a specific purpose.

Making is about the knowledge and understanding of materials, techniques, processes and equipment in order to make quality products for a specific purpose.

In GCSE Design and Technology: Food Technology, you are assessed on your ability to 'design' and your ability to 'make' and this applies to both your coursework and your written exam. The marks are allocated like this:

> *Designing – 40% of the total marks*
>
> *Making – 60% of the total marks*

Coursework and written exam

Your final GCSE grade is made up of the marks that you have gained for your coursework and your exam. Your coursework makes up 60% of your final GCSE grade and your exam 40%.

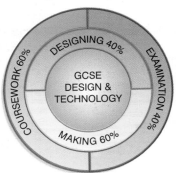

The key to getting a good grade in Design and Technology: Food Technology is to plan your coursework well, to finish it on time and to achieve a high standard. Section I of this book gives you lots of guidance on how coursework is assessed and how to gain high marks.

Foundation and Higher tier papers

Your coursework is not tiered but in the written exam you will be entered for either the Foundation or the Higher tier. The Foundation tier allows you to obtain grades from G to C. The Higher tier allows you to obtain grades from D to A*.

Higher tier							
A*	A	B	C	D	E	F	G
			Foundation tier				

There is no difference in the syllabus content for both tiers. Your teacher will have marked your coursework before your exam entry is finalised. This means your school will have a good idea about which is the most appropriate exam tier to enter you for.

boost your grade

SECTION I
Coursework

CHAPTER 1

RESEARCH

WHAT IS RESEARCH?

At all stages of your coursework project you will need to seek the sort of information that will help you to develop your ideas and also increase your knowledge about how food products are planned and made. In order to collect this information you will need to carry out research.

At the beginning of a project you will not always know exactly what information you are going to need later on but as you work through the project you will probably discover that you need to find out more about various aspects of food technology. Research can take place at any point in your project and you should do your research as and when it is needed, rather than trying to do all of it at the start.

You will need to research information for some or all of the following reasons:

- To develop some ideas for your own product(s).
- To find out about types of products which are already on sale.
- To test products.
- To see what information packaging labels provide.
- To find out what ingredients are used.
- To find out how food products are made.
- To understand how good quality food products are made safely.
- To find out about processing and storage methods.

ANALYSING YOUR DESIGN BRIEF

All projects begin with a design brief. This describes the particular problem you are facing or outlines the need for a new food product or products. Design briefs are written to allow a wide range of responses from students. They are the initial stimulus for research and ideas.

You may be given one design brief by your teacher or you may be given several different briefs and asked to choose one. Once you decide on a brief, you need to analyse it carefully. There will be certain key words in it and it is important that you identify these. Examples of key words include:

special diet   main meal   baked product   cook chill   frozen

children   low cost   low fat   high energy   snack

alternative protein   interesting   well flavoured   sweet

You need to pick out the key words and any other points which you think are important to the brief. This is called **analysing the brief**.

Analysis can be presented in a variety of ways. Examples include spider diagrams, lists, brainstorming sessions, charts, and simple notes.

Your analysis needs to make your own interpretation of the brief quite clear. There is no right or wrong answer. You must proceed with the rest of your project in the light of your own personal interpretation of the brief you have been given.

Figure 1.1 gives an example of the analysis of a design brief. Here a spider diagram has been used to demonstrate how you can quickly pick out the important key words from a brief to highlight which research you need to begin with.

Figure 1.1 *A spider diagram*

INITIAL RESEARCH

To begin with you should only collect information on the topics you have identified during your analysis of the design brief.

For this particular design brief, you would initially need to collect information on special diets, such as:

- diets intended for **diabetics**
- diets intended for **coeliacs**
- diets intended for **vegetarians**
- **low-fat** diets
- **slimming** diets
- **diets for babies**.

Students usually tend to collect and present too much information at this early stage. Only collect information which is *relevant*. For example, for this particular design brief you would only need to find out what people with a special diet are able to eat, not the medical details of the person and the diet.

Now look at Figure 1.2 on page 4 and then read the examiner's comments on it.

EXAMINER'S COMMENTS ON FIGURE 1.2

Good Points
- The student has chosen to look at four different diets.
- A lot of information on each of the diets has obviously been researched by the student but this has been summarised well.
- The summary is in the student's own words and is not a direct copy from books or other sources.
- Only the main facts about specific diets have been given.
- Reference is made to nutritional requirements.
- Some ideas for products are given.
- The information is written in such a way as to help the reader to understand what the student is thinking.

Areas for Improvement
The brainstorm diagram at the bottom right-hand corner is very relevant. It needs to be easier to read. The colours used do not make the diagram stand out clearly enough.

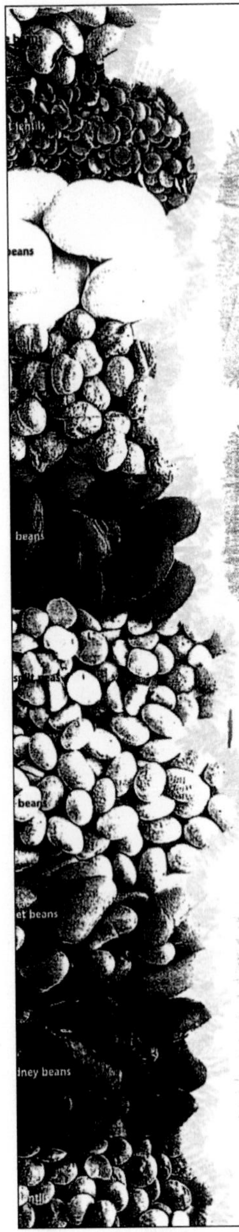

The various diet's which I have decided to look at in a little more detail are opposite. I have brainstormed each explained diet, outlining the main food item's which they can eat, to ensure a healthy diet, or in the case of vegetarian's and vegans which food's they decide to not eat, either for religion reasons or simply because they feel slaughter is a cruel inhumane way to treat animals.

Special diet's are devised and used when people fall ill or require a healthier diet than the one they are following at the minute.

Once I have produced the brainstorms I am going to outline the existing product's available on the market today, which are devised for the consumption of people who require special dietary requirement's.

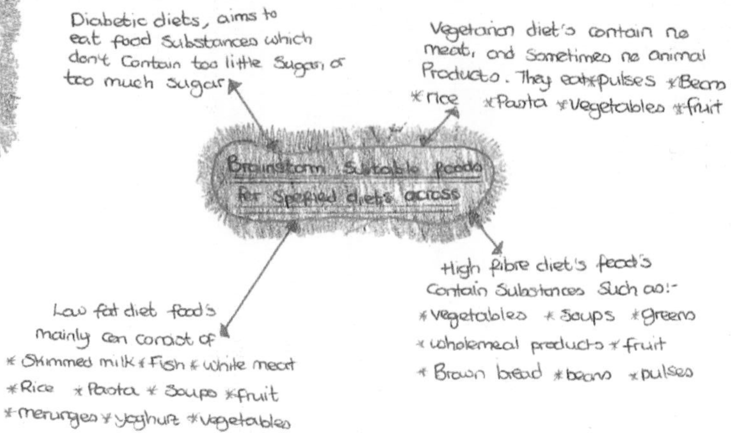

Vegetarian diet's contain no meat, and sometimes no animal Product's. They eat:-
*rice *Pasta *Vegetables *fruit

High fibre diet's food's contain substances Such as:-
*Vegetables *Soups *Greens
*wholemeal products *fruit
*Brown bread *Beans *pulses

Brainstorm. Suitable foods for Special diet's across

Diabetic diets, aims to eat food substances which don't Contain too little Sugar or too much Sugar

Low fat diet food's mainly can consist of
*Skimmed milk *Fish *White meat
*Rice *Pasta *Soups *fruit
*meringues *yoghurt *vegetables

Diabetic diet:- In this diet the amount of insulin produced by the pancreas is inadequate to ensure that glucose from the carbohydrate enters the body's blood stream. The amount of carbohydrate has to be carefully controlled:- food's which have too much sugar are bad, and food's which contain too little sugar are unsuitable. The sugar level has to be carefully balanced

High fibre diet:- This diet is particularly for the prevention of constipation, and other common bowl disorders. Suitable food's include, vegetables, soups etc., and food's like cakes and puddings should be avoided

Low fat diet:- This diet is mainly for people with heart disease, and heart related illnesses. It is also for people who are obese. Any fat consumed by the person should be polyunsaturated. Suitable food's include, rice dishes, pasta, yoghurts, meringues, low fat cheese's etc.. Avoid fried food, and fatty food's

Vegetarianism:- Vegetarianism, is a diet which can consist of two strict regime's. Some vegetarians don't eat any meat, but some vegetarian's prefer to avoid any animal product, which includes, milk, cheese, egg's etc. A vegetarian has to replace any vitamins etc. lost by not eating meat with food's such as protein replacement (quorn etc.)

Figure 1.2 *Looking at special diets*

based on this initial information, you would then choose one of the special diets to study in detail. You would need to ask yourself what additional information is needed. Remember that it is the diet, not the medical condition, that you will be concerned with. For example, if you decided to choose to study a diabetic diet you would need to:

- Find out:
  – what a diabetic can and cannot eat
  – the quantities required
  – about products already available
  – if there is a gap in the market for a particular type of product.
- Design a questionnaire for diabetic people.
- Compare specialist diabetic products with similar non-diabetic products. (Think here about cost, value for money, sensory characteristics, nutritional value, etc.)
- Carry out some blind tasting, e.g. digestive biscuits versus diabetic digestive biscuits.

All of this is **initial research**. Further research would probably be needed later when you have chosen a particular product to develop.

QUESTIONNAIRES

Part of your initial research may involve obtaining information from consumers about existing products. You will need to design a questionnaire that will help you to extract specific information from people. The questions need to be clear and both easy to understand and to answer. It should also be easy for you to collate the results from the questionnaire. You should be able to use these results to generate ideas for products.

The questionnaire in Figure 1.3 was designed as part of the initial research for a design brief to 'design and make a pasta sauce snack which can be reheated in a microwave cooker'.

Look at Figure 1.3 on page 6 and then read the examiner's comments on it.

EXAMINER'S COMMENTS ON FIGURE 1.3

Good Points
- The student has designed a star profile to use for consumer testing of the tagliatelle. The different points which the student wants consumers to comment upon have been clearly thought out.
- The results from the sensory testing are clear.
- The product profile diagrams show the results from the four testers and the differences can be picked out easily.
- The actual disassembly activity which the student has carried out has produced some useful facts about the tagliatelle in terms of ingredients and percentages.

Areas for Improvement
- The student does not comment sufficiently on how the results from the disassembly and the sensory testing will be used to develop ideas for a new product.
- There is no reference to the nutritional information given on the product packaging and whether nutritional value could be improved.

PRODUCT APPRAISAL

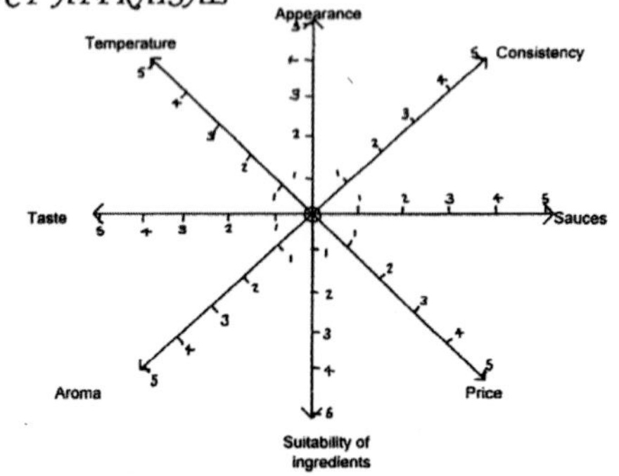

I asked 4 people to complete a product appraisal sheet on the product I disassembled: *Dolmio-Tagliatelle Carbonara*

The results are as follows:

Results from questionnaire

1. Choice of materials
Tricolor Tagliatelle-long and short pieces
Smoked Ham-small squares, all same size, rind left on ham
Mushroom-sliced
Onion-diced

2. Proportion of ingredients
50%-Tagliatelle-green 20%
          -white 20%
          -orange 10%
30%-Cheese sauce
10%-Smoked ham
8%-Mushrooms
2%-Onion

3. Quality of product
The ingredients are fairly well proportioned although there could be more onion and a little less pasta.

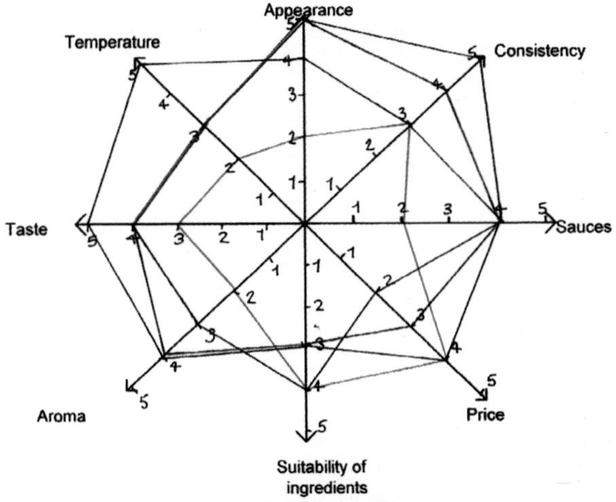

4. Sensory characteristics of product

Sight-Is the product appetising?
1. In my opinion not really, especially the sauce
2. Yes, the sauce makes the dish very appetising
3. Yes, the contrasts make the product appealing
4. A lot of colour, attractive

Smell-Does the product have a pleasing smell?
1. Yes-cheesy smell
2. Yes-the smell is very pleasing although this comes mainly from the sauce
3. No-the smell is bland
4. Yes-very nice cheese smell

Taste-Does the product have an unpleasant, acceptable, or highly agreeable taste?
1. acceptable- not keen on the sauce as it is a bit peppery
2. highly agreeable taste
3. acceptable-not keen on sauce
4. acceptable-a variety of flavours, mainly cheese

Touch-Does the product have an unpleasant or agreeable texture?
1. smooth texture
2. looked nice
3. interesting texture
4. smooth texture
Overall: Average: 7.375 / 10

5. Price-£1.29
6. Overall weight-350g
7. Who would buy the product?
A working person who would not have a lot of time.

Radar chart axes: Consistency, Sauces, Price, Suitability of ingredients, Aroma, Taste, Temperature, Appearance

TAGLIATELLE CARBONARA

PRODUCT APPRAISAL

Radar chart axes: Temperature, Consistency, Appearance, Sauces, Price, Suitability of ingredients, Aroma, Taste

Describe the product using the four headings below:

Sight-Is the product appetising?

Smell-Does the product have a pleasing smell?

Taste-Does the product have an unpleasant, acceptable, or highly agreeable taste?

Touch-Does the product have an unpleasant or agreeable texture?

Overall how many would you give this product out of ten?

    /10

Thank you, for your time. Eve Jenkins 11.T.

Figure 1.3 *Research into a pasta sauce*

ANALYSING INITIAL RESEARCH

All initial research needs to be analysed to help you to produce design criteria, design ideas and specifications.

SHOP SURVEY

- This helped me to see what type of cook-chill products are already on the market. With this I am able to see the variety, so when I make my product it gives me an idea of what to do.
- It also shows the price range of the products that are on the market. So I am able to price my products in the same range as the other products, but still make a profit at the same time.
- The packaging has to be bright and eye-catching to make it stand out from the other products. It also has to give the correct information for the product, so that the buyer can see it straight away.
- The size of the product would depend on who you were going to sell to.

QUESTIONNAIRE

- This has helped me a lot as it tells me what other people would like to see on the market. From this I can see which would be the most popular.
- I have also found out what price range they would prefer. With this I can see what price range would be best to suit my products.
- Also what size portions they would prefer to buy, so that I know what would be best to sell my product.

CONCLUSIONS TESTING SESSION

- Here I am able to try the products that are already on the market.. So with this I can see what types are already being sold.
- Knowing what is on the market already and being able to try them out, this helps me to know what type of thing I want to make with my product.
- When trying the product you know that it has to taste really nice for the customer to buy it again. Also that the product has to look really good too.

LETTERS

- This has helped me a lot with my research as it shows me what the manufacturers have put on the market.
- From the products that the manufacturers have sent me, it shows me the variety that they produce. So with this I can see which products would be the best to produce.
- Also from the information I have been given I am told the different ranges of meals. So I can produce things from soups to desserts.

Figure 1.4 Analysis of initial research

EXAMINER'S COMMENTS ON FIGURE 1.4

Good Points
- The student has looked back at all the research that has been done and has very quickly and simply pulled together the main points from each section of the research.
- Some specific points are identified which will enable the student to produce useful and relevant design ideas.

Areas for Improvement
- The points are very general; e.g. that the questionnaire gives information about the price range which people would prefer. However, the student does not state what the price range is. When the student eventually produces the product specification it should be possible to trace the chosen price back to the research and, in particular, the analysis of the research.

After completing the analysis of your initial research you should begin to get ideas for a new product or products. It is very likely, however, that you will still need additional information at other stages in your project work.

For the pasta sauce snack design brief, further research might be needed at the following stages:

- **design ideas stage** – you might need to research recipes and methods for products and find pictures to illustrate your ideas.
- **development stage** – you might need information on different methods and times for cooking pasta, the characteristics of particular ingredients and their function, e.g. herbs and spices, different methods of sauce making, e.g. white and others. (Look at Chapter 5, page 30.)

MANUFACTURING STAGE

When you begin to think about developing your product in large quantities you might need information on:

- industrial case studies
- manufacturing specifications
- production methods
- hazard analysis critical control points (HACCP)
- packaging and labelling requirements.

Look at Chapter 8 on Industrial Practice (page 53) which shows how further research is needed into the packaging and labelling requirements of a product.

HOW MUCH RESEARCH SHOULD YOU DO?

There is no rule about how much research is needed in a project. However, you must remember that:

- projects have to be completed within a certain number of hours
- research is only one part of the process
- if you spend too long on research it will limit the time you can spend on other aspects and your grade is likely to be affected.

HOW TO PRESENT YOUR RESEARCH

When you have collected and sorted all your information you need to think about how you are going to present it. The presentation of each sheet of research needs to be planned. Always arrange the information on the page before you actually type it out or stick it down. This takes time but will be well worth it. Think about the order in which you are arranging your information. Make sure the page is clear and that you have shown why and how this information is of use. Use a mixture of words and pictures.

The following list gives some ideas to get you started:

- Written summaries, giving the main points, are much better than very long accounts.

- Produce your own work, not long sections copied from textbooks.

- Use:
  - lists
  - bullet points
  - pictures, labels, diagrams, drawings, sketches, photographs (good use of scissors, paper trimmers, guillotines and appropriate glue will be rewarded).

- Include clear labelling for pictures, diagrams and drawings. (A picture of a ready-made, bought lasagne tells someone very little other than that it looks very appealing.) Labels should refer to colour, texture, shape, size consistency, weight, and how the product is assembled and finished, e.g. layers, toppings, decoration, techniques used, etc.

- Include only one sample of a completed questionnaire. Produce your collated results as graphs.

- Write up your conclusions from the results of the questionnaire.

- Summarise the main points from letters and interviews. (It is not necessary to include entire letters and replies as they are often of very little use.)

- Include nutritional information from packages, together with some comments.

- Attach information from manufacturers only if it is relevant.

- If you are fortunate enough to receive information from a manufacturer it is likely that they will send their standard information pack, not a pack made up specially for you. This pack will probably contain only a very small amount of relevant information. You need to cut out useful information and attach it to your design sheet with a brief description of what it says and how it is of use.

- The same applies to information which comes from CD-ROMS and the Internet.

- Produce computer printouts from CD-ROM and the Internet.

Check yourself

QUESTIONS

Q1 Look carefully at all the information you have collected while doing your research.
Based on what you have learned in this chapter, which information can you really use and which is not needed?

Q2 Does all the information need to be presented at the beginning of your project work or would it be better to leave some information until later?

Q3 How are you going to present the information on your sheets of A3 or A4 paper?

Q4 Have you labelled each picture, diagram, sketch, photograph or drawing to show why you are using these examples?

Q5 Will the questions you have written for your questionnaire(s) produce the answers you want and will you be able to collate the results and draw conclusions?

Q6 Can the examiner understand what you are thinking by reading your research sheets?

Q7 Have you arranged the information on each sheet so that there are few gaps?

Q8 Have you written a short conclusion to the research, summarising what you have found out and how you are going to use the information?

TUTORIALS

T1 It is a good idea to obtain a research folder to hold all the information you collect.
When you are at the point of presenting your initial research you need to sort and group the research information from your folder. Think about:
● How each piece of information relates to the design brief you have been given.
● How you will use the information.
● The quantity of information or whether you could you reduce it by giving a summary or a list of important points?

T2 As you sort the information try to organise it into sections. For example, pictures of products could be used to identify particular characteristics of existing products or as examples of design ideas. Recipes could be used for design ideas or to give some knowledge of a particular process at the development stage.

T3 A3 or A4 sheets of paper can be used to present your research. A4 sheets are easy to carry and store but A3 sheets allow you to put a lot more information on each page so that the whole page almost tells a story. You need to plan each sheet, either by dividing the page into sections or by placing information on the page before sticking it down. You need to cut and stick using sharp scissors or a paper trimmer. Use the right type of glue, arrange the information in order and ask someone else to give you their opinion before finally sticking everything into place or producing a final piece of writing. (This is where your teacher can be very useful!)

T4 Labels, pictures and diagrams add interest to project work and can be a simple way of providing information but they are of little use on their own. For this reason you need to make sure that you have labelled or given a brief description of every picture, package, diagram, photograph, etc.

T5 Think about what information you want a questionnaire to produce and how you are going to collate the results. If you ask very open questions, such as, 'What products do you buy?', you are likely to get a vast range of replies which will tell you very little. It is better to ask, 'Which of these products would you buy?', then give a list.

T6 Ask another student, your parent or a teacher to read your research sheets and briefly outline to you what they have understood from them.

T7 Often candidates do not use the space on their paper very well. There should be very little space left on each page – but this does not simply mean using big print, large pictures and wide borders!

T8 The most important part of research is being able to give a brief summary or analysis of it. From this a very clear way forward should be obvious to both you and the examiner.

Remember that a project is assessed on quality not quantity!

WHAT ARE DESIGN CRITERIA?

Whenever a new product is made, regardless of what it is made from, the designer of the product produces a specification for his or her new idea and a maker then uses this specification to produce the exact product that the designer had in mind. With most materials, like wood, plastic and textiles, it is possible to produce an exact specification quite early in the design process because these materials are similar and can be cut, joined, shaped and finished in similar ways. For example, a specification for a storage container might look like this:

> square box with rigid sides, 50 cm x 50 cm
> hinged lid
> two fasteners to attach lid to base
> decoration on lid
> compartments inside to divide box into sections
> able to be attached to a wall
> easy to open
> unit cost £5.

This specification would enable the product to be made in any type of wood, metal, plastic or textile.

Food is not at all like this, however, because it is made up of hundreds of individual materials which all behave very differently. The way food materials are shaped, formed and finished depends on how they have been combined (mixed together) and whether they have been cooked or not. It would be impossible to give the same detailed specification for a range of baked products because the specification for a product like a ginger biscuit, for example, would be very different to that for a sponge cake. However, it would be possible to give some common general points. These points are called the **general design criteria** or **general specification** and it is important that you produce these general points for your product ideas *after* you have completed your initial research.

HOW TO PRODUCE DESIGN CRITERIA

First, you must look back at your design brief and your analysis. You need to make a list of the main points you identified when you analysed the brief you were given by your teacher. You should reread your research, particularly the analysis of your research. You need to home in on particular points that emerge.

For example, if you were asked to produce some ideas for new products for school lunches, your analysis might have brought out the following points:

Your early research might also have produced other information, e.g.:

sweet and savoury

hand-held   hot and cold   nutritious

high energy   low cost   appeal for a teenage market

You will see from this list that a whole range of school lunch products could fit

a need for multi-cultural products   low fat dishes   more fruit and vegetables within products

smaller portions at lower costs   one-pot takeaway products   different foods in summer and winter

cold desserts   more pasta   more interesting flavours   cheaper dishes   more sweet products

your criteria. These points are still very general, however, which is why this stage is called general design criteria.

Check yourself

QUESTIONS

Q1 Have you identified all the points in your design brief?

Q2 Has the research you have done provided you with relevant information for a new product or products?

Q3 Does your list of points enable you to produce ideas for lots of different products?

TUTORIALS

T1 *Look back at the design brief which you were given by your teacher. Select the information from your analysis which relates to the actual food product(s) that you think the brief is asking about.*

T2 *Look at all the research you have done. What sort of things have you found out about the types of products which could be developed. For example:*
- *If you carried out a questionnaire, what types of products did people want?*
- *If you looked at the product ranges which are available in the supermarket, are there any gaps?*
- *If you tested existing products by carrying out some sensory evaluation, what points were emerging?*
- *Were the products too high in additives? If so, one of the general points for your criteria would be to produce a low-additive product.*
- *If the sensory evaluation said that all products seemed very salty, then a general point would be to reduce the salt.*

- *If you examined products and checked the weight and nutritional value, you might conclude that the portion size for teenagers needs to be increased to provide more energy value and protein. You might say in your general specification that a product gives 'high energy value' or provides one third of a teenager's protein requirements.*

T3 *Look at the list of criteria you have made. Are all the points general enough for you to produce a whole range of very different design ideas?*

CHAPTER 3

DESIGN IDEAS

WHAT ARE DESIGN IDEAS?

Design ideas are suggestions for food products that you can draw up when you have:

- studied and analysed the design brief
- produced conclusions from your initial research
- decided upon some general criteria for your product.

At this point a whole range of possible ideas will come to mind. You will need to present them all and then do some extra evaluation to find out which of your ideas will be most suitable for further development.

HOW TO FIND DESIGN IDEAS

1 Look back at your research.

- What products did people prefer when you asked them?
- Did you find any particular gaps in the market?
- Where there any particular groups of people for whom there was a shortage of products?
- Was there a need to consider a particular price range?
- Was there a particular nutritional need?

2 Look in magazines and books. Do any of the pictures or recipes seem appropriate?

3 What types of products have you made before in school? Would any of these be appropriate?

4 Did the design brief indicate that your product should have certain ingredients or mixtures in it? For example, you may have been asked to design a pasta sauce snack, in which case you have been given some very specific information to influence your ideas.

5 Did the design brief indicate that you could consider a wide range of products? For example, you may have been asked to design a product to be included in the menu for the school canteen. In this case you can produce a whole range of very different ideas, both sweet and savoury, using a wide range of ingredients and mixtures.

HOW TO PRESENT DESIGN IDEAS

Whenever you present information in your design folder you must make sure that whoever is reading it will understand:

- what you mean
- why you have included the information
- what made you use the information
- how you intend using the information.

There are many different ways of presenting design ideas. Look at the examples given in this chapter and see how many of them would be suitable for you to use.

SKETCHES, DRAWINGS AND DIAGRAMS

Look at Figure 3.1 and read the examiner's comments on it. This example relates to a design brief for a new range of decorated cakes.

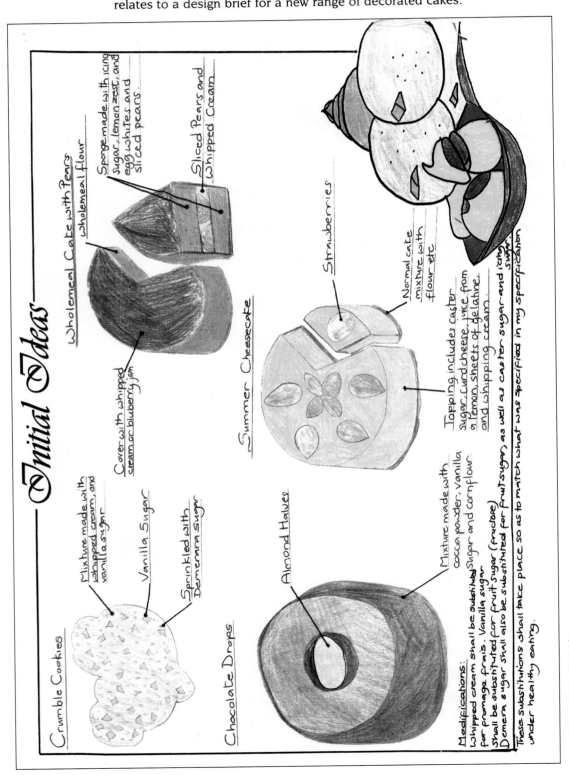

Initial Ideas

Crumble Cookies

Mixture made with whipped cream, and vanilla sugar

Vanilla Sugar

Sprinkled with Demerara sugar

Wholemeal Cake with Pears

Sponge made with icing sugar, lemon zest, and egg whites and sliced pears.

Wholemeal flour

Sliced Pears and Whipped Cream

Cover with whipped cream or blueberry jam

Summer Cheesecake

Strawberries

Normal cake mixture with flour etc

Topping includes caster sugar, curd cheese, juice from a lemon, sheets of gelatine, and whipping cream.

Chocolate Drops

Almond Halves

Mixture made with cocoa powder, vanilla sugar and cornflour.

Modifications:
Whipped cream shall be substituted for fromage frais. Vanilla sugar shall be substituted for fruit sugar (fructose). Demerara sugar shall also be substituted for fruit sugar, as well as caster sugar and icing sugar.

These substitutions shall take place so as to match what was specified in my specification under healthy eating.

Figure 3.1 *Initial ideas*

14

EXAMINER'S COMMENTS ON FIGURE 3.1

Good Points

- Sketches are used to put across new ideas for decorated cakes.
- It is perfectly acceptable for the sketches to be rough ideas and not accurate in size and shape.
- The sketches clearly show various ways in which cakes can be made, shaped, cut, filled, flavoured and decorated.
- Labels on the sketches give additional information which the sketch itself might not make clear.
- Comments link these ideas with previous points in a specification.
- Additional ideas for alterations and improvements are included.
- Colour adds interest to the ideas.
- Design ideas are communicated clearly.

Areas for Improvement

- Alternative shapes could have been suggested.
- Notes and labels could have commented upon any problems which might arise from trying to produce complex shapes.
- Some reference to the different types of base mixtures could have been made.
- Possible problems with substituting ingredients might have been given.

EXAMINER'S COMMENTS ON FIGURE 3.2

Good Points

- Existing recipes are used as the basis for ideas.
- Only a basic recipe is given and not the method.
- Reasons for selecting the recipes have been included.
- Reasons link back to initial research and use information about different target groups, storage methods, cost, nutritional value and alternative ingredients.
- Four concise ideas have been presented on one page and clearly convey the thought process of the student to the reader.
- Some alternative ideas for ingredients are given to meet design criteria that have already been identified.

Areas for Improvement

- More adaptations for each recipe idea could have been given.
- Some brief outline ideas for future development could have been included. These might have referred to carrying out investigations into the suitability of the product for freezing.
- Possible development for a whole range of products could be added.
- A clear indication should be given of whether or not the ideas are to be made and sensory tested.
- The use of nutritional analysis for each recipe could have led to the production of a model of the idea.

RECERPES FOR SUITABLE PRODUCTS WHICH YOU HAVE OR COULD MAKE

Look at Figure 3.2 and then read the examiner's comments on it on page 15. These ideas relate to a design brief for a low-cost frozen meal product.

Figure 3.2
Design ideas

Design Ideas

7) Pancakes with grated carrot and sweetcorn
100g plain flour
1/4 tsp salt
1 egg
300ml semi-skimmed milk
2 large carrots
200g sweetcorn (canned)

Reasons for choice
This dish is really simple and because of the nature of the ingredients it will also be quite cheap. I think my target audience would enjoy this as pancakes are normally served as a "fun food". The pancake batter contains milk which would give the children protein and calcium. The carrot and sweetcorn would provide vitamin A.

8) Turkey stew
450g skinless turkey breast
350g potatoes
1 large onion
2 carrots
1 tbsp olive oil
1 tsp dried thyme
1.2litres chicken stock
150g curried sweetcorn
150g frozen peas

Reasons for choice
This dish uses turkey which is different from normal "everyday" meats and it is also a cheaper alternative to others. It has a nice variety of vegetables and would be very filling. I think this dish would provide my target group with beneficial nutrients and I believe it would freeze well.

9) Quiche lorraine
350g shortcrust pastry
1 tsp olive oil
1 large onion
4 rashers lean back bacon
3 eggs
75ml semi-skimmed milk
200ml low fat creme fraiche

Reasons for choice
This dish would be good as I would be able to show off some of my skills, such as in pastry making. It contains ingredients which would appeal to my target audience and ones which I think would react well to freezing and re-heating. Although it would provide the child with a lot of protein and calcium there may be too much fat from the pastry and cheese. I'm also not sure whether this dish would end up being low cost!

10) Baked potatoes with tuna
4 large potatoes
50g butter
300g tinned tuna in brine
100g tinned sweetcorn
50ml natural yoghurt

Reasons for choice
Potatoes can be bought very cheaply, thus this dish could be very low cost, as only a small quantity of topping would be needed on the potato. The potato would provide the diner with a burst of carbohydrate which is good for energy. The tuna would provide protein and the sweetcorn gives vitamin C. Instead of using mayonnaise to mix the topping, natural yoghurt offers a low cost, low fat alternative.

OTHER WAYS TO PRESENT DESIGN IDEAS

- Put together a montage of pictures from books or magazines, showing products or ingredients which depict colour, eye appeal, shape, size, texture, quality, flavour.
- Show the results of nutritional analysis of a recipe. This is a way of modelling an idea without actually making it. It is a good way of checking to see if a product meets the nutritional requirement of the brief or of your own design criteria.

You must always ensure that your design ideas are fully explained. You can do this by:

- labelling diagrams and pictures
- listing the main ingredients
- describing/listing the particular characteristics or features of the product
- commenting on each idea
- relating ideas back to aspects of your research or the design criteria which you have produced
- using sensory testing to evaluate some of the ideas which you have actually had a go at making
- producing a summary of the sensory characteristics of each product.

EVALUATING ALL OF YOUR DESIGN IDEAS

You need to consider all the ideas you have presented because you will need to select the most suitable one or ones. You cannot decide to select an idea just because you like it; it is the cheapest; your family would buy it; you are good at making this type of product.

You must evaluate it in terms of:

- Does it fit the brief?
- Does it match the findings from your research?
- Does it meet your general specification?
- Does it fit the nutritional profile?
- Can it be stored according to the requirement of the brief?
- Has it the correct sensory characteristics, e.g. taste, texture?
- Can it be developed in a variety of ways, e.g:
  – Can it be produced in different shapes and sizes?
  – Can taste, texture, flavours be changed?
  – Can different ingredients and components be used?

You will need to reach your conclusions by looking back at what you said and produced in the earlier parts of your project; testing your ideas; carrying out sensory evaluation.

Look at Figure 3.3 and then read the examiner's comments. This gives you some guidelines for evaluating your own design ideas and presenting your conclusions. This evaluation of design ideas relates to the production of a low-cost frozen meal product.

EXAMINER'S COMMENTS ON FIGURE 3.3

Good Points
- Each design idea has been evaluated against the original design brief.
- Reference is made to findings from research which relate to target consumer groups and their possible nutritional needs.
- It is clear that any ideas which did not match the brief or research findings have been discarded.
- The student is not deviating from the requirements of the original brief.
- Evaluation refers to storage methods and their suitability. This is important because the product has to be frozen.
- Ideas for development are also indicated.
- The evaluation makes a direct link back to the brief, the research and the design criteria which have already been carried out.
- The route for future development is clear.

Areas for Improvement
- More specific reference to the nutritional content of each product would have been useful as this could be matched more closely to the target group needs. Development could then have used this information.
- Possible changes to the recipes could have been more detailed and linked to sensory characteristics.

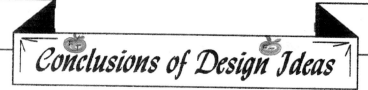

Conclusions of Design Ideas

After completing my original design ideas and looking at these I have decided the three appropriate dishes to take further would be:

Potato and Sausage Bake

Cottage Pie

Potato and Carrot Casserole

I shall make these, freezing and reheating them as the design brief states. They should be low cost so I shall cost the ingredients and this will therefore enable me to work out the cost per portion. I will also look at how well the dishes fulfil the nutritional requirements of my target group.

Potato and Sausage Bake

I shall trial the potato and sausage bake because, as I stated in the design ideas, the dish would provide a change from the usual children's meals. I don't think that this dish contains any ingredients which would be too over-powering for children yet it isn't just bland and uninspired.

I think that this dish will be able to fulfil the design brief, as the main ingredient is potato which is one of Britain's staple foods, therefore it is plentiful, readily available and cheap. I think that the dish would end up not being too expensive and I think that it would freeze and reheat well. Also, I could make it up into a range easily, for example by using a different type of sausage or replacing the sausage with other products such as beefburger or chicken.

Cottage Pie

I shall trial this dish because I think that it would be popular with my target group. Again I am using traditional ingredients, which, if proportioned properly, will be low cost as, like my other chosen ideas, it uses potato. I think, also, that this dish could be made into a range by using different bases. It contains carbohydrate as well as protein and so would enable a parent to have a complete meal quickly. Frozen vegetables or tomato could be added as a serving suggestion to provide vitamin C.

Potato and Carrot Casserole

I decided to trial this dish because I think that it is different from the type of frozen meals on the market at the moment. I think that children would enjoy it as it doesn't use any ingredients which they may dislike. I think that it doesn't really use any expensive ingredients so the final dish will be low-cost. It does not contain any ingredients which may not freeze well. I believe that there is a lot of scope to make this dish into a range, perhaps using a different type of vegetable or by adding a meat alternative or using different toppings.

I have decided to make the cottage pie first.

Figure 3.3 *Conclusions of design ideas*

Check yourself

QUESTIONS

Q1 Have you read all the information you have put into your design folder?

Which parts of the brief and the research will you need to use to produce relevant design ideas?

Q2 Look back at your design criteria/general specification and make sure each idea matches this.

Q3 Have you made your design ideas clear?

Do you need to add any labels or comments to your ideas?

Have you presented your ideas in different forms – pictures, sketches, recipes?

Which design ideas would you actually want to make? What would be the purpose of making them?

Q5 Would someone who has not been working with you in the classroom know what you were thinking about?

Q6 Have you looked at each idea and thought about how you could evaluate it to meet the needs of the brief and research?

How did you decide on your best idea?

TUTORIALS

T1 You need to read what you have written to remind yourself of the main points about the project. The whole purpose of being given a design brief and carrying out research is to produce information which can be used to stimulate design ideas. Often students spend a lot of time on their research but then never look back at it or use it. Look back at Chapter 1 on research (page 2) to remind you!

T2 Anyone who is making a product needs to be given a set of rules about what it should look or taste like. Look at the design criteria you produced and, on rough paper, write down a list of products that immediately come into your mind which would fit those criteria. Look in recipe books for other ideas.

T3 What is going to be the best way of presenting your ideas. You might like to use several different ones. Writing is not always the best way. Can you find pictures from magazines, packets and leaflets to which you can add your own labels and comments about size, shape, ingredients and possible changes and adaptations. Sketches and drawings add interest, particularly if you can use colour, Clipart, etc. You do not need to be the best artist in the world. You are not going to be assessed on your artistic ability but on the way in which you can convey your ideas to someone else. Often these types of sketches do not just give ideas but also give you the opportunity to show where you can make changes.

T4 When carrying out a food technology project there is the opportunity to make some products at the design ideas stage. This enables your making skills to be assessed further and gives you the chance to carry out some sensory testing. Sensory characteristics cannot be defined in a picture and without actually making a product you cannot make changes for improvement.

T5 Ask someone else to look at your design ideas. Get them to list and describe the ideas you have produced and to comment on the particular characteristics of each one.

T6 Make a list of the points each idea will be evaluated against. You must make it clear why you rejected some and kept others. Always produce a detailed summary of your findings.

WHAT IS A PRODUCT SPECIFICATION?

When you have evaluated your design ideas and chosen the most suitable idea for further development you will need to produce a product specification. If your design brief asks you to design and make more than one product, you will need a product specification for each product that you are going to develop.

Even though you are carrying out your project work in school, you are actually working in a similar way to a professional food technologist employed in a real test kitchen in the food industry. Food technologists design product specifications and then use ingredients and methods to make a '**product prototype**' which matches each specification. A prototype is a model from which copies can be made.

A product specification does not cover very general points like the design brief. Instead, it describes **very specific characteristics** which a product must have. At this stage it would be too general to say, 'The product must have an edible container.' Instead, you would need to say, for example, 'It must have a pastry container.'

HOW TO DESIGN A PRODUCT SPECIFICATION

The following list gives some examples of specific characteristics that might be found in a product specification:

- indication of portion size, e.g. an individual serving
- approximate sale cost, e.g. 'Would sell for £1.50'
- type of outcome, e.g. pastry product, pasta product, filling encased in pastry, vegetables served in sauce, filled and covered cake, protein mixed with spicy sauce
- approximate energy value, e.g. number of calories to be generated
- storage conditions, e.g. to be sold chilled or frozen
- serving requirements if appropriate, e.g. suitable for serving hot or cold
- cooking/reheating requirements, e.g. suitable for traditional and microwave cooking
- specific sensory properties, e.g. crispy topping, variety of colours, soft filling and crisp base
- other nutritional requirements, e.g. percentage of protein, vitamin C content, iron content
- healthy option product, e.g. low in sugar, high in fibre, low in fat
- specific target group, e.g. suitable for children
- type of product, e.g. savoury main meal, sweet, snack.

Look at Figure 4.1 and read the examiner's comments on it. This design specification relates to the production of a low-cost frozen meal product.

Design Specification

I am now at a stage where I can make my design criteria more specific.

- My dish will be based on potatoes.
- It will contain a variety of different vegetables.
- It will be suitable to add other ingredients to in order to make a range.
- It will be suitable for freezing.
- It will be suitable for reheating.
- It will cost no more than 20p per portion at the ingredient stage.
- It will contain nutrients suitable for children aged between 6 – 10.
- It will weigh around 175 g for a one child portion.
- It should have good sensory qualities such as flavour, texture, colour and so forth.
- It will be packaged in material suitable for the method of reheating.
- It will be able to go on sale at a local retail outlet.

I shall take these points into account when making my dish.

Figure 4.1 *Design specification*

EXAMINER'S COMMENTS ON FIGURE 4.1

Good Points
- Specific ingredients are identified.
- Points which were in the original design brief have been covered. For example, the brief said the product had to be frozen.
- The target consumer group is referred to, i.e. children.
- Research has been done on cost and portion size.
- As the product will be part of a range of dishes the specification provides the basic information and states that it will be possible to add other ingredients.
- No decision has been made as to the method of reheating but in the specification this is stated as a distinct requirement for both the product and the packaging.
- General reference has been made to sensory qualities.
- There is sufficient flexibility in the specification to allow a good range of development work to take place and enough specific points are made to enable evaluation to take place as the product develops.

Areas for Improvement
- Some additional information on the main nutrient needs of children could have been included.
- Sensory qualities could have been more specific. For example, as the product is for children it could have said 'colourful, crunchy textures'.
- It is not clear if the product is an individual child's portion or a family-size product. This would make some difference at the development stage.

WHAT IS A MANUFACTURING SPECIFICATION?

In the food industry when the food technologist has completed the development work the **final prototype** is ready for manufacturing in large quantities. To enable the prototype to be copied exactly the food technologist will have to provide the food manufacturer with a **manufacturing specification**. This gives the exact detail that the manufacturer will need to produce an exact replica of the prototype. To say that a product should have a 'pastry case' would be too vague for the manufacturer. The food technologist needs to tell the manufacturer about the type of pastry to use, the ingredients that should be in the pastry, the thickness to which the pastry should be rolled, the exact shape and size of the pastry case, i.e. its dimensions and measurements, and the sensory characteristics of the pastry, e.g. 'crisp short texture, baked to a light golden colour, free from fatty taste, crumbly when broken'. In addition to written details the manufacturer is often provided with a labelled diagram.

HOW TO DESIGN A MANUFACTURING SPECIFICATION

The following list gives you some ideas of what to include in a manufacturing specification:

- specific dimensions (with a sketch), i.e. weight, size, shape
- specific qualities of ingredients, e.g. percentage of fat in meat, size of glacé cherries
- names of ingredients with weights and proportions to use, e.g. '200 g butter, 450 g flaked haddock'
- specific tolerances, e.g. thickness of pastry, viscosity (runniness) of sauce
- the size to which ingredients must be cut, e.g. the exact shape and size of pieces of fruit and vegetables, the nozzle size for mincing meat, the slicing grade for carrots, the grating size for cheese
- types of cooking methods and cooking temperatures with critical control points (see Chapter 7 page 42 and Chapter 22 pages 156 and 157)
- cooling times and methods
- finishing techniques, e.g. 'Brush with whole egg glaze before baking', 'Fill centre of cake with fresh whipped cream to a thickness of 2 cm', 'Decorate with six slices of tomato and one teaspoonful of mixed herbs before cooking', 'Cover surface of biscuit with white rolled icing to a thickness of 0.5 cm'
- specific details of packaging requirements, e.g. 'micowavable dish with sealed film covering in crushproof sleeve'
- wording for the label which will provide information for the consumer about ingredients, nutrition, the name of the product, storage and cooking/reheating instructions, shelf life, etc.
- sometimes a photograph is used to help a manufacturer to meet the specification. This would normally still need additional written information but is useful in large-scale catering where a meal is being assembled on a plate from bought components.

Look at Figure 4.2 and read the examiner's comments on it.

Manufacturer's Specification

In order to have my final dish manufactured correctly commercially I have come up with the following points for the manufacturer(s):

- The potatoes and carrots will be grated so that they result in strips 1.5 cm × 0.5 cm.
- The leeks will be sliced so that they are 0.5 cm thick and 2 cm in diameter. They will be sliced in half across the diameter if above 2 cm in diameter.
- The Cheddar cheese will be grated so that it results in strips 0.5 cm × 1.5 cm.
- The quantity of each ingredient shall be multiplied by a common factor for large scale production. This factor will depend on demand for the product.
- The filling will be packaged in low density polythene containers 15 cm × 12 cm × 7 cm.
- The filling will be in the containers to a depth of 6 cm.
- 50 mls of sauce will be added to the base. The sauce will be spread so that it is 1 cm from the edge of the dish at all times.
- The dishes will be cooked in the oven (before topping) for 20 mins at a temperature of 180°C.
- The "breadcrumbs" will be finely made with margarine and plain flour. They will have no lumps and each crumb will be approximately 2 mm in diameter.
- 6.4 g of the topping will be put onto each dish. It will be spread evenly over the dish ensuring it goes to the edge.
- The dish will be recooked for a further 10 mins in the oven.
- The dish will undergo a rapid chill to 1°C within 1.5 hrs.
- The dish will then be blast frozen to −30°C in a space of 6 hrs.
- The dish shall then be heat sealed with low density polythene.
- The dish will then be packaged in card boxes.

Figure 4.2 *Manufacturer's specification*

EXAMINER'S COMMENTS ON FIGURE 4.2

Good Points
- Very detailed information is given.
- Measurements, weights and sizes are very specific. The size of individual ingredients is important to ensure consistency between the end products.
- The candidate has given the depths, coating methods and weight of topping which will ensure quality and consistency in large-scale production.
- Cooking temperatures and times are given.
- Cooling, chilling and freezing times and temperatures are given.
- There is information on the type of packaging and the method of sealing.

Areas for Improvement
- There is little reference to specific ingredients and the production methods which the manufacturer should use. For example, the quantity for sauce is given but not the ingredients or method.
- No indication is given of the thickness of the sauce.
- No order/instructions for assembling the product are given.
- No labelled diagram of the finished product is provided.
- No nutritional information is given for the label.

Check yourself

QUESTIONS

Q1 Look at the design idea which you have chosen to develop. List the characteristics of the product or the characteristics which you want it to have.

Q2 Will it be possible to change ingredients, methods, shapes, sizes, flavours to achieve the product specification?

Q3 Have you really provided exact information on your manufacturing specification?

Q4 Could the information you have given about the product enable anyone, anywhere, to produce the same outcome?

TUTORIALS

T1 *When looking at a recipe, a picture or a sketch some of the characteristics will seem very obvious. For example, 'coated with sauce, crisp brown top, enclosed in pastry, covered in cheese' etc. Other characteristics are not so obvious, e.g. 'high in vitamin C, provides 450 calories, spicy flavour'.*

T2 *When you make your final product you do not have to get it right first time. When you look at 'development' in the next chapter you will see how important it is to change, adapt and amend parts of your product to meet the specification.*

T3 *It is important that you give exact measurements, shapes, quantities and details about methods. For example, you need to say, 'Roll biscuit dough to a thickness of 1 cm, cut into circles measuring 6 cm in diameter.'*

T4 *This is the ultimate check on a manufacturing specification.*

CHAPTER 5

DEVELOPMENT

WHAT IS DEVELOPMENT?

Development is the stage in the design process where changes are made to an idea to enable it to meet the requirements of the design brief, the information which has been gathered during research and, most important, the product specification. Development is the process used to ensure that the product will:

- be of good quality
- be good to look at, and enjoyable and safe to eat
- provide value for money
- meet the appropriate nutritional profile.

Development should form one of the larger sections of your project work. It is also a section in which you can show a good range of making skills.

The majority of development work usually takes place when the final product idea has been chosen but it is possible to include some development work at the design ideas stage before a final idea is selected. Development is all about **changing**, **testing**, or **modifying** all or part of a product until a desired outcome, which meets the product specification, is achieved.

IDEAS FOR DEVELOPMENT WORK

You need to record development work in your design folder. Long sections of writing are not needed. Here you will find some ideas for development work and different ways of recording it in your design folder.

INVESTIGATIONS

You need to state what you are doing, why you are doing it and what you have found. The easiest way to do this is to write it up in a similar way to a science experiment.

You must always remember to show how you are using the results of your investigation. This is where the examiner will be able to give you credit.

It would be possible to carry out a simple investigation, e.g. to find out which is the most suitable type of pastry for a product. Small quantities of ingredients would be used to make small samples. Results presented in a chart would record your findings.

TESTING

A chart recording the findings of any test is the quickest, simplest and most meaningful way of presenting information relating to testing. You must make sure that the information is clear and must know how you will use the results.

USING DIFFERENT INGREDIENTS AND METHODS

If you are beginning your development work from an existing idea or recipe, there is good opportunity for you to change or substitute ingredients and methods. The use of different vegetables, fruits, flavourings, sauces, fillings, flour, fat, spices or herbs can completely change an idea. These ingredients can be evaluated in terms of their effect on the sensory characteristics of the product or on its nutritional value.

Changing the methods for making products will also produce different outcomes. When making pastry, for example, the use of different methods and ingredients will significantly alter the final texture, appearance, taste and nutritional composition. Bases for pizza can be made by a variety of methods. The texture, flavour and keeping qualities of cakes depend upon the methods used in making them.

Development gives you the opportunity to try out such changes and **evaluation** enables you to make appropriate decisions. Simple notes, charts or diagrams with comments are adequate ways of recording your results.

Look at Figure 5.1 (page 28) and read the examiner's comments on it.

LOOKING AT SIZE, SHAPE AND CONSISTENCY

At the development stage it is possible to try out different sizes of a product, in terms of both weight and volume. These can then be evaluated against the nutritional requirements. For example, in the case of individual hand-held products, such as biscuits, cakes and pastries, appearance will influence size.

Consistency relates to the thickness or thinness of a liquid or mixture. Different consistencies are required for different functions. Some liquids are needed to bind, coat or moisten other ingredients. For example, the softness of a cake mixture will influence the texture of the cake.

Storage methods and times will dictate the consistency required. You can carry out some testing to find out the effects of freezing, chilling and reheating on different consistencies. For example, if a sauce product is to be made for the freezer, the sauce needs to be made thinner than if the product was to be consumed immediately. The reason for this is that freezing causes starchy liquids to thicken up.

It is possible to write up these activities as investigations or experiments.

Adaptations to the Ingredients

The following changes were made to the recipe for the Italian Pasta Soup to improve the overall appearance/texture/taste etc. of the product :-

Original recipe	Final recipe	Reasons for change
75g butter	75g low fat margarine	less fat
1 onion	1 onion	
400g chopped tomatoes	400g chopped tomatoes	
100ml semi-skimmed milk	200ml semi-skimmed milk	to make the soup thinner
100ml water	200ml water	thinner soup
10g tomato puree	25g tomato puree	improve colour
100g pasta shells	75g macaroni	pasta shells were too bulky
40g sweet corn	40g sweet corn	
Italian herbs(as desired)	Italian herbs(as desired)	
Mixed herbs(as desired)	Mixed herbs(as desired)	

75g butter- 75g low fat margarine
This change was made to reduce the amount of fat present in the soup.It would work just as well and wouldn't really affect the flavour.

100ml semi-skimmed milk- 200ml semi-skimmed milk
This change was made as the soup was far too thick.The milk serves as a binder but also as a liquid thinner.

100ml water- 200ml water
This change was also made to thin out the soup.

10g tomato puree- 25g tomato puree
This change was made to improve the colour of the soup and also to make the flavour just that little bit stronger.

100g pasta shells- 75g macaroni
I made this change because the pasta shells were too bulky to be served in a take-away container and using macaroni also helps the overall look of the soup as it is smaller. You don't need as much macaroni either.

EXAMINER'S COMMENTS ON FIGURE 5.1

Good Points

- The aims of the development are given, i.e. 'to improve the overall appearance/taste/texture'.
- Details of changes to the original recipe are provided.
- Reasons for changes are given.
- A knowledge of the nutritional effects of changing ingredients is shown, i.e. the use of low-fat margarine.
- A knowledge of the effects of adding different or extra ingredients is shown and linked to the use of the ingredient, i.e. milk is used as a thinner.
- Development is linked to the original brief and uses earlier observations, e.g. 'The soup is to be sold in a carton therefore the size of the pasta is very important and also the quantity.'

Areas for Improvement

- Evaluation of the development should be included on the same page if possible.
- The results of sensory evaluation could have been included.

Figure 5.1 *Adaptations to ingredients*

CHANGING SENSORY CHARACTERISTICS

This is perhaps the most common form of development and, unfortunately, students often see this as the *only* type of development which they need to carry out. None the less, it is a very important part of product development and needs to be done to meet the sensory characteristics which the product specification has outlined. Changes to taste, texture or appearance can be done throughout the development process, with fine modifications made to the very final product. Sensory characteristics will be achieved by the use of seasoning, herbs, spices; addition of different ingredients to alter both flavour and texture; use of different production methods; addition of fillings, toppings, decorations.

A table showing the ingredient or method, together with the resultant effect, is a good recording strategy, especially when combined with a conclusion.

APPLYING DIFFERENT FINISHING TECHNIQUES

The application of a glaze, nuts and seeds, icings, grated cheese, sliced fruits or vegetables, piped cream or potato, spices or herbs to products will affect appearance, taste and texture.

DEMONSTRATING KNOWLEDGE OF FOOD MATERIALS AND PROCESSING

The ability to understand scientific principles and their application to food production is an essential part of development work. Look at Figure 5.2 (page 30) and then read the examiner's comments on it.

EXAMINER'S COMMENTS ON FIGURE 5.2

Good Points
- The student understands the effects that mixing and cooking will have on the choice of ingredients for the two parts of the product.
- The specification states that the product will contain crunchy vegetables and the composition and cooking of vegetables achieves this.
- The candidate demonstrates the necessary knowledge and understanding of the effects of cooking on potato to achieve the desired result.
- A very clear explanation of gelatinisation is shown for sauce making.
- The candidate explains how the required consistency of sauce is achieved and how ratios and proportions affect the degree of gelatinisation
- Clear understanding of making techniques are also given and can be applied to faults which might occur in a mixture.

Areas for Improvement
- Some actual testing of different vegetables could have been added, particularly for obtaining the best results in terms of cooking methods, the size of individual pieces and critical time controls in cooking.

Scientific Principles

I have decided to discuss the scientific principles behind my dish. This shall enable me to see exactly what happens during cooking.

During cooking potatoes go through a process of gelatinisation. The starch molecules in the potato take up water and swell as the following diagram shows:

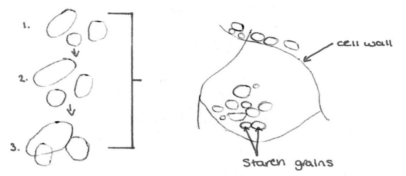

Potatoes need to be cooked long enough for complete gelatinisation of starch otherwise they will have an uncooked taste and texture.

My dish is primarily based on vegetables. Changes occurring in the texture of vegetables during cooking are due to the softening of the cellulose and the gelatinisation of the starch. Overcooking makes the vegetables soft and 'mushy'. The vegetables should be cooked only until tender but firm. This means that some of the crispness of the raw vegetable is retained. The cooking time of vegetables is determined by the amount of cellulose the vegetable contains, e.g. carrots require a longer cooking time than green vegetables.

If overcooked, some flavour can be lost from the vegetables. This is due to the loss of volatile acids in cooking. To combat this I only cooked my vegetables as long as absolutely necessary and did not use more liquid that required.

In my final dish I have a sauce. The sauce was made using the roux method. As in all sauce making gelatinisation occurred. This process thickens a liquid such as a sauce. When starch is mixed with a liquid the granules are suspended in the liquid. As the mixture is heated the liquid begins to penetrate the starch granules causing them to soften. The granules swell to about five times their normal size until they nearly touch each other. This makes the liquid thick and we say that a gel has been formed. The degree of gelatinisation is affected by the proportion and type of starch, the temperature of the liquid and the effect of other ingredients.

The process of gelatinisation is important in all starch thickened liquids, if this process is not correctly done the mixture may be unpleasant, be of the wrong consistency or may become lumpy. Lumps will form in a starch thickened mixture if:
- Dry starch is mixed with warm or hot liquid. On immediate contact with dry starch the hot liquid will gelatinise the outer starch granules. These granules act as a barrier and the liquid is unable to penetrate to the remaining uncooked starch inside.
- The mixture is not stirred whilst heated. The starch granules will not remain in suspension unless the mixture is stirred. They simply settle in groups at the bottom of the saucepan. The starch granules in contact with the liquid gelatinise and prevent the liquid from penetrating the remaining starch.

Figure 5.2 *Scientific principles*

DESIGNATED TOLERANCES, RATIOS AND PROPORTIONS

The manufacturing specification will need to contain very accurate information about these three factors. Development gives you the chance to try out such things as different thicknesses of dough for pastry, biscuits, scones or bread, different viscosity of sauces, icings or fillings, different sizes of fruits or vegetables, pieces of meat or fish.

The results of your investigations will provide you with a good quality product and the information that is needed for manufacturing it. This could be presented by giving the base recipe with amendments noted in an adjacent column, showing where and how modifications were made.

CARRYING OUT FURTHER RESEARCH

Chapter 1 pointed out that research can be done at any stage in a project. Often, when students reach the development stage, they realise that they still need some specific information on types of ingredient or processes which it was not possible for them to know about at the beginning of the project.

Look at Figure 5.3 (page 32) and read then the examiner's comments on it.

EXAMINER'S COMMENTS ON FIGURE 5.3

Good Points

- A need for some knowledge of sauce making has been identified by the student.
- A sauce product has been specified in the design brief, therefore the student has found it necessary to discover how sauces can be used in products.
- Different methods for making sauces have been researched.
- Thickening agents have been identified.
- Some scientific understanding is demonstrated, which the student will apply later during making.
- Sources of information are given.

Areas for Improvement

- The need for the information has been related to the design brief but a more specific need may become apparent as a result of the student's design ideas. This should be shown.
- The student must show clearly how this information is to be used.

SAUCES RESEARCH

- I referred to cookery and recipe books to obtain information on making all types of sauces.

A SAUCE IS a thickened, flavoured liquid added to a food or dish for any of the following reasons:

1 To enhance the flavour of the food which it accompanies.

2 To provide a contrasting flavour to an otherwise mildly-flavoured food, e.g. cheese sauce with cauliflower.

3 To provide a contrasting texture to particular solid foods, e.g. poultry or fish.

4 To bind ingredients together for dishes such as fish cakes or croquettes.

5 To add colour to a dish, e.g. jam sauce with a steamed sponge pudding.

6 To contribute to the nutritional value of a dish.

7 To reduce the richness of some foods, e.g. orange sauce with roast duck, apple sauce with roast pork,

8 To add interest and variety to a meal.

A SAUCE can be served as;

a coating for vegetables, meat, or fish

part of a meal

an accompaniment.

It is important to stir a sauce continuously while it is cooking to prevent it sticking to the bottom of the pan or becoming lumpy.

Consistencies of sauces

Pouring - A pouring sauce, at boiling point, should just glaze the back of a wooden spoon, and should flow freely when poured.

Coating - A coating sauce, at boiling point, should coat the back of a wooden spoon, and should be used as soon as it is ready, to ensure even coating over the food.

Binding - A binding sauce or panada should be thick enough to bind dry ingredients together, so that they can be handled easily to be formed into rissoles, cakes, etc.

SAUCES should be carefully flavoured and should be *tasted* before serving, so that adjustments can be made. A badly flavoured sauce can ruin an otherwise perfectly good dish.

THICKENINGS FOR SAUCES
Starch, in flour, cornflour, arrowroot, etc.
Protein, from eggs.
Emulsification of oil and water.
Puréed vegetables or fruits.

All sauces should be free from lumps and should not be overcooked, as this may spoil their flavour.

EMULSIFICATION OF FAT

If oil and water are thoroughly mixed, they become an emulsion. To prevent seperation, egg yolk, which contains the emulsifier lecithin, may be added. This is the method used to thicken and stabilize the oil and water (in the vinegar) of a mayonnaise.

EGG PROTEIN

The coagulation temperature of a yolk is 70°C.

When egg is used to thicken a sauce it should be added to other ingredients while they are cool and then gently heated to reach this temperature. Once the sauce is thickened, it should be cooled rapidly to stop the coagulation.

Example: egg custard sauce.

CORNFLOUR

Cornflour may be used to thicken sweet sauces such as chocolate, lemon, and butterscotch. It contains starch the granules of which, when mixed with cold water and heated to 60°C, begin to absorb the water and swell. On heating further to 85°C they will swell to five times their normal size and thicken the liquid. If heating continues, some of the granules will rupture, releasing starch which will form a gel with the water. On cooling, the gel will set, and the sauce will become solid.

PUREES

Cooked or raw fruit or vegetables can be puréed to produce a smooth sauce, by rubbing them through a sieve or by liquidizing.
Examples: apple sauce and tomato sauce.

ROUX SAUCES

A roux is sometimes used as a method of thickening a sauce with the starch contained in flour. (See Cornflour).

Method

Melt approximately 12g fat in a pan and add to it the same amount of flour. Stir until well mixed and heat gently for one minute. During this time the starch granules will begin to soften and the starch will start to cook. The fat and flour mixture form the roux which is the basis of a sauce using approximately 275ml of liquid.
Examples : *white, cheese, mushroom, onion, and parsley sauces.*

Sauce-based Product

Figure 5.3 *Sauces research*

THE NUTRITIONAL PROFILE

The product specification will show the nutritional profile that is required. The only way to match the product to the specification is to carry out some **nutritional analysis**. By producing a series of computer printout summaries as you carry out changes, you will be able to see how your product is matching up to the specification. Changing ingredients or quantities of ingredients will have a significant effect on the product's nutritional value.

COSTING

Costing is often a major priority in a product specification. Costing tables will show the effects of changing ingredients and quantities but changing ingredients to reduce cost can be detrimental to the successful making of the product. You need to comment on this.

Check yourself

QUESTIONS

Q1 Are there distinct parts to your product idea?

Q2 Could you make changes or give alternatives for each part?

Q3 Think about the different types of development that you could carry out.

Q4 Have you carried out nutritional analysis? How are you using the results?

Q5 Are you satisfied with the final product? Does it need fine tuning?

Q6 Do your design sheets show everything that you have done? Will the reader understand?

Q7 Have you made sure that your knowledge about food and the effects of mixing, shaping, cooking and storing is evident?

TUTORIALS

T1 Look carefully at the idea for your product. Is it possible to divide the product into separate parts, such as flan case and filling, pasta and sauce, cheesecake base, topping and glaze, pasty and filling, pizza base and topping, bread and filling?

T2 Once you have identified the different parts of the product, brainstorm ideas for changes. These could include changes to ingredients, methods, shapes, sizes, finishes, storage methods, flavours, textures.

T3 For each idea give some details about the development. For example, if you are making small cakes, one idea could be to carry out an investigation into the use of different fats to meet certain dietary needs and preferences. You should produce a list of possible fats and the methods to be used. Some thought also needs to be given to the method of recording the results and how the result are to be used.

T4 Part of your specification might have made some reference to nutritional requirements. One way to check the effects of making changes to a recipe is to carry out computer analysis of the changed recipe. The printout of the results is good evidence to put in your design folder, accompanied with some comments of your own.

T5 You will eventually make a final product. Look at it, taste it and ask other people to do the same. Are any small, simple changes needed to improve it?

T6 Make sure all the work you have done has been recorded in your folder. It is very important that the evidence is clear and the detail shows the changes that you have made.

T7 You will be given credit if you can show that you understand the effects of mixing foods and how the changes which take place during cooking and processing affect the finished result.

CHAPTER 6

EVALUATION

WHAT IS EVALUATION?

Evaluation is all about making judgements. It is a very important part of designing and making and should be done at all stages of the design process so that you will be able to make the right decisions for the next step in the process. Evaluation is a way of looking back at what you have already found out and using this information to help you produce criteria and ideas and eventually to make a food product which fits the design brief. Evaluation does not just happen at the end of a project. It is the process which enables you to find ideas and adapt and improve a product.

TYPES OF EVALUATION

- looking at and tasting existing products
- reading and summarising relevant points from various sources of information
- considering ideas in the light of consumer preferences
- matching ideas to criteria
- testing products against a specification
- testing products for particular sensory characteristics – sensory evaluation
- carrying out nutritional analysis
- making judgements about the suitability of particular ingredients or methods
- judging the effects of different methods of storage or processing on ingredients, mixtures or complete products
- looking at different packaging materials and judging which would be the most suitable for your product
- making a final evaluation against the original design brief.

WHEN AND WHERE SHOULD YOU CARRY OUT EVALUATION?

THE INITIAL RESEARCH

1 You should examine and taste existing products to assess what is good or not so good and if an alternative or better product could be made.

2 At the initial research stage you should also evaluate the information you have collected and draw together points from questionnaires.

THE DESIGN IDEAS STAGE

1 You should look carefully at the ideas you have produced and select the most appropriate ones which match your design criteria and the requirements of the design brief. You should choose the most promising idea and think about how this idea could be developed. (Look back at Chapter 3, page 13.)

2 You should carry out **sensory testing** (see Chapter 30, pages 217–221).

THE DEVELOPMENT STAGE

1 You should evaluate and compare similar products which you have made but where you have changed one or more ingredients. Look at Figure 6.1 (page 36) and then read the examiner's comments on it. This work is related to a brief which asks for the production of a healthy option cake.

EXAMINER'S COMMENTS ON FIGURE 6.1

Good Points
- Specific sensory characteristics are identified.
- Useful comparisons are made of characteristics between full fat and low fat.
- Some observations are made about the appearance of the product at different stages of making.

Areas for Improvement
- No clear objectives for the comparison are given.
- No conclusion is made about the results.
- No comments are made which show the candidate's knowledge and understanding of food, i.e. the fact that low-fat spread results are different because of their water content.
- No reasons are given for the different characteristics of the two cakes.
- The photographs need annotating and specific comments should be made about the size and shape of different products.
- No indication is given as to how these results will be used or how and why further testing might be needed.

2 At this stage you should also test the products which you make against the product specification.

3 You also need to test parts of the product that you are making. Look at Figure 6.2 (page 37) and then read the examiner's comments on it. Here the student has carried out some development work on part of the product.

6. Bake at 350-375° (Gas mark 4-5) for about 20mins until firm to touch.

VERDICT

Full-Fat chocolate fairy cakes.

Texture:- The Full-fat cakes were very dry in the mouth, they crumbled easy when bit into.

Taste:- The Full-fat cakes had plenty of flavour, they were buttery and tasted of "real" chocolate.

Smell:- The cakes, when they just came out of the oven smelt really good, they smelt of hot chocolate and an excellent aroma came from them.

Appearance:- The cakes were a light brown colour, they looked like Rock-cakes on top but were light and Puffy inside.

Any other comments:- When I was beating the butter and sugar together it took a very long time to cream, as the butter was quite firm. The full-fat cakes definitely tasted the best.

Low-fat chocolate fairy cakes.

Texture:- The Low-fat cakes were really light and fluffy in the mouth, they were moist and didn't crumble at all in the mouth.

Taste:- The cakes tasted very different to the Full-fat ones, they were chocolaty, but they tasted more of dark chocolate rather than milk. They were just as nice to eat as the Full-fat ones, and are healthier to eat to.

Smell:- When the cakes come out of the oven they smelt different to the Full-fat ones, they were a much stronger aroma, and you could smell the "carob" coming out.

Appearance:- The cakes were much darker in colour than the Full-fat cakes, they were smooth on top a looked like "bread buns" rather than "rock cakes".

Any other comments:- When I was beating the cakes (butter + sugar) they creamed together really easily, and the butter (low-fat spread) looked much lighter in colour.

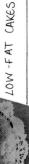

FULL-FAT CAKES.

LOW-FAT CAKES.

51

Figure 6.1 Verdict

36

In my third development I decided to trial different toppings for my chosen dish, potato and carrot casserole. I didn't use my chosen sauce in this testing because I didn't want anything to detract from the focus of this development: toppings.

I decided to trial the following toppings:

Plain crumble topping: This is a topping made simply from flour and margarine. It is made by rubbing the margarine into the flour until it resembles breadcrumbs. It will be relatively cheap and won't alter my nutritional structure much.

Cheese topping: This topping is made from actual breadcrumbs mixed with cheese and put on the top of the dish. This will also be low cost and won't drastically affect the nutritional values.

Onion topping: This is the same as the cheese topping yet with chopped onion instead of cheese.

Toast topping: This is bread toasted and then put on the dish. It too is cheap and won't alter the nutrients much.

Crisp and breadcrumb topping: This is simply breadcrumbs with crumbled crisps. It will be reasonably cheap and, like all the other toppings, I don't think it will alter the nutritional analysis greatly.

Overall my toppings went well and I was able to complete them well within the time allowed.

The toppings didn't add large costs onto the original cost of the casserole:

1. Plain crumble topping = 3p for 320g worth of potato casserole (which is two portions). This increases the overall cost of the product to 15p per portion.

2. Cheese topping = 5p for 320g worth of casserole. This increases the overall cost of the product to 16p per portion. I may not need to use extra cheese, as before putting the topping on, I put additional cheese onto it, so I could use this cheese in the topping instead.

3. Onion topping = 3p for 320g worth of casserole. This increases the overall cost of the product to 15p per portion.

4. Toast topping = 2p for 320g worth of casserole, This increases the overall cost of the product to 14.5p per portion.

5. Crisp topping = 25p for 320g of casserole. This increases the overall cost of the product to 25p per portion.

Evaluation - Toppings

As you can see, the most expensive topping is the crisp one and the least expensive is the toast topping.

All the dishes turned out well, the only problem I faced was that the toast burnt, but I was able to rectify this using a fresh piece of bread. In large scale production this is a potential problem.

All the toppings looked very appetising, they added to the appearance and presentation of the dishes. When tasting all the different toppings, they were all delicious. They were crunchy which added to the texture and mouthfeel of the casserole and, I believe, improved it.

I didn't do an ordinary sensory evaluation as I thought it would be better to ask my target group which topping they preferred. As you can see, the favourite was the crumble topping, which I would agree with, as once the dishes cooled down, the crisp and toast toppings went a little soggy. I think that with all the cheese already present in the dish, the cheese topping produced an over-powering taste, as did the onion one. I feel this would be particularly true for my target group.

After freezing and reheating there were no major changes in the consistency, taste, flavour, etc. of the dishes. They all reacted reasonably well. The toast and crisp toppings became even soggier in the microwave, in fact all the toppings weren't as crisp as they were prior to reheating. This is due to the absorption of liquid when in the freezer. I think that to combat this I would state that the dish should either be reheated in the oven or reheated in the microwave and then crisped under the grill. This would improve the texture of the topping.

I decided not to do a nutritional analysis for this development as the toppings were added in such small quantities the nutritional structure of the dish wouldn't be altered too much.

EXAMINER'S COMMENTS ON FIGURE 6.2

Good Points

- A good range of alternative or possible toppings is explored.
- Some reference is made to the effect on nutritional value of adding a topping.
- Costing is considered.
- Comments are made about the sensory effects of adding toppings.
- Using a target group for evaluation is a very good strategy.
- The need for some testing of storage methods has been noted.
- The student demonstrates good knowledge and understanding of processing methods, i.e. the effects of freezing and microwaving.
- The student understands why and when nutritional analysis is required.
- It is very clear how the student is going to use the results of their development work.

Figure 6.2 *Evaluation of toppings*

4 You also need to test the effects of different temperatures and storage methods on parts or all of your product.

5 Finally, you need to evaluate your end product against the product specification and the design brief. Look at Figure 6.3 and then read the examiner's comments on it. This final evaluation refers to a brief which asked for a range of low-cost meals for the freezer.

EXAMINER'S COMMENTS ON FIGURE 6.3

Good Points
- All development work has been included in the final evaluation.
- Clear objectives are given for the final evaluation.
- Some evaluation of the student's own personal achievement and progression is included.
- Previous development work and testing are referred to and the student's own knowledge is made clear.
- Points which were outlined in the original brief have been looked at.
- Nutritional analysis results have been used and relate to the consumer group needs.

Areas for Improvement
- Some reference could have been made to the value of the research which was done and how existing products were used.
- A short comment relating the final result to the product specification would be useful.
- A statement saying how this information would be used in a manufacturing context could be added.

SUMMARY OF EVALUATION

◼ You must always have clear objectives for your evaluation. In other words, you must be very sure of what it is you want to find out.

◼ When you write up your evaluation you must make it clear what you have found out, how successful you have been, and what is right and what is wrong.

◼ You must make it clear how you are going to use the information gathered from your evaluation.

◼ Your evaluation should guide you towards the next step in your work.

◼ The end product which you make will be the result of ideas which you have changed and modified. The final product may be very different from your first ideas. This will be the result of evaluation.

For further help on evaluation see Chapter 30 on Sensory Analysis (page 214).

Evaluation - Final Product

For my final practical I decided to put all my developments together in order to see exactly how successful my dish would be. I wanted to see how all my ideas combined together so I used my chosen topping, sauce and vegetable shape.

The dish was finished within the time allowed, and I completed it without any major problems. I tried to complete my work tidily and hygienically.

Overall I found that I was able to show a range of skills, such as vegetable preparation and sauce making. Perhaps the most complex part of the dish was making the "Béchamel" sauce, as one has to be careful to make sure that it does not go lumpy! The scientific principles behind sauce making are explained later.

I found that the dish worked well with all the developments together. Previously the dish had been a little bland and hadn't allowed me to incorporate many of my skills. This dish has improved that greatly.

The final product looked very appealing as the crispy topping made it look very appetising and it added more interest. The sauce moistened the dish and the topping added a crispy texture, which creates a better mouthfeel as it contrasts with the texture of the vegetables.

After freezing I found that the dish reacted well. From my previous trials I knew that I had to have a thinner consistency of sauce, so that it didn't become too thick after reheating. I also knew that it would be better to reheat the dish in the oven or in the microwave and then "crisp-up" the topping under the grill. I found this dish is suitable for freezing and reheating.

After reheating my dish I carried out a sensory evaluation to assess the acceptability of my final idea. I asked five people to complete my evaluation. As you can see it was pretty popular, although as some of the comments suggest, I should have perhaps added more salt, which I realised at the time of making my dish. I was also pleased to see that the marks for texture and mouthfeel increased as these are where the problems were in my previous trials of the dish.

The dish was obviously improved in the opinion of the tasters.

Overall my dish has worked out reasonably cheaply. The total dish costs 90p for six portions which means that it costs 15p per portion; this is satisfactory because my design brief states that it should be a low cost dish.

I did a nutritional analysis of my final product in order to see how all the developments affected the nutritional content. This dish isn't seriously lacking in any nutrients. I would have expected the dish to be higher in carbohydrates as these are found in starchy foods such as potato, however this isn't the case. It is high in protein; this is due to the high presence of dairy products like milk and cheese. Vegetables also contain protein. I could advertise this dish as 'protein and calcium rich.' This may create extra custom as many parents are concerned that children don't have enough calcium, as a lack of it may result in conditions such as osteoporosis, in later life.

Figure 6.3 *Evaluation of the final product*

Check yourself

QUESTIONS

Q1 Look back at the research which you carried out at the beginning and at various other stages in your project. Have you evaluated all the information you collected? How did the information help you produce design criteria?

Q2 After producing your design ideas did you really check that the idea or ideas which you decided to develop actually matched the design criteria and the design brief?

Q3 When you began to carry out the development of your chosen product or products did you make it clear how you were using the results of any tests or investigations. Could this be clearly seen both in your design folder and in the making activities which followed?

Q4 Did you have clear objectives for your sensory evaluation? Were the results meaningful and were you able to carry out some modification to your product as a result?

Q5 Did you make checks as you went along and implement modifications or improvements as a result?

Q6 Have you included a final evaluation at the end of your project?

TUTORIALS

T1 Chapter 1, on research (page 2), tells you to collect, sort, sift and present information. Look at the final research which you presented and also at the examples of other students' work shown in Chapter 1. Make sure that you have collected and presented the main points from your research which you then used in your design criteria and ideas.

T2 You can produce a whole range of design ideas. Each one can be quite different. However, you must make sure that the design ideas fit the brief and the design criteria which you have drawn up. An idea which you like but which does not fit cannot be given credit.

T3 Each time you carry out testing or investigations you will collect results. These results are very important because they will have an effect on the next activity you do. However, testing is not an activity which you should include unless there is a real reason for doing it. You must make sure that any tests or investigations are written up in your folder work and that any conclusions which lead to changing ingredients, methods or quantities are incorporated in the making activities which follow.

T4 Most students really like doing sensory evaluation but often they are not quite sure why it is being done. In other words, they have not given enough thought to the objectives and purpose of the sensory evaluation.

Often the people used as tasters are not given sufficient guidance. When this happens results can be meaningless and of little use in changing or improving a product. Inappropriate words may be used, e.g. 'good', 'nice', 'like', 'dislike'. Make sure you receive information which enables you to modify your product.

T5 Always write up your evaluations as you go along so that they appear in the appropriate section of the folder. This is the only way to make it clear how you are using evaluation to guide the next stage in the process.

T6 A final evaluation is very important at the end of the project. This uses all the observations you have made throughout the project but also comments on how the final product meets the original brief, where ideas have been developed, how problems have been overcome, and on the success of the end result.

WHAT ARE SYSTEMS AND CONTROL?

A **food-making system** can be broken down into the several different parts which make up a food production method and result in a finished food product. The system ensures that the final product:

- fulfils the purpose for which it was intended
- is of good quality
- is safe to eat
- is cost effective to make
- is suitable for manufacture in large quantities
- has made the most efficient use of people and equipment.

Control is the range of checks and procedures which are built into the system to ensure that it works as it should.

All systems are based on the same model: **input → process → output**.

Input is everything that goes into the food system: ingredients, effort, time, money.

Process is what happens to everything that goes into the system: weighing, mixing, shaping, forming, cooking, cooling, finishing, checking.

Output is the end product and any by-products: the food product, its packaging and labelling, plus any leftover waste materials or recyclable materials.

Systems and control are very important in food production because they:

- ensure a good quality product is made. This includes:
  - nutritional content
  - sensory characteristics
  - weight and size
  - meeting a specific need
  - value for money.
- ensure a food product is safe to eat.
- enable large quantities of products to be made to a consistent standard.
- maintain cost effectiveness.
- meet legislation requirements.
- reduce waste.
- increase the speed at which products are made.
- reduce the time spent on repetitive, tedious tasks.
- control complex processes.
- reduce the risk of human error.

THE IMPORTANCE OF FEEDBACK

Feedback means keeping a check on what is happening. It provides information or evidence which is collected as the system operates. Feedback is given at various points in the system. It is very important because it tells you if you need to make changes in order for the system to work better.

- Weighing scales provide feedback about exact quantities.
- Weighing and measuring parts of a food product as it is made ensure consistency in such things as thickness of dough, weight of bread loaves, viscosity of sauce.
- Checks on oven temperatures ensure accurate cooking temperatures and times.
- Visual checks ensure the appropriate colour and quality of products at both the input and the process stages.
- Sensory testing gives feedback about flavour and texture.
- Computer systems provide feedback through the use of sensors such as a metal detector or a temperature gauge.

HAZARD ANALYSIS AND CRITICAL CONTROL POINT (HACCP)

HACCP is a system of risk assessment and safety checks (see Chapter 22, pages 156 and 157).

If your final product were going to be manufactured commercially, the manufacturer would have to design an HACCP procedure for it. As part of your project you will need to design an HACCP procedure for your final product and place it in your design folder. The following points will help you:

Figure 7.1 *Information must be fed back to make sure all parts of the production system are working properly*

- Produce a list of all the stages involved in the production process. This will include every step from the purchase of ingredients to point of sale of the final product. You will find that a **flow chart** is the best way of recording this.
- For each stage that you have named think about any **hazard** which could occur at that point.
- Describe how this hazard could be prevented or eliminated.
- Decide on a specific **control point** for each stage. For example, during the storage of raw materials cross-contamination of different components or ingredients has to be prevented. A control point would be to separate raw and cooked components.
- Show how each control point will be **monitored**. For example, regular monitoring would be used to check that storage areas are clean and storage temperatures are constant. The written HACCP would state that the refrigerator temperature would be monitored by checking every 60 minutes
- Indicate where and why records of the monitoring procedures will be kept.

Look at Figure 7.2 and read the examiner's comments on it.

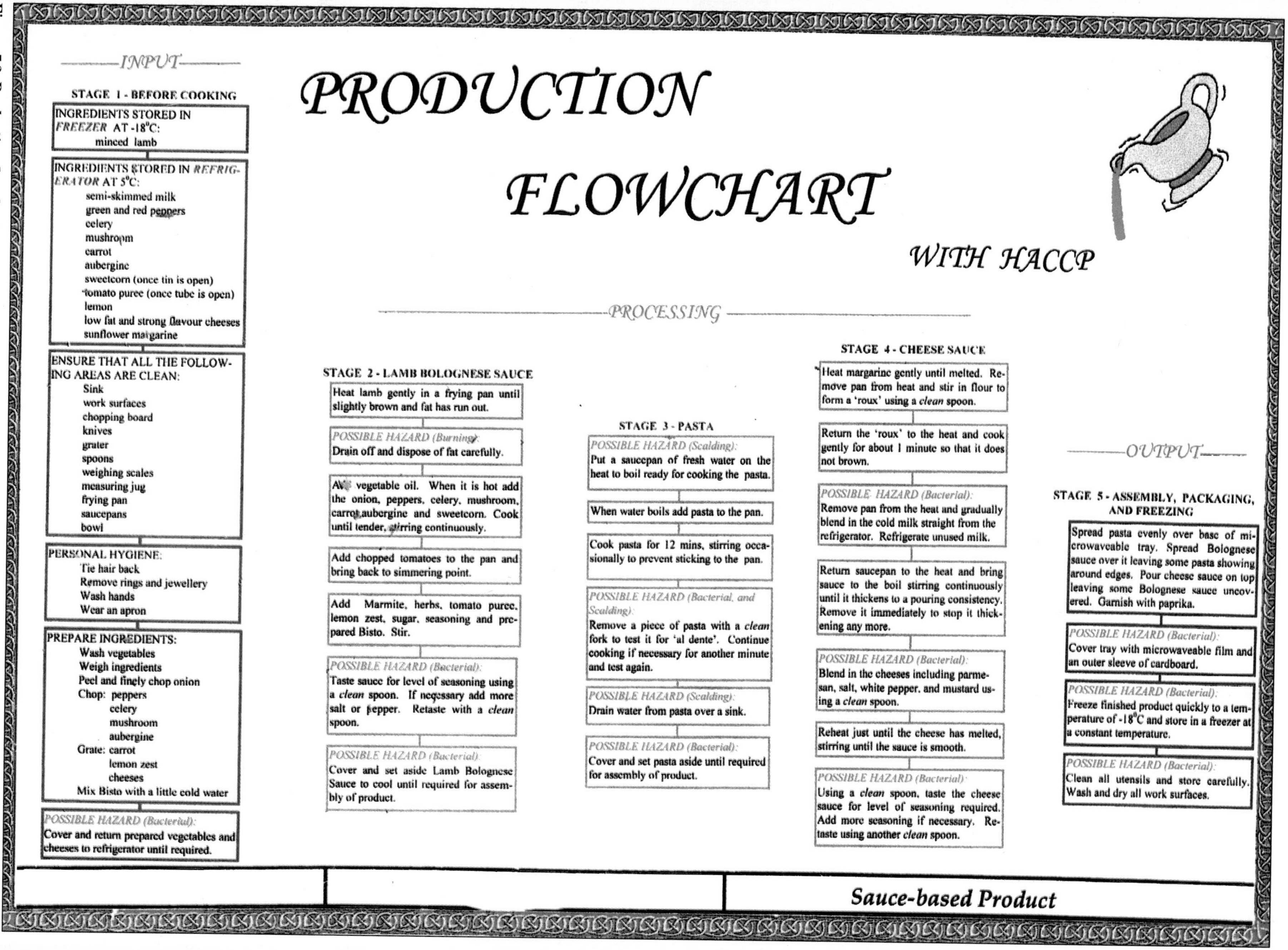

PRODUCTION FLOWCHART

WITH HACCP

— INPUT —

STAGE 1 - BEFORE COOKING

INGREDIENTS STORED IN
FREEZER AT -18°C:
minced lamb

INGREDIENTS STORED IN REFRIG-
ERATOR AT 5°C:
semi-skimmed milk
green and red peppers
celery
mushroom
carrot
aubergine
sweetcorn (once tin is open)
tomato puree (once tube is open)
lemon
low fat and strong flavour cheeses
sunflower margarine

ENSURE THAT ALL THE FOLLOW-
ING AREAS ARE CLEAN:
Sink
work surfaces
chopping board
grater
knives
spoons
weighing scales
measuring jug
frying pan
saucepans
bowl

PERSONAL HYGIENE:
Tie hair back
Remove rings and jewellery
Wash hands
Wear an apron

PREPARE INGREDIENTS:
Wash vegetables
Weigh ingredients
Peel and finely chop onion
Chop: peppers
        celery
        mushroom
        aubergine
Grate: carrot
        lemon zest
        cheeses
Mix Bisto with a little cold water

POSSIBLE HAZARD (Bacterial):
Cover and return prepared vegetables and
cheeses to refrigerator until required.

— PROCESSING —

STAGE 2 - LAMB BOLOGNESE SAUCE

Heat lamb gently in a frying pan until
slightly brown and fat has run out.

POSSIBLE HAZARD (Burning):
Drain off and dispose of fat carefully.

Add vegetable oil. When it is hot add
the onion, peppers, celery, mushroom,
carrot, aubergine and sweetcorn. Cook
until tender, stirring continuously.

Add chopped tomatoes to the pan and
bring back to simmering point.

Add Marmite, herbs, tomato puree,
lemon zest, sugar, seasoning and prepared Bisto. Stir.

POSSIBLE HAZARD (Bacterial):
Taste sauce for level of seasoning using
a *clean* spoon. If necessary add more
salt or pepper. Retaste with a *clean*
spoon.

POSSIBLE HAZARD (Bacterial):
Cover and set aside Lamb Bolognese
Sauce to cool until required for assem-
bly of product.

STAGE 3 - PASTA

POSSIBLE HAZARD (Scalding):
Put a saucepan of fresh water on the
heat to boil ready for cooking the pasta.

When water boils add pasta to the pan.

Cook pasta for 12 mins, stirring occasionally to prevent sticking to the pan.

*POSSIBLE HAZARD (Bacterial, and
Scalding):*
Remove a piece of pasta with a *clean*
fork to test it for 'al dente'. Continue
cooking if necessary for another minute
and test again.

POSSIBLE HAZARD (Scalding):
Drain water from pasta over a sink.

POSSIBLE HAZARD (Bacterial):
Cover and set pasta aside until required
for assembly of product.

STAGE 4 - CHEESE SAUCE

Heat margarine gently until melted. Remove pan from heat and stir in flour to
form a 'roux' using a *clean* spoon.

Return the 'roux' to the heat and cook
gently for about 1 minute so that it does
not brown.

POSSIBLE HAZARD (Bacterial):
Remove pan from the heat and gradually
blend in the cold milk straight from the
refrigerator. Refrigerate unused milk.

Return saucepan to the heat and bring
sauce to the boil stirring continuously
until it thickens to a pouring consistency.
Remove it immediately to stop it thickening any more.

POSSIBLE HAZARD (Bacterial):
Blend in the cheeses including parmesan, salt, white pepper, and mustard using a *clean* spoon.

Reheat just until the cheese has melted,
stirring until the sauce is smooth.

POSSIBLE HAZARD (Bacterial):
Using a *clean* spoon, taste the cheese
sauce for level of seasoning required. Retaste using another *clean* spoon.

— OUTPUT —

STAGE 5 - ASSEMBLY, PACKAGING,
AND FREEZING

Spread pasta evenly over base of microwaveable tray. Spread Bolognese
sauce over it leaving some pasta showing
around edges. Pour cheese sauce on top
leaving some Bolognese sauce uncov-
ered. Garnish with paprika.

POSSIBLE HAZARD (Bacterial):
Cover tray with microwaveable film and
an outer sleeve of cardboard.

POSSIBLE HAZARD (Bacterial):
Freeze finished product quickly to a temperature of -18°C and store in a freezer at
a constant temperature.

POSSIBLE HAZARD (Bacterial):
Clean all utensils and store carefully.
Wash and dry all work surfaces.

Sauce-based Product

Figure 7.2 **Production flowchart**

EXAMINER'S COMMENTS ON FIGURE 7.2

Good Points
- Clear steps in the production process are identified.
- Hazards are identified and recorded in colour on the chart, which makes them easy to identify. This would be useful for personnel who have the responsibility of checking during production.
- Some ways of eliminating hazards are given. For example, 'Cover and return prepared vegetables and cheese to refrigerator until required.'
- Some critical control points are given. For example, 'Freeze finished product quickly to a temperature of −18 degrees and store at constant temperature.'
- The layout of the chart is clear.
- The HACCP procedure has been put on one page in the design folder which makes it easier to read and understand.
- The student has also included information on input, process, output, which shows their understanding of systems and control in food technology.

Areas for Improvement
- Some critical control points have been left out. For example, not all temperatures and timings are given
- Little mention is made as to how the control points are to be monitored, e.g. temperature checking, metal detection, bacterial control.
- No reference is made to any monitoring procedures and how records of checks will be made, kept and used.
- The chart could have been improved by drawing it as a flow diagram with lines, arrows and symbols, i.e. terminator, process, decision symbols.

USING THE COMPUTER

It is possible to use software to design an HACCP procedure for your product. Investigate the software available in your school. You may find that you can look at an existing HACCP procedure for a product which the software company has produced. Often you can reuse this diagram by removing existing information and substituting information about your own product. This is an effective way of designing HACCP procedures as it saves you time and provides you with a check at each stage of the product development.

INPUT, PROCESS, OUTPUT

You could produce a table, diagram or chart to show the specific areas of input, process and output within the production system for your product prototype. Look at Figure 7.3 and read the examiner's comments on it.

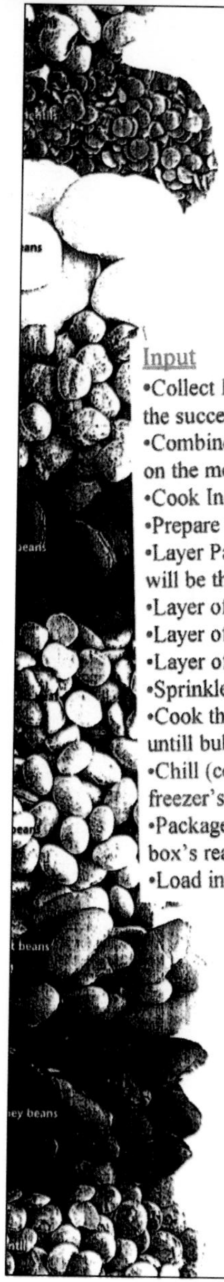

Input, Process and Output process sheet

Input

- Collect Ingredients which are needed for the successfull production of the lasagne
- Combine the ingridents together as described on the method
- Cook Ingredients
- Prepare and make Cheese Sauce (roux method)
- Layer Pasta in Appropiate cooking dish which will be the final dish used for transportation
- Layer of Ingredient (meat-substitute)
- Layer of Pasta
- Layer of Cheese Sauce
- Sprinkle of Cheese on top
- Cook the lasagne in oven (gas mark 6) untill bubbling and thoroughly cooked
- Chill (cook-chill method) in industrial freezer's untill below -18 c
- Package with final Cover and pack into box's ready for transportation to shop's
- Load into Freezer wagon's and transport

Process

- Wash and prepare the ingredients so that they are clean and ready for cooking
- Mix the ingredients together thoroughly, to ensure even distribution on product
- Cook ingredients in large frying pan (or industrial equivalent) - Ensure cooking throughout process
- Make Cheese sauce (roux method) stirring constantly to avoid lumpiness (this could be a job on the production line - to make cheese sauce constantly also a control point)
- Put pasta into tub, ensuring it fit's properly and snugly in the tub
- Layer ingredients (meat sub) on top of the pasta - ensure it is evenly spread
- Place another layer of pasta on top of the meat sub, again ensuring it is even
- Pour cheese sauce over pasta - ensure it is covering pasta and of correct consistency
- Sprinkle cheese on top - a light covering (2grams) for colour and flavour
- Cook Finished lasagne in industrial oven for 30 minutes
- Chill lasagne in industrial freezer until temp of lasagne is -18 c
- Finally pack product with outer-covering then into box's
- Load quickly into freezer's to avoid defrosting and bacteria build up

Output

- Cleaned and well-prepared ingredients which reduces the risk of bacteria and other micro-organisms entering the food product
- Well mixed ingredients ensures equal quantity spreading and distribution
- Well cooked and coloured ingredients which means taste and appearance improves
- No lumps in cheese sauce - sauce add's moisture and flavour to the product
- Well proportioned ingredients mean's a well produced product for retail
- as above
- as above
- as above
- Cheese sauce should cover pasta ensues even cooking and moisture distribution
- Sprinkled cheese add's colour to product
- Cooking kill's bacterium in the food product and reduces chances of salmonella organism's expanding
- Chilling also kill's the chances of micro-organism's expanding
- Packing add's security to product for when it is transported - also gives vital and informative information
- Freezer van's keep the product chilled through the journey

The work above, show's the various input, process and output process's that should be taken into account when producing the vegetarian lasagne. The chart's give information on check's that should be made to ensure standard's are kept to the maximum level to retain the quality of the product

Figure 7.3 *Input, process and output process sheet*

QUALITY SYSTEMS

One of the main aims in the production of a food product is to provide quality. Both **quality control** and **quality assurance** systems are used in industry to ensure a good quality end product.

QUALITY CONTROL

Quality control is the method used to check and test a product as it is made.

When your product prototype goes into production you need to ensure that the following checks are made:

- quality of ingredients
- working to designated **tolerances**
- sizes/thickness/quantities
- shape
- texture
- colour
- uniformity.

In your design folder you can show how quality control is achieved by:

- identifying the stages in the production of your food prototype
- using the list given above to prompt ideas for checks
- thinking about how you can carry out checks for quality at each stage
- describing the checks that you will make
- showing how you will correct problems after checks have been made.

A simple chart, table or diagram is the best way of presenting this information. Look at Figure 7.4 and read the examiner's comments on it.

MANUFACTURING SYSTEMS

A food manufacturer needs to decide which method of production will be most suitable for a food prototype. In your design folder you can discuss the advantages and disadvantages of different methods of production for your particular prototype. You need to know about the different production methods.

Consider the following production systems:

- one-off production
- batch production
- mass production
- continuous flow production.

You can illustrate the production sequence by diagrams, sketches or computer graphics with labels or simple comments (see Figure 7.4).

COMPUTER-AIDED MANUFACTURING SYSTEMS (CAM)

On your production diagram show where some or all of the following CAM systems would be used:

- use of sensors to detect weight changes – used for the measurement of ingredients. (The sensors send information back to a central computer which responds and makes changes.)
- use of flow rate devices for adding liquids or fillings to products
- use of timing devices for accurate cooking and cooling processes
- use of temperature sensors for achieving and maintaining constant temperatures for cooking, cooling and storage
- use of metal detectors (often magnets) to identify the presence of metallic foreign bodies
- use of sensors to control thickness of dough
- use of sensors to detect colour changes as a product is cooked.

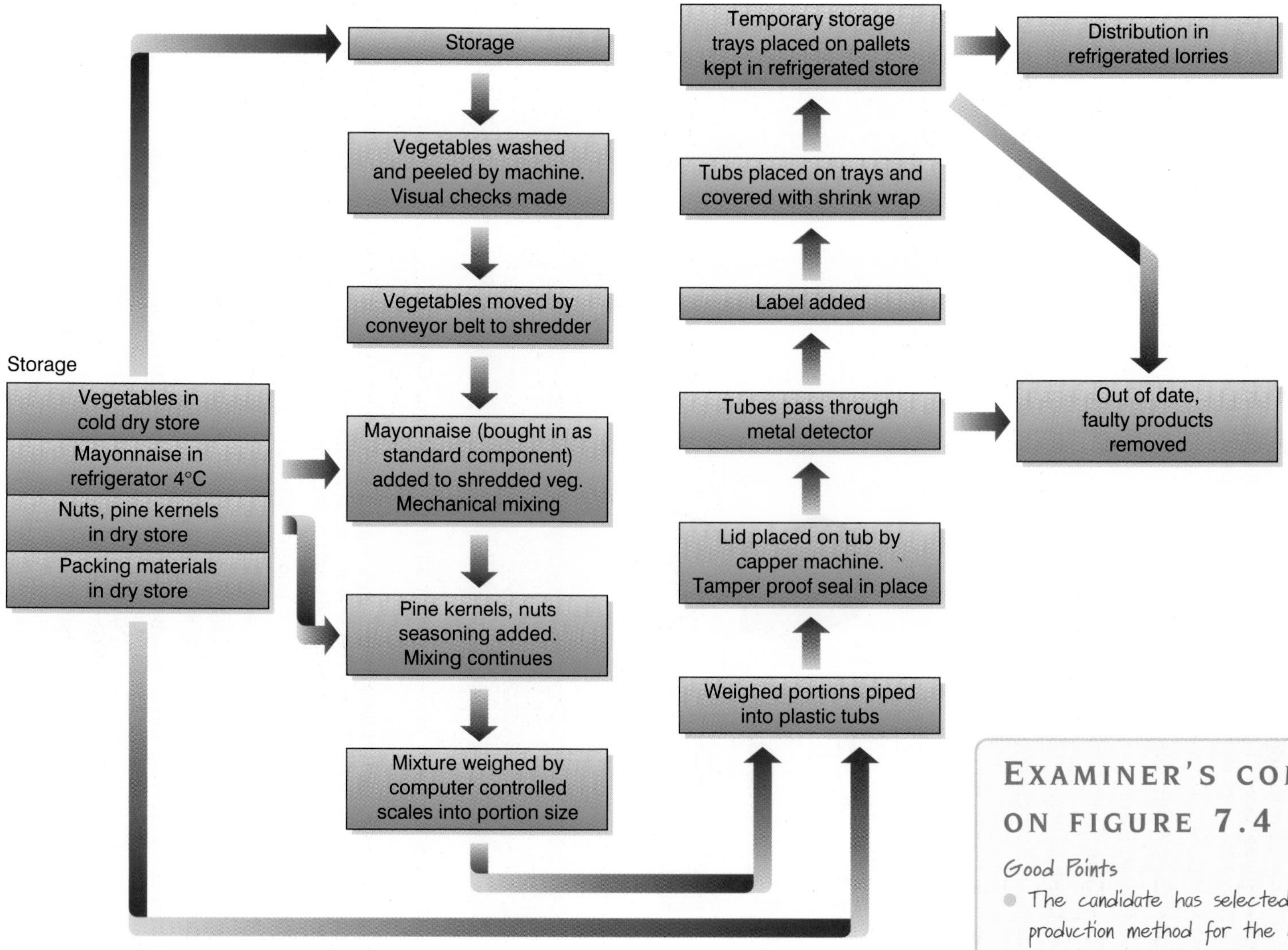

EXAMINER'S COMMENTS ON FIGURE 7.4

Good Points

- The candidate has selected an appropriate production method for the coleslaw.
- Clear steps in the process have been identified.
- Some control points have been identified, such as temperature and weight.

Figure 7.4 A simple production sequence

Storage

- Vegetables in cold dry store
- Mayonnaise in refrigerator 4°C
- Nuts, pine kernels in dry store
- Packing materials in dry store

Storage

Vegetables washed and peeled by machine. Visual checks made

Vegetables moved by conveyor belt to shredder

Mayonnaise (bought in as standard component) added to shredded veg. Mechanical mixing

Pine kernels, nuts seasoning added. Mixing continues

Mixture weighed by computer controlled scales into portion size

Weighed portions piped into plastic tubs

Lid placed on tub by capper machine. Tamper proof seal in place

Tubes pass through metal detector

Label added

Tubs placed on trays and covered with shrink wrap

Temporary storage trays placed on pallets kept in refrigerated store

Out of date, faulty products removed

Distribution in refrigerated lorries

Check yourself

QUESTIONS

Q1 Have you decided which method of production would best suit your product prototype?

Q2 Can you separate the different parts of the production process for your product into input, process, output?

Q3 At which points will you get feedback? Make sure you highlight these points.

Q4 Have you included an HACCP procedure for your product prototype?

Q5 Does the HACCP include all the hazards and controls?

Q6 Have you included specific information on the HACCP, e.g. critical temperatures and times?

Q7 How have you planned to make a quality product?

Q8 If the product were to be mass produced, how would you ensure it could be made to a high standard as regards quality?

Q9 Could parts of the production process be controlled by computers?

TUTORIALS

T1 Read the information in Chapter 20 on manufacturing processes. What are the advantages and disadvantages of each method. Look at examples of food products which are made by each method. Consider the similarities of your product prototype with these products. Select an appropriate method.

T2 Working in rough, divide a page into three boxes. Using the headings INPUT, PROCESS, OUTPUT, fit the information about the materials and methods which you are using for making your product into these boxes. Produce a finished, clear diagram which you can include in your design folder.

T3 Remember that feedback is information which you obtain as a system is working. When you are making your food product you will need to ensure that you have identified the stages where information about your product is provided. Look at your systems diagram and add the points where feedback is essential. This might be related to visual appearance, certain tolerances, sensory characteristics, time, temperature, etc.

T4 Look back at all the information given on HACCP on page 42. Think about all the different stages in the manufacture of your product, right from the source of ingredients to the point of sale. Does your flow diagram include all these stages? Are there high-risk foods in your product? Have you considered the critical control of these? If you cannot remember specific critical temperatures, do some further research to ensure you include accurate information.

T5 As you made the prototype you will have worked carefully and accurately to make something which looks and tastes good. Sometimes it is easy to produce a very good quality product as a 'one off' but not as easy if you are making hundreds or thousands of the same product. You must think about how identical-quality products can be made. Every production run must produce identical products. When the consumer buys the products they expect them to look and taste the same each time and the manufacturer's continued sales depend on this.

T6 Look at the flow diagram which you have produced and at the examples of methods of computer-aided manufacture which were given earlier. Which of these could be used in your product manufacture and where in the process would they be used? For example, metal detection might occur at the storage stage, after mixing, and again when the product has been packaged.

Remember always to include the appropriate symbols on your flow diagram.

CHAPTER 8

INDUSTRIAL PRACTICE

WHY DOES INDUSTRIAL PRACTICE MATTER IN YOUR COURSEWORK?

You must make sure that you show evidence of industrial practice in your food technology project. Most of the previous chapters have included examples of industrial practices which are actually carried out in the food industry. If you have taken notice of them and applied similar practices to your own work then you have already begun to build up your evidence.

EVALUATING EXISTING PRODUCTS

This is a common method which is often used in industry by food retailers who are looking for ideas for new products. The food manufacturers buy competitors' products and carry out 'in house' testing on them.

The tests used include **sensory evaluation** and **identification of ingredients**. Judgements are then made about portion size, value for money, etc. When you are doing your own research you will have the opportunity to include this type of industrial practice. Look at Chapter 1 (page 6), for ideas and methods.

GATHERING INFORMATION

Food retailers need to collect a range of information both about food products which already exist and also about ideas for new products. They use many different sources to provide this information, such as **market research**, **taste-testing** in supermarkets and **questionnaires**. Look at Chapter 1 (page 5) and decide if a questionnaire would be an appropriate method for you to use.

Figure 8.1 *Taste-testing is often done in supermarkets*

SENSORY EVALUATION

This is used at all stages in food product development. Examining existing products, producing design ideas and developing a **prototype** are all good opportunities to include sensory evaluation.

Look at Chapter 30, on Sensory Analysis (pages 219–221) and decide which methods would be appropriate for you to include in your work. Include a range of different methods if possible.

USING STANDARD COMPONENTS

In the food industry manufacturers buy in standard components from other food manufacturers. (Look at Chapter 16, pages 120 and 121, to check that you understand what a component is.) When you are developing your own prototype you will actually make each part of your product yourself. However, if the prototype is to be manufactured in quantity, the commercial food manufacturer will find it more cost effective to buy in some ready-made parts of the product, e.g. bases for pizzas, stuffing for meat, icing for cakes, pastry cases for savoury flans, etc. You need to identify which parts of your final food product, could be bought in ready made. This is a very relevant way to mirror industrial practice.

The following example shows how you can illustrate the use of standard components in your design folder:

> The final result, after carrying out all the development work, is to be a Caribbean Sponge Surprise. The development has shown that this dessert consists of a biscuit base with a layer of exotic fruits on the top covered by a topping of sponge. I have made all the different parts of the product in order to make decisions about size, weight, sensory characteristics, suitable storage methods, effects of storage, packaging and labelling information. However if this prototype were to be manufactured I would suggest that the biscuit base and the exotic fruit filling are bought in as standard components. This would mean that less capital is required for the purchase of equipment and machinery to produce these components of the dessert. The manufacturer would then only need to make the sponge topping and the packaging. A cake manufacturer who already has the plant and machinery for making sponge cakes could manufacture the dessert.

DEVELOPING A PROTOTYPE

Within a commercial company in the food industry there is always a **product development team**. One member of the team is a **food technologist** who has the knowledge and skills to develop recipes for a wide range of products and who will develop different methods for making these products. The food technologist will also carry out testing on recipes at the development stage and is later responsible for making the product prototype and supplying the manufacturer with information for the manufacturing specification.

When you are working on a food technology product you are working in exactly the same way as a professional food technologist and you will also be responsible for making a product prototype. This is another good example of industrial practice but you need to make it clear in your design folder that you know prototype development is an accepted industrial practice. This could be done by writing a paragraph about this topic at the end of the development section. A short piece of text like the one printed below will do the job.

Figure 8.2 *A food technologist will carry out taste-testing on products*

> Throughout my development work I have tried to think about all the characteristics that my final product would need to have. I have used different ingredients, quantities and methods to check that the combination of these ingredients will still produce an acceptable product. I have developed and tested products of different shapes, sizes and weights and have carried out nutritional analysis to check that the product is meeting the nutritional profile given in the product specification. I now have exact information about the amounts and types of ingredients which need to be used. The tests which I have carried out have also given me information about suitable storage methods and storage times. I am now in a position to pass my information to the manufacturer for production.

TESTING PRODUCTS

Within any industry making any product, from motor cars to ice cream, testing is a critical part of the process in order to ensure the end product is safe to use, able to do the job for which it was made, is of good quality, works efficiently and meets legislative requirements.

All the time a food product is being developed, various forms of testing are carried out. Look back at the chapters on Research (page 2), Development (page 26) and Systems and Control (page 41). Identify where you have carried out any kind of testing.

Will it be clear to someone reading your work that you have deliberately included these aspects of testing to ensure that your product prototype is safe to eat, is of good quality, looks good, tastes good, is stored in an appropriate way, is packaged correctly, and meets food safety legislation?

CARRYING OUT TRIALS

When a new product is first developed, often relatively small numbers of it are made. These are usually sold in carefully chosen areas of the country as 'trials'. The results from sales, sensory testing carried out in supermarkets, and directly linked market research are all forms of trials for new products. You might like to consider how, where and why trials for your product prototype would take place and comment on this in your design folder. You would also need to say what you would expect to happen as a result of the information produced by the trials.

USING STANDARD EQUIPMENT

Figure 8.3 Pastry can be made by hand or by using an electrically operated mixer

Equipment is a very important tool in product development. As far as food technology is concerned you need to demonstrate the correct use of appropriate equipment in your work, but in terms of industrial practice the type, size and use of equipment is of very great significance. For this reason, you should show the use of equipment in your practical work but not in a normal domestic situation, rather more in line with its use in industry. You should look for opportunities to use equipment when you are making a food product and choose to use a piece of equipment to overcome problems of human error, to ensure consistency and to save time and labour costs. For example, if pastry were to be rubbed in by hand the following problems could occur:

- Different people have different techniques.
- Judgements about when the mixture has achieved the right consistency vary from person to person.
- Even if one person were to do all the rubbing in, the temperature of their hands might vary and the rubbing in process would then vary in length.
- The process would take a long time.

If a piece of equipment were used to do the job:

- The mechanical action is the same each time.
- The process can be timed exactly.
- The equipment can be kept at the same temperature.
- The whole process can be controlled to ensure the pastry crumbs are consistently the same size.
- The process can be done quickly.

PACKAGING

The packaging of a food product is one of the things which make a bought product most obviously different from one made at home. The packaging of a food product is an industrial practice and has to meet all food safety requirements.

The main GCSE Food Technology syllabuses do not ask you to make packaging for your food product. However, you will need to consider the type of packaging which would be suitable for the product you have designed and give reasons for your choice. You need to look at Chapter 29, on Packaging Materials (pages 208–212).

Figure 8.4 *Looking at packaging*

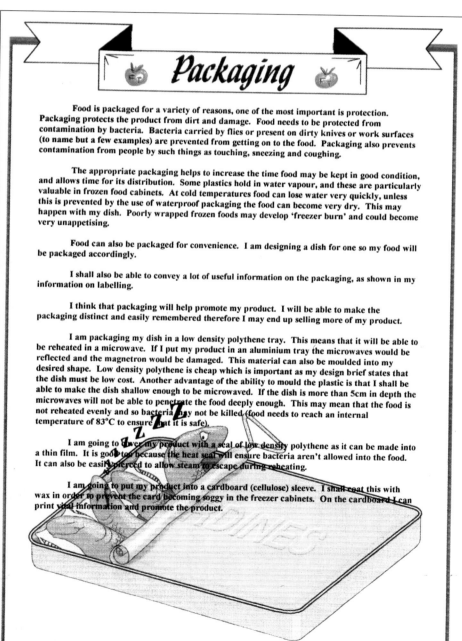

Packaging

Food is packaged for a variety of reasons, one of the most important is protection. Packaging protects the product from dirt and damage. Food needs to be protected from contamination by bacteria. Bacteria carried by flies or present on dirty knives or work surfaces (to name but a few examples) are prevented from getting on to the food. Packaging also prevents contamination from people by such things as touching, sneezing and coughing.

The appropriate packaging helps to increase the time food may be kept in good condition, and allows time for its distribution. Some plastics hold in water vapour, and these are particularly valuable in frozen food cabinets. At cold temperatures food can lose water very quickly, unless this is prevented by the use of waterproof packaging the food can become very dry. This may happen with my dish. Poorly wrapped frozen foods may develop 'freezer burn' and could become very unappetising.

Food can also be packaged for convenience. I am designing a dish for one so my food will be packaged accordingly.

I shall also be able to convey a lot of useful information on the packaging, as shown in my information on labelling.

I think that packaging will help promote my product. I will be able to make the packaging distinct and easily remembered therefore I may end up selling more of my product.

I am packaging my dish in a low density polythene tray. This means that it will be able to be reheated in a microwave. If I put my product in an aluminium tray the microwaves would be reflected and the magnetron would be damaged. This material can also be moulded into my desired shape. Low density polythene is cheap which is important as my design brief states that the dish must be low cost. Another advantage of the ability to mould the plastic is that I shall be able to make the dish shallow enough to be microwaved. If the dish is more than 5cm in depth the microwaves will not be able to penetrate the food deeply enough. This may mean that the food is not reheated evenly and so bacteria may not be killed (food needs to reach an internal temperature of 83°C to ensure that it is safe).

I am going to cover my product with a seal of low density polythene as it can be made into a thin film. It is good too because the heat seal will ensure bacteria aren't allowed into the food. It can also be easily pierced to allow steam to escape during reheating.

I am going to put my product into a cardboard (cellulose) sleeve. I shall coat this with wax in order to prevent the card becoming soggy in the freezer cabinets. On the cardboard I can print vital information and promote the product.

EXAMINER'S COMMENTS ON FIGURE 8.4

Good Points

- The student has included information which shows he or she understands about the function of packaging materials.
- These general functions are applied to their own product.
- The student also demonstrates that he or she understand about microwave cooking and the need for certain materials to be avoided.
- A very good point is made about cost. The choice of packaging materials takes account of the fact that the student is making a low-cost product.
- Some reference to food safety is made.
- The shape of the container is linked to the student's chosen method for reheating and specific temperatures are given.
- Overall, the explanation and descriptions about packaging are very clear. They are made very specific to the product which the student has developed and details from the design brief have been taken into consideration.

Areas for Improvement

- A labelled sketch of the packaging used, particularly the dish, would have reduced the amount of writing.
- The illustration used is not appropriate to the product in question and it serves no purpose. In fact, it is misleading and confusing on first glance.

LABELLING REQUIREMENTS

As a professional food technologist you would need to supply certain information to the packaging department about the food product which you have designed and made as a prototype.

Look at Chapter 28 on Labelling (page 198). Use the information from your final recipe and from the final nutritional analysis which you carried out to produce a list of ingredients and the nutritional information to be printed on the packaging. Some computer software actually allows you to produce nutritional information in the form of a label which looks very similar to the information you see on the packaging of a commercially produced food product.

You will also need to produce cooking/reheating and storage instructions and any special claims for the product.

This information needs to be a part of your design folder work. Remember that this should be done towards the end of your project when you have made the final product and when you are giving information about its manufacture in large quantities.

You can supply the information as narrative or headed paragraphs or actually put it onto a packaging net. This does not need to be to scale. It can be a shape which you think seems appropriate.

Labelling

Food labelling is important for many reasons. Many things have to be included by law, for example ingredients and quantity. The labels can also be used to promote and advertise the product. Useful information such as barcodes can also be added. The following is a plan for what I would include on a label for my product.

The name of the product is very important. The brand name means that the product can easily be recognised and chosen by the customer. The name must also include a description of the product, however it mustn't be misleading. If, for example, you have a "strawberry yoghurt", if it is only strawberry flavoured this must be stated. It can only be called "strawberry" or "strawberry flavoured" if the flavour derives from real strawberries. This is very important because if the customer is misled then legal action may be taken against the company.

I would call my dish, "Crisp & Crunchy Potato Casserole". I would describe it as a shredded potato and carrot casserole with a creamy white sauce and crunchy cheese topping. I do not feel that this would mislead the customer in any way.

The net quantity of the food must be included so that the customer can see exactly how much they are paying for. The net weight for my product would be 265g.

The list of ingredients must be included so that the customer can see if they are allergic to any of them or if they don't want to eat any of them. They must appear on the label in descending order of weight and additives must be included on the ingredients list. The following list would be written on my label: Potatoes, semi-skimmed milk, natural yoghurt, carrots, cheddar cheese, leek, wheat flour, onion, margarine, salt and pepper.

Most foods now have to carry a date mark. This is necessary so that retailers can keep their stocks up to date and helps consumers to use food while it is still at its best. This prevents the risk of things like food poisoning. I have made a freezer product so the product will have to be labelled accordingly. In some refrigerators freezer foods may be stored for up to 3 months if three black stars are present. The dish will, however, be best if kept in a freezer where it will be able to last for 3 months, if not longer, at a temperature of -18°C. The British Standard symbol of a white star in front of a the 3 star refrigerator symbol denotes this:

As I previously stated, my food is to be stored in a freezer so this information will have to be included on the label. All foods in freezers should be kept at -18°C. They will have to be kept at this temperature so that harmful bacteria can not survive. They find it easier to survive. Bacteria can be responsible for making people ill. Also if this low temperature food will remain in a similar state as when it first went into the freezers, as soon as the temperature starts to rise the decomposition may start to occur.

Figure 8.5 *What labelling does*

Labelling

The name and address of the manufacturer needs to be included because they are responsible for the original condition of the food and may need to be contacted if something goes wrong.. I would also put my name and address on it. The place of origin needs to be included in case the customer is likely to be misled, for example, "Cheddar cheese" from New Zealand.

The instructions for use are necessary on the product so that the customers can prepare the food to the best of their ability. This may include how it has to be defrosted and then reheated. It could also include serving suggestions, however these are not vital. My instructions would be as follows:

Take out of cardboard packaging, prick the plastic seal with a fork and put the dish in the microwave for 1½ mins on high power. It can then be served or put under the grill for a couple of minutes to crisp the topping. Alternatively the dish can be heated in the oven for 15 mins at a temperature of 180°C. I would have to include which method I would recommend. The dish has to reach an internal temperature of 83°C so that all bacteria are killed.

Other details that may be useful to the consumer are nutrition labelling, number of servings and serving suggestions. I could also put on a bar code for retailers. This is not only convenient for cashiers but can help the retailer keep stocks high and also see which brands sell the most and so forth.

The nutritional information which would be included on my dish →

NUTRITION INFORMATION		Values per portion
Energy	Kcal	335
Fat	g	15
Carbohydrate	g	30
Fibre (NSP)	g	3
Calcium	mg	419
Iron	mg	1
Vitamin C	mg	9

EXAMINER'S COMMENTS ON FIGURE 8.5

Good Points

- The student demonstrates knowledge and understanding about labelling
- Some reference is made to information that is required by law and to consumer information.
- The student has taken general information and converted it into information for his own food product label.
- Previous information from research and results from tests and development work are incorporated into the label, e.g. a list of ingredients from the recipe used, storage temperatures from research on freezing, and the weight of the product also links with the specification and preparation instructions.
- Some nutritional information is given.
- Special claims are referred to.

Areas for Improvement

- Insufficient attention is given to the nutritional information. Only values per portion are given and not per 100 grams. No protein value is given.
- There is no indication of where on the package the labelling information would be found. A rough sketch showing the positioning of this information would have been useful.
- This student used a software package for the production of the nutritional information. This could have been imported onto a packaging net and would have demonstrated a good use of ICT.
- The student has not made it clear which information is required by law and which is consumer information.

USE OF ADDITIVES

A wide range of food additives are used in the manufacture of food products. See Chapter 27 on Additives (page 190). Although it is unlikely that your product prototype will contain additives, there may be good reasons for the use of these in products which have to be kept stored for some time without deteriorating. This is known as the shelf life of a product.

Look at Chapter 27 which gives the functions of additives (pages 192–195). Consider the need for and value of using additives in your product if it were to go into commercial production. Would additives give your product better quality, appearance and taste, and would they prolong its shelf life?

Produce a list of additives which you think might be used in the manufacture of your product and give a reason for using each one. Include this information in the section on manufacturing in your design folder.

Check yourself

QUESTIONS

Q1 Make a list of all possible industrial practices outlined in this chapter. Which ones have you already included in your work? Can you use any others?

Q2 Have you provided information on the type of packaging needed for your product?

Q3 Check that you understand about using standard components. Look at Chapter 16 if you need to.

Q4 Have you produced the information for the nutritional label, the list of ingredients used and the cooking, re-heating and storage information?

TUTORIALS

T1 *Read through your folder and write down every example that you think is used in industry. If you have a fairly good list of examples, you are probably providing sufficient evidence.*

T2 *Look at the design brief. Did it give information about the storage/cooking method for your product, e.g. cook-chill, microwavable? If so, then this will guide you about the type of packaging required. If there is no direct information in the design brief, has your research identified a specific storage method for the product? Will the packaging need to be moisture-proof or crush-proof, e.g. if the product is for a vending machine then being crush-proof is essential. Think about how the product is to be transported, stored, both in the shop and at home, how a long shelf life can be achieved and how the product is to be cooked and eaten.*

T3 *Look at the final product you have made. Can you divide it into separate, distinct parts? Even if you have made all these parts yourself, would or could the manufacturer make them all or might they buy some in already made?*

T4 *You need to have carried out some nutritional analysis on your final product. This needs to be printed in a format which can be understood by the consumer. Use software which produces a label similar to the ones found on actual packaging. You need to consider nutritional requirements for the whole product, for a serving, or for 100 grams. A list of ingredients in descending order of quantity needs to be given. This can be done by referring to your final recipe. Provide storage and cooking instructions.*

CHAPTER 9
**USING
INFORMATION
COMMUNICATION
TECHNOLOGY
(ICT)**

WHY IS ICT IMPORTANT?

All the food technology projects you work on need to show evidence of your use of ICT. You need to think about how you will use ICT and how you can include different aspects of it in your work. However, there should be a genuine reason for using ICT, not just because it makes your work look better, although producing a well-presented, high quality design folder is also very important. However, you must not spend more time on using ICT for presentation purposes than you spend on your actual designing and making work.

EVIDENCE IN YOUR PROJECT WORK

The following list gives some ideas of what sort of thing you can use ICT for, although it may not be possible or even practical to include them all.

- obtaining, handling and presenting information
- exploring ideas which other people have already produced
- collecting, collating and presenting data
- drawing and designing
- modelling ideas
- producing high quality results
- simulating a manufacturing process or industrial practice.

USING ICT IN WORD PROCESSING/ DESK TOP PUBLISHING

To produce neat and well-presented:

- blocks of written text
- lists
- bullet points
- labels.

Look at Figure 9.1 on page 59 and then read the examiner's comments on it.

EXAMINER'S COMMENTS ON FIGURE 9.1

Good Points
- The student has summarised all her research information and displayed it on one side of a sheet of A3 paper.
- The use of lists and bullet points and the arrangement of the text, in terms of both size and the style of lettering chosen, enhance the work and make it easy to read.
- The reader's attention is instantly drawn to the most important aspects of the work.

RESEARCH ANALYSIS

• Company Research

- Recipes

Many sauces are made with vinegar that helps to form an emulsion with egg. A skin sometimes forms on the sauce once it is left to stand. This can be avoided by lightly dabbing some butter or margarine on the surface, or covering with greaseproof paper. Lots of herbs and spices such as parsley, basil, chives, stem ginger, mint, garlic and tarragon are used in the sauces to add flavour, along with seasoning. All the recipes mix colour and texture in an effort to appeal to the consumer.

- Development

A flowchart is usually drawn by the supplier showing precisely what happens to the ingredients. The flow process is broken down into stages. A Critical Control Point is the step in the making process where hazards must be controlled. The HACCP system aids safe food production. Freezing should be done quickly, as slow freezing results in large uneven ice crystals which break through the cells on thawing and affect the flavour of the food. Modifications must be made to recipes to ensure that the end product is acceptable.

• Research What is already on the market?

There are many products already on the market that are frozen and sauce-based, although very few of these are pasta dishes. The average price of a frozen sauce-based product is 66p per 100g.

• Disassembly Research

The product I disassembled "Delmio-Tagliatelle Carbonara" had been made to a very high standard and scored on average of 7.4 out of a possible 10 marks. The people I asked to taste the product found its appearance, consistency, taste and temperature satisfactory. The only areas where the product did not receive full marks were aroma, suitability of ingredients, price and sauces. The product I disassembled was aimed at working people who would not have sufficient time to prepare the product themselves; it was microwaveable and easy to re-heat quickly.

• Packaging Research

A package must contain certain labels by law:

List of ingredients	Instructions for use
Lot/Batch number	Nutritional information,
Name of product	Use by date or best before date,
Storage instructions	Name and address of manufacturer,
Weight in grams	Particulars of the place of origin if the name might be misleading
Price	Statement that food has been irradiated or contains irradiated ingredients (if applicable)

Other additional labels may be added:

Serving suggestions,

Customer guarantee

The most common material used for microwaveable and freezeable products is a plastic inner tray covered by a thin plastic film, which is pierceable. The outer package displaying the labels is made of cardboard: a cardboard sleeve or a box.

• Pasta Research

Costs of types of pasta:

Tagliatelle-26.4p per 100g	Farfalle-10.4p per 100g
Lasagne-24.8p per 100g	Penne rigate-9.8p per 100g
Fusilli-13p per 100g	Conchiglie-9.8p per 100g
Macaroni-12.8p per 100g	Penne-3p per 100g
Spaghetti-11p per 100g	

Tagliatelle, although the most expensive at 26.4p per 100g, is the favourite according to my consumer questionnaire. Spaghetti was the second type of pasta preferred by the consumers and has a fairly low price of 11p per 100g. Lasagne the third favourite is almost as expensive as Tagliatelle at 24.8p per 100g. Penne meanwhile, although not a consumer favourite, is only 3p per 100g. The other types of pasta are neither cheap nor consumer favourites and, as such, should no longer be considered for my product. All the types of pasta stated above are ideal for a sauce-based product.

• Sauces Research

Sauces should be carefully flavoured and tasted before serving. A sauce can be thickened by starch, egg protein, emulsification or pureeing. A sauce must be stirred continuously while it is cooking to prevent it sticking to the bottom of the pan or becoming lumpy. A roux sauce would be most suitable for a cheese sauce. Cornflour would be most suitable for thickening a tomato or bolognese sauce. A pouring sauce at boiling point should just glaze the back of a wooden spoon, and should flow freely when poured. A coating sauce, at boiling point, should coat the back of a wooden spoon, and should be used as soon as it is ready to ensure even coating over the food.

• Consumer Research

Pasta -Tagliatelle was the preferred type of pasta, followed by Spaghetti and Lasagne.

Savoury sauces - Cheese sauce was the favourite followed by tomato and bolognese.

Desserts - Treacle sponge was the preferred dessert, followed by Crème Caramel, Peach Melba, and Lemon Double Delight.

Sweet sauces - Chocolate was the favourite type of sweet sauce, followed by Lemon and Brandy.

Prices - The maximum price people were prepared to pay for a sauce-based product for one person was £1.50.

• Healthy Eating Research

<u>Sodium</u> - should be eaten in moderation: no more than 1% grams per day. Adding large amounts of it to food should be avoided.

<u>Sugar</u> - should be eaten in moderation, and a healthy balanced diet should contain more starchy carbohydrates than sugars.

<u>Vitamins and minerals</u> - are very important and should be eaten as often as possible to avoid deficiencies.

<u>Fibre</u> - both soluble and insoluble, is important. As a nation we do not eat enough of this important substance, as we should be eating around 18g per day. Pasta is a good source of fibre and carbohydrate.

<u>Fat</u> - should be reduced in our diets. For an average woman the consumption of fat per day should not exceed 75g and for an average man no more than 100g.

As a result of my research I should include mostly carbohydrate and fibre in my product and ensure that there are enough vitamins and minerals. A dessert with sauce would be too unhealthy so I shall make a savoury dish with a sauce instead.

Sauce-based Product

Figure 9.1 *This work on research analysis was produced on a word processor*

CHARTS, TABLES AND GRAPHS

Figures 9.2, 9.3 and 9.4 show how the use of ICT can make information easy to read and will often take up less space than hand-written charts and tables.

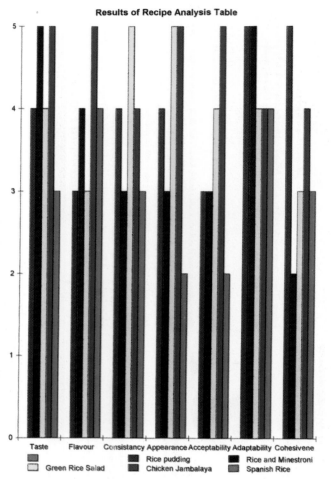

Results of Recipe Analysis Table

Figure 9.4 *A bar chart used to show the results of a recipe analysis table*

Experiment	Control cake	Variaton from control	Comment
1 Soft margarine at room temp	Packet margarine at room temp	Soft margarine at room temp	Sloppy
2 Granulated sugar	Castor sugar	Granulated sugar	Sloppy
3 No additional raising agent	1 × 2.5 ml baking powder	Omit baking powder	Lovely
4 Under-mixed	Beat ingredients together for 2 minutes by hand	Beat ingredients together for ½ minute by hand	Oily
5 Over-mixed	Beat ingredients together for 2 minutes by hand	Beat ingredients together for 10 minutes	White, not firm
6 Electric hand mixer	Standard all in one method by hand	Beat ingredients together using an electric hand mixer	Stodgy and white
7 Low baking temperature	Middle shelf: temp. 160°C	Middle shelf: temp. 140°C	Under cooked and sloppy
8 Low baking temperature	Middle shelf: temp. 160°C	Middle shelf: temp. 220°C	Over cooked

Figure 9.2 *A table used to give details of the all in one creaming method*

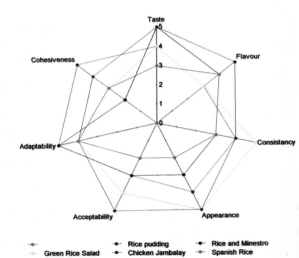

Figure 9.3 *A radar graph used to show the results of a tasting panel*

EXAMINER'S COMMENTS ON FIGURES 9.2, 9.3, 9.4

Good Points
- These are good examples of how results can be presented in a clear and concise way.
- These tables and graphs are much easier to read than hand-written work.
- They give an instant and clear picture of the results, which a written description would not do.

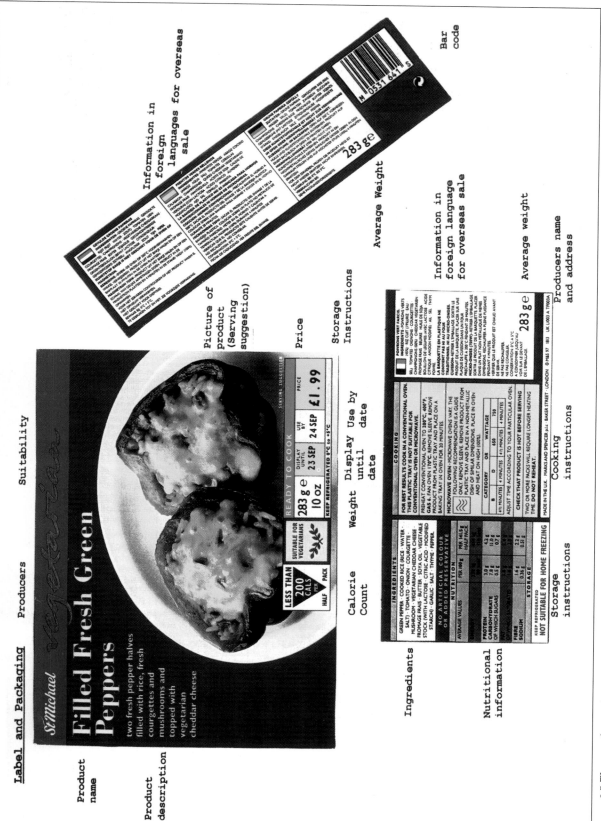

Figure 9.5 *The use of scanning*

61

ADDING PICTURES TO TEXT

Clipart

You will find pictures of food ingredients or food products within some software programs, while floppy discs or CD-ROMs also often have such pictures on them. Ask your teacher if your school has access to these resources. You might also find it useful to speak to the teachers who teach information technology. If your school does not have any of these resources, they may be willing to get them for you.

Scanned images

> **EXAMINER'S COMMENTS ON FIGURE 9.5**
>
> *Good Points*
> - By scanning the packaging the student has been able to add extra information to the image.
> - Different parts of the product's packaging have been scanned and the student has also labelled each section to provide additional information.

Digital photographs

> **EXAMINER'S COMMENTS ON FIGURE 9.6**
>
> *Good Points*
> - This student has used a digital camera to take photographs of the products she has made.
> - The product has been shot from different angles and the results reviewed before printing. These photos show all the products grouped together and also some close-up shots.
>
> *Areas for Improvement*
> - Better use might have been made of the digital camera if the student had added comments about the appearance, shape, smell, taste texture, etc. of the dishes.
> - The student could have used the camera to make comments on the effects of using ingredients which can be seen in the photographs or which are hidden in the mixtures.

Figure 9.6 *The use of digital photography*

USING CAD PACKAGES

You can use CAD packages to produce **drawings** or to use **images** in an interesting way in:

- spider diagrams
- product profiles
- packaging nets
- food labels
- design ideas.

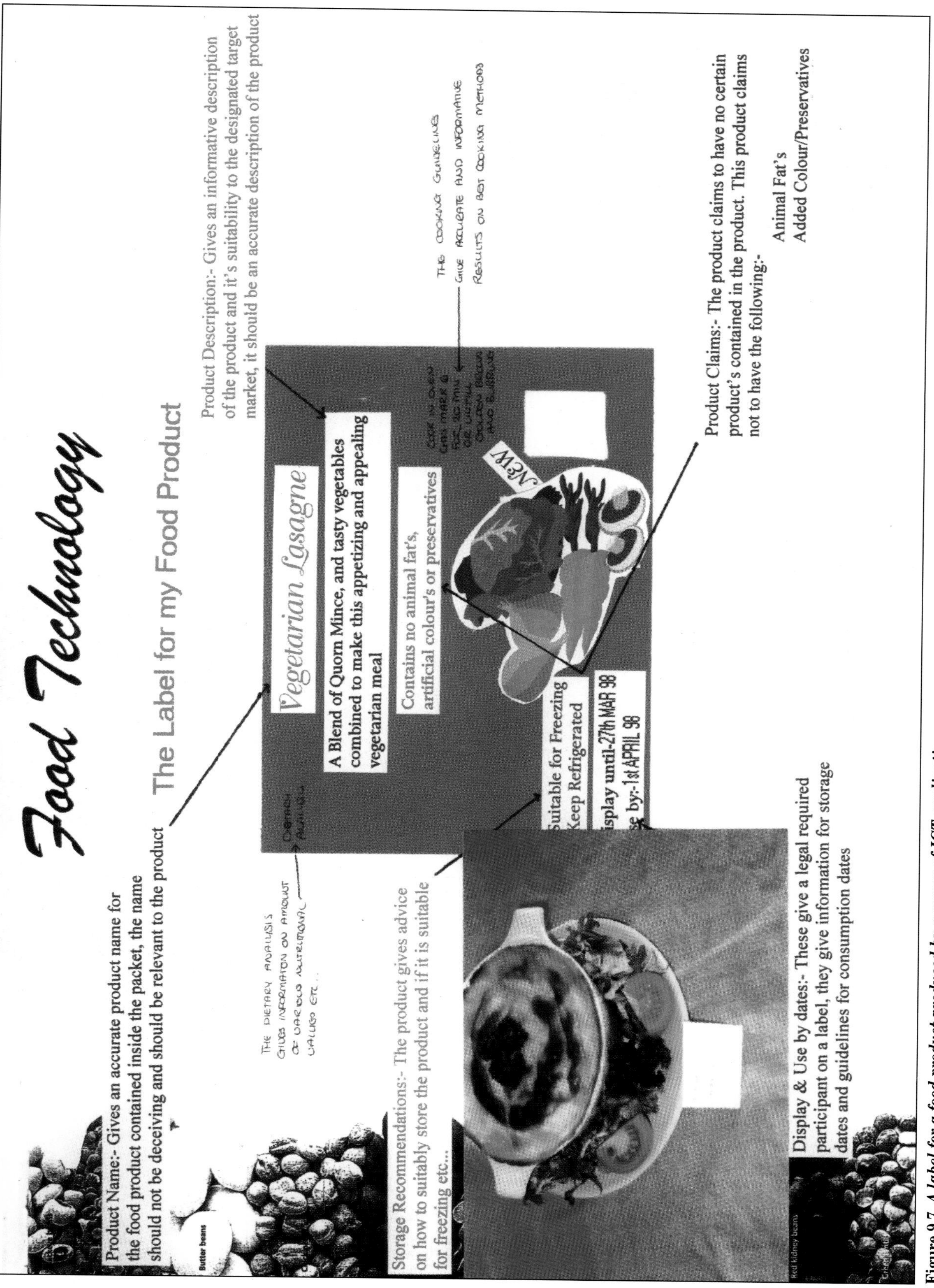

Food Technology

The Label for my Food Product

Product Name:- Gives an accurate product name for the food product contained inside the packet, the name should not be deceiving and should be relevant to the product

Product Description:- Gives an informative description of the product and it's suitability to the designated target market, it should be an accurate description of the product

Product Claims:- The product claims to have no certain product's contained in the product. This product claims not to have the following:-

Animal Fat's
Added Colour/Preservatives

Storage Recommendations:- The product gives advice on how to suitably store the product and if it is suitable for freezing etc...

Display & Use by dates:- These give a legal required participant on a label, they give information for storage dates and guidelines for consumption dates

THE DIETARY ANALYSIS GIVES INFORMATION ON AMOUNT OF CARBOHYDRATE CALORIES ETC...

THIS COOKING GUIDELINES GIVE ACCURATE AND INFORMATIVE RESULTS ON BEST COOKING METHODS

Vegetarian Lasagne

A Blend of Quorn Mince, and tasty vegetables combined to make this appetizing and appealing vegetarian meal

Contains no animal fat's, artificial colours or preservatives

COOK IN OVEN GAS MARK 6 FOR 20 MIN OR UNTIL GOLDEN BROWN AND BUBBLING

NEW

Suitable for Freezing
Keep Refrigerated

Display until-27th MAR 98
Use by:-1st APRIL 98

Butter beans

Red kidney beans

Figure 9.7 A label for a food product produced by a range of ICT applications

EXAMINER'S COMMENTS ON FIGURE 9.7

Good Points

- This student has used a mixture of Clipart, scanned images, digital photographs, word processing and desk top publishing to produce a packaging design for the final product idea. The final idea has been well developed.
- The inclusion of a label provides clear information about the design and also demonstrates that the student understands about the packaging and labelling of foods products.

DATABASES

Databases allow the production, collation and presentation of questionnaires and their results. Look at Figure 9.8 on page 65 and then read the examiner's comments of it.

EXAMINER'S COMMENTS ON FIGURE 9.8

Good Points

- This student has worked out certain clear aims before carrying out his questionnaire research and has designed the questions to allow the answers to be collated easily.
- The results, which have been collated using software, give a picture of the main points which need to be taken into account in the development of a vegetarian product.
- By using ICT, the results can be presented in different forms and reduced in size to present them on one sheet. This looks clearer and more accurate than trying to collate and present results by drawing and writing by hand and, of course, it takes less time to produce a professional-looking result.

Questionnaire

My aims with this questionnaire are to find out as many details and requirements of vegetarians as possible. I will gain information about how often they buy convenience foods and the variety. Cost is an important factor as there is no point producing a product which is too expensive for the consumer. I hope to question 10 people from different age ranges to discover their needs and to choose a specific or general age target group.

1) How old are you?   15-20
                       20-25
                       25-30
                       30+

2) How long have you been vegetarian?   1-3yrs
                                         3-6yrs
                                         6-9yrs
                                         Other

3) Why did you decide not to eat meat?   Religion
                                         Health
                                         Animal Welfare
                                         Taste
                                         Environmental
                                         Other

4) Which alternative protein do you mostly eat?   T.V.P
                                                  Quorn
                                                  Tofu
                                                  None

5) How often do you eat ready made meals?   Every day
                                            2-3 times
                                              per week
                                            Sometimes
                                            Never

6) What makes you buy a ready made product?   Convenience
                                              Interesting
                                                recipes
                                              Cost
                                              Other

7) Do you buy/Would you buy any of the following?
   Stuffed Veg.
   Pasta dishes
   Rice and pulse
      dishes
   Pastry dishes
   Dishes with TVP,
      quorn, tofu

8) How much are you prepared to pay for a ready made meal?   £1
   £1.50
   £2
   More

9) Do you find specific products for this diet expensive and easy to find?   Yes
                                                                              No

Results

How old are you?

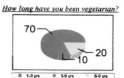
How long have you been vegetarian?

Why did you decide not to eat meat?

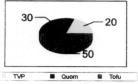
Which alternative protein do you mostly eat?

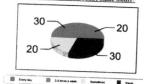
How often do you eat ready made meals?

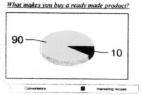
What makes you buy a ready made product?

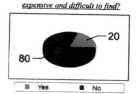
Do you find specific products for this diet expensive and difficult to find?

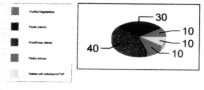
Do you buy/Would you buy any of the following products?

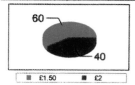
How much would you pay for a ready made meal?

Conclusions

The results from the questionnaire have allowed me to come up with the following conclusions.

Question 1
The majority of vegetarians I asked were teenagers (40%) which demonstrates the current trend of many young people following a meat free diet. The next largest age group was 20-25 which is also made up of young people. There is clearly a generational opinion between choosing to be a vegetarian. The population of those excluding meat from their diet is younger than that of those who eat it.

Question 2
The length of time which people have been vegetarian is between 1 and 3 years. This time span is very short which illustrates the idea that choosing to become a vegetarian may have been influenced by BSE scares, health warnings and food poisoning outbreaks.

Question 3
The vegetarians I asked had excluded meat from their diets for one of three reasons:- health, animal welfare or environmental issues. They considered that the treatment of animals during purposeful breeding for slaughter is inhumane and unjustifiable. medical research has shown that certain health problems could be prevented by eating less or no meat.

Question 4
The most popular alternative protein was shown to be TOFU although the others were also used.

Question 5
Although a high proportion of people buy ready made meals on a regular basis, there is still 30% which never do. This is therefore a challenge for me to design a product which will appeal to them.

Figure 9.8 *A questionnaire about vegetarianism*

USE OF THE INTERNET

The Internet can be used to:

- carry out research
- collect information, pictures, data
- visit web sites to research:
  - food manufacturers
  - recipe ideas
  - product ideas
  - information on specific diets/nutritional needs
  - information on ingredients.

MODELLING IDEAS

You can use software to carry out nutritional analysis.

Figure 9.9 *Nutritional analysis of a turkey bolognese dish*

Comparison with Dietary Reference Values

Total Energy for this list = 5084 kJ 1215 kcals

% Protein	24
% Fat	32
% Carbohydrate	44

Energy: Current dietary guidelines recommend that a MAXIMUM of 35% of Energy is supplied by fat.

Comparison of your list with the DRVs for a man aged 19–50 years old

		Your Diet	EAR	% of EAR
Energy	(kJ)	5085	10600	48
	(kcals)	1215	2550	48

		Your Diet	RNI	% of RNI
Protein	(g)	72.7	55.5	131
Fibre (NSP)	(g)	7.21	(adults approx. 18 grams/day)	
Sodium (Na)	(mg)	1151	1600	72
Calcium (Ca)	(mg)	990	700	141
Iron (Fe)	(mg)	5.11	8.70	59
Vitamin A	(ug)	1027	700	147
Vitamin B1	(mg)	0.63	1.00	63
Vitamin B2	(mg)	1.06	1.30	81
Niacin	(mg)	21.0	17.0	123
Vitamin C	(mg)	147	40.0	367
Vitamin D	(ug)	6.45	No RNI data for this group	

DRV = Dietary Reference Values. EAR Estimated Average Requirement. RNI = Reference Nutrient Intake. NSP = Non-starch polysaccharides.

ou can use spreadsheets for costing and scaling up quantities for production.

Ingredients	1 tray	10 trays	50 trays	100 trays	500 trays	1000 trays
Cooking Chocolate	0.15 kg	1.5 kg	7.5 kg	15 kg	75 kg	150 kg
Caster Sugar	0.1 kg	1 kg	5 kg	10 kg	50 kg	100 kg
Egg	£1.00	£10.00	£50.00	£100.00	£500.00	£1,000.00
Margarine	0.05 kg	0.5 kg	2.5 kg	5 kg	25 kg	50 kg
Dessicated Coconut	0.1 kg	1 kg	5 kg	10 kg	50 kg	100 kg
Self-raising Flour	0.005 kg	0.05 kg	0.25 kg	0.5 kg	2.5 kg	5 kg
Ground Almonds	0.025 kg	0.25 kg	1.25 kg	2.5 kg	12.5 kg	25 kg
Glacé Cherries	0.075 kg	0.75 kg	3.75 kg	7.5 kg	37.5 kg	75 kg

Ingredients	1 tray	10 trays	50 trays	100 trays	500 trays	1000 trays
Cooking Chocolate	£0.74	£7.40	£37.00	£74.00	£370.00	£740.00
Caster Sugar	£0.11	£1.10	£5.50	£11.00	£55.00	£110.00
Egg	£0.08	£0.80	£4.00	£8.00	£40.00	£80.00
Margarine	£0.06	£0.60	£3.00	£6.00	£30.00	£60.00
Coconut	£0.67	£6.70	£33.50	£67.00	£335.00	£670.00
Flour	£0.02	£0.20	£1.00	£2.00	£10.00	£20.00
Ground Almonds	£0.28	£2.80	£14.00	£28.00	£140.00	£280.00
Glacé Cherries	£0.33	£3.30	£16.50	£33.00	£165.00	£330.00
Total	£2.29	£22.90	£114.50	£229.00	£1,145.00	£2,229.00

able 9.1 *Costing and scaling up quantities*

CONTROL

Software can be used to model process flow charts and HACCP procedures which show critical control points and give feedback on the production process.

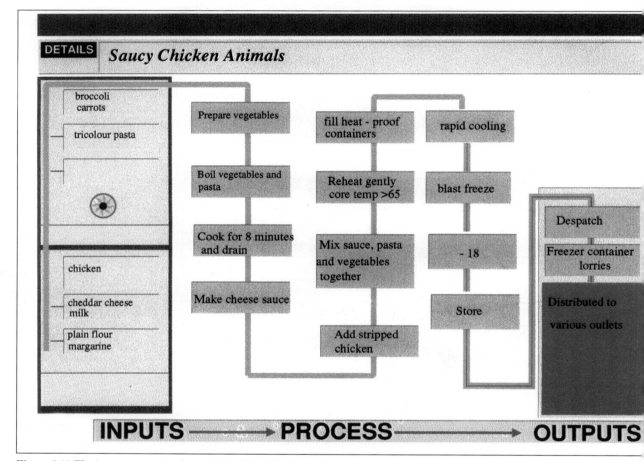

DETAILS *Saucy Chicken Animals*

INPUTS ──────▶ PROCESS ──────▶ OUTPUTS

Figure 9.10 *The input, process and output for Saucy Chicken Animals*

EXAMINER'S COMMENTS ON FIGURE 9.10

Good Points

- This student has used software to produce a flow diagram which identifies a process, the various stages in the process and the points in the process where specific checks need to be made.
- These checks might be related to quality, time or temperature but are all essential to the safe production of a product.
- In industry this process would also be used to pre-plan the production procedure of all products, identifying where and when hazards could occur and how these could be eliminated.
- By using this type of software this student has produced a clear production plan which is of good quality.
- The use of software programs saves time. The programs also give prompts as they are used which make sure that the users will not omit critical points in the process.

HOW DOES THE FOOD INDUSTRY USE ICT SUCH CAD AND CAM?

If your product prototype were to be mass produced, which parts of the production process could be controlled by computer? Look back at Chapter 7 on Systems and Control (page 44) for ideas

Check yourself

QUESTIONS

Q1 Look back through all the work you have presented in your design folder and list the different aspects of ICT which you have used.

Q2 Does your list use a range of different applications or is the use of ICT always the same?

Q3 Does ICT really improve your work? In what ways?

Q4 Could you add any other ICT to your design work?

Q5 Where might commercial food manufacturers use ICT?

Q6 How could ICT be used to make a quality product?

TUTORIALS

T1 Use of ICT has to be planned. As you plan each design sheet or activity, think about how you might use ICT. Before you finally present the work for each section of your project, check that there are no lost opportunities for using ICT.

T2 Remember that when you use ICT, in addition to improving the appearance of your work, it should have a real purpose. You may decide that all your work will look better if it is computer generated rather than being hand written. This is fine providing that you have time to produce the work and also access to a computer whenever you need it. A project which contains hand-written work but which also includes specific aspects of ICT which were used because they are the most suitable way of presenting information, applying a particular technique or simulating an industrial process, will get just as much credit and often more credit than a project which is all computer generated but only uses a limited range of ICT applications, most of which are for presentation purposes only.

T3 Look critically at all the ICT work you have included in your design folder. You should be quite convinced that your use of ICT has been the best way of dealing with each particular aspect of the work you have produced.

T4 Look at the list of ways in which you can include ICT in your work. Examine all the design sheets which you have produced and identify any gaps where you could have added any ICT applications to improve your work?

T5&T6 Look at the sections of your folder work which relate to industrial practice, systems and control, and manufacturing. Have you included ICT work which reflects these processes, for example CAM applications, HACCP simulations and flow diagrams with control points?

CHAPTER 10

MAKING SKILLS

HOW IMPORTANT ARE MAKING SKILLS?

While you are carrying out your coursework project you will be assessed on designing and making.

In the majority of syllabuses these two topics are given equal importance but in some syllabuses 'making' is given more importance and can be worth twice as much as 'designing'. You will see from this, therefore, that making is a very important part of your project work.

Many students spend a lot of time producing their design folder and work hard on the designing parts of their project work, often at the expense of the making work. You need to show a wide range of making skills in your project work and you also need to show that you have spent a good proportion of your project time on making. If you make only one food product and use only one or two hours of project time to do this, it would be an insufficient use of your time and would not balance the time spent on making in other materials in your Design and Technology work. You must remember that a making grade is awarded on the basis of the amount of time spent, the quality of the result produced, the knowledge displayed and the demand, in terms of skill, of the making tasks which have been undertaken.

WHAT IS 'MAKING' IN FOOD TECHNOLOGY?

Making refers to practical activities which you use to provide information, results and outcomes as part of the process of the development of a food product. You can carry out making at various stages in the design process. If you look back at Chapter 1, on Research (page 2), Chapter 3 on Design Ideas (page 13), and Chapter 5 on Development (page 26), you will see that many examples of making are given.

The following list includes examples of making activities:

- evaluating existing products
- comparing products
- sensory analysis
- preparation skills
- cookery skills
- changing ingredients
- altering methods or processes
- using alternative ingredients or substitutes
- mixing
- moulding
- forming
- rolling
- shaping
- manipulative skills
- organisational skills
- using equipment, both hand-held and large electrical equipment
- controlling temperature
- adapting recipes
- applying finishing techniques.

Figure 10.1 *Equipment can be used in making*

PROVIDING EVIDENCE OF MAKING IN YOUR PROJECT WORK

You need to think of different ways in which you can provide evidence of your making/practical work other than just by making a complete product. On the other hand, you must remember that it is not just the quantity of your making which you should show but also the quality.

PHOTOGRAPHS

These are only useful if the quality and detail of the product or experiment result can be seen clearly.

Photographs of the process can be very informative, e.g. rolled out pastry, chopped vegetables, sauce in a pan, dough being shaped, scones cut out on a baking tray, cream being piped, etc. They can show the examiner the skills which you used and the quality of the work you did. For example, if you show a pastry dough rolled to a regular shape and to an even thickness, this shows that the pastry was well made, of a good consistency and that you could control the rolling out process in terms of keeping both the shape and also the thickness regular.

A digital camera can be very useful. You can view the picture before printing and this is a very appropriate use of ICT.

Figure 10.2 *Mixers can save a lot of time*

ACTUAL RECIPES

Including dozens of recipes and methods is unnecessary and very time consuming. A recipe on its own is not evidence that you have actually made the product.

It is much more sensible to refer to a recipe when you are testing a finished product particularly where you are suggesting improvements, either by using different ingredients or commenting on sensory characteristics. This shows that you have actually made the product.

SENSORY EVALUATION

Charts, star diagrams and comments which inform the examiner about specific products are all evidence of making. (See also Chapter 6 on evaluation, page 34, and Chapter 30 on Sensory Analysis, page 214.)

Figure 10.3 *A photograph can show evidence of 'making'*

RESULTS AND CONCLUSIONS FROM EXPERIMENTS

You need to make conclusions from experiments in order to make decisions about ingredients, methods and processes. However, the way you carry out the experiment and the control and procedures which you use are also important evidence for the examiner to assess. This will be proof of your making skills. You should give the aim of the experiment, a brief description of the method used, the results obtained and how you have used these to draw conclusions. All of this information should be concise and on the same page. (See also Chapter 5 on Development, page 26, and Chapter 9 on Information Technology, page 58.)

EVALUATIONS OF YOUR OWN AND EXISTING PRODUCTS

Any activities which relate to the evaluation of products can be counted as making provided that they involve sensory testing and some preparation and cooking skills. You might have the chance to compare products, e.g. to compare a ready made product with your own version.

PLANNING YOUR MAKING ACTIVITIES

You will be assessed on your ability to plan your making activities. Time management is a very important part of this. You will need to think and plan carefully both for individual practical lessons and for the overall project. There is no need to include a time plan for every practical that you carry out. In fact, this would be a poor use of project time and would reduce the time left for other, more important aspects of your designing and making work. Students often produce a plan *after* they have carried out a making activity but this gets no credit. You need to make a plan *in advance* and then, after completing the making activity, comment on the plan's use and accuracy, adding where and why changes were necessary. Your evidence of good planning could take the following forms:

- a time plan which includes accurate procedures, the dovetailing of tasks and an evaluation. One or two of these are quite sufficient for an examiner to see the process which you have used.

- the breakdown of a product into different parts and suggestions as to how you will make and combine each part. This would be very useful for managing your time in short lessons and for producing a sequence of tasks within the development of a product.

- a flow diagram for a complete product, showing where and how control would be applied. It is likely that this will be appropriate at a later stage of development.

You need to include some specific comments about where and why you are including making skills in your project. You could, for example, add these before evaluating a product, or after carrying out an investigation. Remember that you need to show the examiner what you are thinking and why you are carrying out the various making tasks in your project.

Check yourself

QUESTIONS

Q1 As you work through your project and begin to look at the different sections of the design process, are there opportunities for making?

Q2 Have you considered looking at existing products and carrying out comparisons as part of your research?

Q3 Can you include some making when you are thinking about design ideas?

Q4 Does your project include experiments and investigations?

Q5 Have you modified existing recipes by changing and substituting ingredients, shapes and sizes.

Q6 Where will an examiner find evidence of your making work?

TUTORIALS

T1 The sections of your project work where there is likely to be some opportunity for making are research, design ideas and development. When you are planning these sections of work always remember that you can include making activities.

T2 One practice which is used in the food industry is to look at products which already exist within the product range which is being considered. If you include this type of activity in your project work, provided that it involves sensory testing it can be used as evidence of making. It may be that you will need to carry out some preparation and/or cooking of an existing product as part of the testing process.

T3 Look back at Chapter 3 on Design Ideas (page 13) and consider ways in which you can adapt existing recipes and products by adding or changing ingredients and methods. To make decisions based on the effects of these changes it would be necessary to make products and then evaluate them.

T4 You must remember that it is not always necessary to make the whole product and that parts of your chosen idea can be developed. Small quantities of ingredients can be used to set up an experiment or an investigation. This would all be classed as making.

T5 As a result of experiments, investigations and sensory testing, it may be necessary to change ingredients. Also, after making a product you will need to consider if the shape and size of the product are appropriate. Much time and money is spent on this in the food industry in order to provide a product which is cost effective, meets nutritional requirements, looks attractive and is something entirely new. It may be that a new shape would be the critical selling point for a new food product, or that size is an essential factor if producing a product for a child.

T6 There are two main ways of providing evidence of making:

- work which you have recorded in your folder
- information which your teacher will give to an examiner about your work, in particular the way in which you have carried out making activities.

Do not spend unnecessary time writing out time plans, recipes and methods. These do not provide evidence that you have actually made something. However, results from tests, experiments, investigations and sensory evaluations give clear evidence of what you have done. Photographs are another good source of evidence but will only show the quality of your work if they are good. Food photography is difficult. You need to use good background colours, close up shots and different angles. A digital camera is an excellent tool because you can view the photo before printing it.

SECTION II

Knowledge and Understanding

CHAPTER 11

FOOD COMMODITIES

WHAT ARE FOOD COMMODITIES?

Today a vast range of food products are made from a small number of raw foods. These are processed in many different ways to produce products that meet the needs and preferences of consumers everywhere.

For the food products that you have designed and made you will have used both raw foods, e.g. fruit and vegetables, and processed foods, e.g. flour and sugar. Foods can be classified into two main groups:

- **primary source** – raw food materials, e.g. milk, fruit, vegetables, wheat grain, sugar beet
- **secondary source** – processed food materials, e.g. butter, jam, flour, sugar.

The changes made to raw foods to make them more edible are known as **food processing**. Food processing involves changes to raw materials which improve:

- appearance
- texture
- palatability
- nutritive value
- ease of preparation
- keeping properties.

Food processing is classified into two main areas:

- **primary processing**
- **secondary processing**.

Figure 11.1 *Primary source foods*

Figure 11.2 *Secondary source foods*

PRIMARY PROCESSING

This involves changing or converting the raw food materials into:

- foods that can be eaten immediately
- ingredients that can be used to produce other food products.

It could involve processes such as:

- washing salad vegetables, e.g. spring onions, radishes
- sorting, shelling, peeling vegetables, e.g. potatoes, peas
- squeezing fruit, e.g. fruit juice
- chopping, slicing, cutting, e.g. meat, poultry.

Or it could involve more complex processes such as:

- heat treatment, e.g. pasteurisation of milk
- milling, rolling, sieving, e.g. cereals such as wheat, corn, rye
- refining, e.g. sugar beet and sugar cane
- extraction and refining, e.g. vegetable oils.

SECONDARY PROCESSING

This involves changing or converting the primary processed foods into other food products. It may involve combining one or more food ingredients, e.g:

- flour, sugar, butter, eggs to make cakes
- wheat-durum semolina, water, and sometimes eggs, to make pasta.

Many different techniques and processes can be used during secondary processing, e.g:

- mixing, kneading and proving in bread manufacture
- boiling and crystallisation in sweet manufacture
- aeration and drying in the manufacture of meringue
- mixing and extrusion in the manufacture of pasta.

Figure 11.3 *Pasta being made in a factory*

Foods are processed from a primary to a secondary source and then into other food products. Check the chart below for a few more examples and then write out others based on the food materials you have used during your course.

Primary Source Raw Foods →	Primary Processing converted into →	Secondary Source Food Ingredients →	Secondary Processing manufactured into →	Food Products →
olives	→	olive oil	→	salad dressing
sugar cane	→	caster sugar	→	cakes
corn (maize)	→	cornflour	→	sauces
wheat	→	flour	→	pastry
milk	→	cheese	→	pizza

Table 11.1 *Using primary and secondary sources to make food products*

You will need to understand that raw foods are processed to provide a wide range of food products. During your course you will have studied at least one food commodity and you should be able to identify:

- the food processing stages, i.e. from primary source to secondary source. It is often helpful to draw a flow chart to show these stages
- the range of food products that can be obtained from a primary source food material.

Cane sugar and olives are two good examples of this.

CANE SUGAR

Figure 11.4 *Sugar crystals made from refined sugar*

Table 11.2 *Processing sugar cane*

Processing Stages
↓
raw material – **sugar cane** from tropical countries, e.g. Cuba, West Indies
or **sugar bee**t from temperate countries, e.g. Europe, USA
↓
harvested by large harvesting machines or cut by hand labour
↓
Sugar Cane
cleaned, chopped, shredded
↓
crushed between heavy rollers
↓
heated with lime to separate out all impurities
↓
filtered to remove all unwanted particles
↓
boiled in a vacuum drum to form a thick syrup
↓
crystals – **raw sugar** and syrup – **molasses**
↓
separated by spinning in a **centrifuge**
↓
brown raw sugar crystals refined to produce pure sugar crystals.

Figure 11.5 *Different types of sugar*

Refined Sugar

All white sugar is refined and there is no difference between beet and cane.

Unrefined Sugar

This is only part-purified and will contain some molasses which will affect the texture, aroma, colour and taste. All unrefined sugars comes from sugar cane. They are identified by the word 'raw' or 'unrefined' on the packet label.

The range of secondary source sugar products obtained from this primary source include: icing sugar, caster sugar, crystal sugar, cube sugar, demerara sugar, granulated sugar, golden granulated sugar, molasses, muscavado sugar, preserving sugar, soft brown sugar, golden syrup, treacle.

USING SUGAR IN OTHER FOOD PRODUCTS

Sugar has several important functions in the manufacture of food products:

- as a **sweetener** – commonly used to sweeten sweet and some savoury products, e.g. cakes, fruit juice, tomato sauce, baked beans

- as a **preservative** – it inhibits the growth of micro-organisms (bacteria, yeast and moulds), e.g. in fruit tinned or bottled in sugar syrup

  – it acts with pectin to form a gel in jams and marmalades.

- as a **stabiliser** – it helps to maintain consistency and texture, e.g. in frozen/chilled desserts

- in **aeration** – together with fat, sugar entraps air to aid the rising and aerating of cakes and yeast products

- in producing **colour** – colour comes from the type of sugar used, e.g. muscavado sugar is dark brown, while caster sugar is white –

  – colour also comes from **caramelisation**, which happens when the sugar turns brown when heated, e.g. in baked products such as cakes or sweet pastry, or in boiled sugar, e.g. in toffee and caramels

- in **thickening** – which helps to produce the correct texture in sauces and custards

- to provide **texture** – this helps to soften gluten and prevents the overdevelopment of gluten in cakes and pastries

- to retain **moisture** – sugar helps to retain moisture and delays products from drying out and becoming stale.

Figure 11.6 *Sugar is used in baking*

OLIVES

Olive oil is one of the oldest natural ingredients used as a food. The main areas of cultivation are in Spain, Italy, Greece, Portugal, France, Turkey, Morocco and Tunisia, which together produce 95% of the world's olive harvest. There are several different kinds of olives. Black olives contain most oil.

Figure 11.7 *Harvesting olives in Italy*

Table 11.3 *Processing stages in making olive oil*

Harvesting is a labour-intensive process in which the olives are 'combed' onto umbrella-like nets to avoid bruising the fruit.
↓
The olives are transported to processing plants within three days to avoid oxidising and the lowering of the yield of oil.
↙   ↘

Modern Extraction –
↓
Washed four times
↓
Crushed into a paste using stainless steel cutters
↓
Resulting oil, water and solids mixed in large stainless steel chamber – heated to 30°C
↓
Oil extracted by spinning in a centrifuge
↓
Oil separated from the water and solids
↓
Oil filtered, tested, graded, and bottled for sale

Traditional Extraction – known as 'cold pressing'
↓
Olives are washed once
↓
Crushed to a pulp by stone mills
↓
Pulp spread over synthetic mats which are stacked on top of each other under a hydraulic press
↓
Pressure slowly builds up, squeezing the oil out
↓
Oil separated out from water by spinning in a centrifuge

A range of secondary source oil products are obtained from the primary source, e.g. olive oil in a wide range of flavours, aromas and colours, such as extra virgin olive oil, virgin olive oil, olive oil.

Figure 11.8 (left) *Olive oil being processed in an oil press*

Figure 11.9 (right) *Different types of olive oil*

USING OLIVE OIL IN OTHER FOOD PRODUCTS

Olive oil has several important functions in the manufacture of many food products:

- to add flavour – each variety of olive oil has a distinct characteristic with sensory descriptors such as 'floral', 'nutty', 'hot and peppery', 'grassy'
- it is used to add flavour by pouring/trickling over salad vegetables, potatoes or pasta
- it is used in marinades made from a mixture of olive oil/lemon juice/herbs, etc. to tenderise or add flavour to meat or fish
- olive oil is stable at high temperatures and is therefore a good frying medium e.g. for sauté potatoes or stir fry vegetables
- it adds moisture and flavour when used in cakes, bread and pastry
- it is used in emulsions, e.g. as a mixture of olive oil/wine vinegar/pepper/salt/garlic/mustard to form a vinaigrette dressing for salads. Also used to stabilise emulsions, e.g. mayonnaise
- it has a natural resistance to rancidity and will keep unrefrigerated for at least 18 months
- it is a good source of low saturated fats.

Figure 11.10 *Stir fry vegetables*

PRODUCT DIVERSITY

Many products can be developed from a single food commodity such as wheat, maize, sugar cane or milk. Think of all the products that are made from wheat. In the past approximately 13 staple plant foods were used to feed the world's population. These were wheat, corn, rice, potatoes, rye, oats, cassava, sweet potatoes, millet, yams, plantain, teff and taro. Today approximately 50 staple cereals, oilseeds and legumes are used to produce over 20,000 products. Table 11.4 shows the range of products, which are processed from raw milk.

Table 11.4 *Milk products (from cows, sheep and goats)*

Heat-treated milk	Milk products	Butter	Cream	Cheese	Yogurt
pasteurised ultra heat treated (UHT) sterilised	skimmed semi-skimmed homogenised dried evaporated condensed	salted unsalted clarified buttermilk	single whipping double clotted creme fraiche soured	soft – no rind, e.g. cottage; ripened, soft, e.g. brie; semi-hard, e.g. stilton; hard cheese, e.g. cheddar; very hard, e.g Parmesan	set stirred flavoured or natural Greek style

Figure 11.11 *Milk products*

KEY WORDS

These are the key words. Tick them if you think you know what they mean. Otherwise check on them.

appearance	**combining**	**commodity**
complex	**conversion**	**edible**
extraction	**harvesting**	**manufacturing**
nutritive value	**palatability**	**primary processing**
primary source	**product diversity**	**raw material**
secondary processing	**secondary source**	**simple**
texture		

Check yourself

QUESTIONS

Q1 An important primary source food material is wheat grain. It is milled to produce flour. Briefly describe the two main types of flour which are produced during the primary processing stages.

Q2 White flour is a popular secondary source material. It is used to make many different baked food products. List three types of white flour and give examples of food products they could be used to make.

Q3 Sugar is used in many food products. You will associate sugar with familiar products such as cakes, biscuits, meringues, etc. However, sugar is also added to some food products that you may not immediately think of. Look at the following lists of ingredients.

1 Which food products do you think are made from each list of ingredients?
2 What is the function of the sugar in each of these products?

> **Beans, Tomatoes, Water, Sugar, Salt, Modified Cornflour, Spiriy Vinegar, Spice Extracts, Herb Extract**

> Sugar, Water, Vinegar, Apples, Orange juice (made from concentrate), Apricots, Dried apricots, Modified Cornflour, Dried onions, Mango chutney, Dried onions, Red pepper, Stem ginger, Gherkins, Turmeric, Orange peel, Spice extract, Sultanas, Salt, Carrots, Dates

Figure 11.12

REMEMBER! Cover the answers if you want to.

ANSWERS

A1 Two main groups of flour are:

- wholemeal flour
  - all the grain is milled, giving a 100% extraction rate
  - contains fibre in its bran content so it has a high NSP (non-starch polysaccharide) content
  - is brown in colour with a nutty flavour.
- white flour
  - the bran and germ, i.e. 30% of the wheat grain, are not milled, giving a 70% extraction rate.
  - contains less fibre so it has a lower NSP (non-starch polysaccharide) content
  - is whitish in colour.

TUTORIALS

T1 *Steel rollers are used in modern roller milling and two types of flour result from the primary processing stages carried out during the roller milling of wheat grains. To produce white flour an extra stage is needed to separate the bran and germ part of the grain from the endosperm which is then milled. There is also a traditional method of milling wheat. This is called stonegrinding. It involves grinding the grains between two rotating heavy circular stones to produce stoneground flour.*

ANSWERS

A2

Your answer could include:

● Strong white flour – this has a high gluten content which helps to create high volume, open-textured products, e.g. white bread, Yorkshire pudding.

● Plain white flour – often called all-purpose flour. It contains less gluten and is used for shortcrust pastry, biscuits, and for thickening sauces and gravies.

● Self-raising flour – this has a chemical raising agent evenly mixed into it, e.g. baking powder. It is used to create an aerated texture in cakes, scones, etc.

● Soft cake flour – this has a chemical raising agent evenly mixed into it and it is made from wheat with a lower protein content. Additional sieving in the processing produces a fine soft flour used for sponge cakes.

A3

● Ingredient list 1 is for tinned baked beans in tomato sauce.
Function: The sugar is added to sweeten the sauce and counter the sharp (acidic) taste of the vinegar.

● Ingredient list 2 is for a jar of fruit chutney.
The sugar is a main ingredient. Note the position of sugar in the list. Refer to Chapter 28 which explains that ingredients are listed in descending order of weight.
Function: The sugar has several functions in the chutney:
– as a preservative to inhibit growth of micro-organisms
– as sweetener to sweeten the fruit (apples) and to balance the sharp taste of the vinegar
– as colour – brown sugar is often used in chutney to add flavour and colour.

TUTORIALS

T2

Gluten is a protein found in wheat flour. It is not present in other cereals, e.g. maize, barley, oats. Gluten is formed from two proteins – glutenin and gliadin. When mixed with water they give the dough an elastic stretchy working characteristic. The mixing and kneading process in bread-making strengthens the gluten. The dough has the capacity to stretch and hold the carbon dioxide produced by the raising agent. Salt also strengthens gluten. It coagulates when baked in a high temperature (e.g. when bread is baked at 220°C) to form a high volume open texture.

Other products such as cakes, rubbed-in pastry such as shortcrust, and some biscuit mixtures do not require this stretchy elastic property. A flour which contains less gluten is needed to provide a short crumbly texture, e.g. shortcrust pastry or shortbread, or a soft fine risen texture, e.g. sponge cakes.

Many products can be developed from a single food commodity. This produces product diversity. Many products are made from processing maize. Can you think of other single food commodities that are processed to make several more food products for us to use?

T3

Figure 11.13

Beans, Tomatoes, Water, Sugar, Salt, Modified Cornflour, Spiriy Vinegar, Spice Extracts, Herb Extract

Sugar, Water, Vinegar, Apples, Orange juice (made from concentrate), Apricots, Dried apricots, Modified Cornflour, Dried onions, Mango chutney, Dried onions, Red pepper, Stem ginger, Gherkins, Turmeric, Orange peel, Spice extract, Sultanas, Salt, Carrots, Dates

This is another example of how a single food commodity is used to manufacture products which meet the needs and preferences of consumers. In response to the National Guidelines on Dietary Targets some people try to eat less sugar. As well as cutting out familiar sugary foods such as sweets, cakes, biscuits and sugar added to hot drinks or sprinkled on breakfast cereals, it is necessary to reduce the intake of 'hidden' sugars, i.e. those foods which are not usually linked to sugar, e.g. baked beans, tomato sauce.

HOW DO FOOD MATERIALS DIFFER?

During your course you will have used a wide range of food materials to design and make food products. You need to know and understand the working characteristics of the main food materials and what happens when these are combined by different processing methods.

EGGS

Eggs are one of the most useful and versatile food ingredients. They can be used to:

- make a range of egg meals, e.g. scrambled, poached, boiled, omelette
- incorporate their working characteristics in a wide range of food products, e.g. cakes, biscuits, sauces, cold desserts, savoury pastry products.

Figure 12.1 *Eggs are a versatile food ingredient*

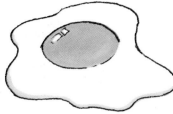

Composition

Eggs have two main parts – the white and the yolk.

Nutritional Components

- protein with a high biological value
- vitamins A, D + B$_2$
- fat and iron in the egg yolk.

Working Characteristics

Egg proteins have three main properties:

1 Egg protein coagulates when heated and this is used for:

- setting into a firm structure, i.e. liquid to a solid, e.g. scrambled, poached, boiled eggs or baked meringue
- binding – holding dry ingredients together, e.g. burgers, croquettes
- coating/enrobing – holding dry coatings such as breadcrumbs onto a surface and forming a barrier during cooking processes, e.g. fried breaded fish
- thickening – setting a liquid (one medium egg will set 125 ml liquid for egg custard, savoury flan, etc.)
- enriching – thickening a sauce and also adding colour and improving the nutritional profile
- glazing – beaten egg or egg and milk brushed over baked savoury products. As the egg coagulates the surface bakes to a shiny golden brown.

The temperature range for coagulation of egg proteins is:

- egg white 62°C to 70°C
- egg yolk 65°C to 70°C.

2 Egg proteins stretch when beaten and hold air in the structure.

- Whisking air into liquid egg white or whole egg creates a foam. Whole egg foam is used in sponge cakes and egg white foam is used to make meringues which, when baked, change to a solid foam. (See Chapter 13 page 97.)

3 Egg yolk proteins are good emulsifying agents.

- Egg yolk contains lecithin, which is an emulsifying agent. Lecithin stabilises emulsions of oil and water, e.g. in mayonnaise. (See Chapter 13 page 95.)

Figure 12.2 *Milk is made into a variety of products*

MILK

Milk is widely available. It is processed to form several milk products. Cows' milk is the main source, with milk from sheep and goats also used for some products. Milk forms the basis of butter, cheese, cream, yogurt and ice cream.

Composition

Milk is an emulsion of two liquids, e.g. oil in water. This is visible when the liquids separate and the cream collects (as fat droplets) at the top of a bottle of milk.

Nutritional Components

- protein of high biological value
- fat – whole milk 3%, semi-skimmed 1.6%, skimmed 0.1%, Channel Island 5.1%.
- sugar in the form of lactose
- vitamins A and D; a little vitamin B_1, B_2 and C
- calcium and phosphorus

Milk provides ideal conditions for the growth of micro-organisms. Most milk sold in the UK is heat treated to destroy harmful bacteria and improve its keeping quality. The main methods of heat treatment include:

- ultra-heat treatment, sterilisation, pasteurised milk, all sold in bottles and cartons
- condensed and evaporated milk, both sold in cans.

To find out more about the effect of heat on milk, see Chapter 25, page 180.

Working Characteristics

- Milk is used to give flavour, colour and consistency to sauces, soups, batters, etc.
- In some food products milk binds ingredients together.
- It contains the proteins lactalbumin and lactoglobulin which coagulate when milk is heated. Together they form a skin on the top of boiled milk, custards, sauces and milk puddings. Stirring the milk or milk mixture helps to break up the mass of coagulated proteins.
- To prevent a cream line forming, pasteurised milk can be processed through fine sieves which break the fat globules into very fine droplets which are then dispersed throughout the milk. This is known as **homogenisation**.

BUTTER

Butter is a water in oil emulsion made from churned cream. It is a solid, firm fat, sold salted or unsalted. It is used for:

- flavouring – in sauces, desserts, cakes and biscuits etc.
- shortening – it combines with flour to prevent gluten forming so that a short crumbly texture is obtained in shortcrust pastry, shortbread biscuits, etc.
- aeration – when butter is creamed with sugar, air is incorporated to form an air in fat foam. When heated the air acts as a raising agent in creamed cakes and biscuits
- extending shelf life by holding moisture in cakes, scones, etc.
- cooking – used to shallow fry and add flavour, e.g. omelettes.

Figure 12.3 *Different kinds of butter*

CHEESE

There are many different types of cheese, all made by different methods of production and with different types of milk. The main method of cheese production is when a lactic acid starter is added to pasteurised milk. An enzyme rennet is then added to clot the milk and form curds (solids) and whey (liquids). Different moulding and ripening periods then produce a wide range of cheeses. e.g:

- firm cheeses such as Cheddar, Cheshire, Parmesan, mozzarella, feta, Danish blue, stilton
- ripened soft cheeses such as brie, camembert
- other types of cheese, including cream cheese, curd cheese, cottage cheese, Quark.

Nutritional Components

This varies with the type of cheese. Firm cheese contains protein, fat, water, vitamins A and D and calcium. Other cheeses may have a different profile. For example, cottage cheese is low in fat; cream cheese is high in fat.

Working Characteristics

- Cheese is used to add flavour, texture and colour to sauces, savoury fillings and cold desserts.
- When heated cheese melts, so it is often grated to mix thoroughly with other ingredients. If it is overheated the protein coagulates and squeezes out the fat and water. This is known as **syneresis**. At this stage the cheese can become tough and rubbery.

Figure 12.4 *Different kinds of cheese*

CREAM

Cream is made from the fat content of milk. It is an oil in water emulsion. Cream is available in several forms, e.g. double cream 48% fat; whipping cream 35% fat; single cream; creme fraiche; fromage frais; soured cream.

Working Characteristics

Cream is used to:

- give flavour, texture and volume to both sweet and savoury products, e.g. chilled desserts, soups, sauces

Figure 12.5 *Different kinds of cream*

- decorate sweet products, e.g. cakes or cold desserts, and to garnish starters and soups
- some cream with a high fat content, e.g. double and whipping cream, can be whisked to incorporate air and form a foam. The stable structure of whipped cream is used to decorate cold desserts and to add volume to mixtures such as chocolate mousse.

YOGURT

Figure 12.6 *Different kinds of yogurt*

Yogurt is made from either cows' or ewes' milk. A culture of lactic acid bacteria is added to whole milk, semi-skimmed or skimmed milk. The proteins coagulate between 37°C to 44°C to set the yogurt. It is then cooled and stored below 5°C.

Working Characteristics

The yogurt can be sold as natural yogurt with no flavouring added. The texture will vary according to the milk used and whether it is set yogurt or stirred yogurt. Yogurt may be flavoured by adding syrup or pieces of fruit or nuts to make whole or real fruit yogurt.

Yogurt can be used as:

- a food product to eat for breakfast, a cold dessert or as an accompaniment to puddings and fresh fruit
- an ingredient in cold desserts or an alternative to cream, e.g. in cheesecake
- a thickening agent in sauces, soups, salad dressing and dips
- an ingredient to add creamy and acidic flavour and texture, e.g. to casseroles, soups.

MEAT

Figure 12.7 *Raw meat and poultry*

Meat and poultry are the muscle tissue of animals and birds. They can be cooked in many ways and used in a wide range of fresh, frozen, cook-chilled and part-prepared food products.

- **animal meats:** beef, lamb, pork, veal, venison
- **poultry meat:** chicken, duck, turkey, goose, ostrich
- **offal:** (internal organs) heart, liver, kidney, ox-tail, tongue

Composition

The muscle tissue is made up of long thin muscle fibres. The fibres are held together in bundles by connective tissue. There are two types of connective tissue:

- collagen which holds the bundles of muscle fibres together. It is a soluble protein and dissolves to gelatine when heated
- elastin which binds the muscle together or to a bone. It is tougher than collagen, insoluble and slightly yellow in colour. It provides elasticity and strength.

Nutritional Components

- protein of high biological value
- fat according to type and cut
- iron
- vitamins B, thiamin B_2 riboflavin

Working Characteristics

Meat is used to make many food products that reflect British or worldwide cuisine. It is made appetising and palatable by preparation and cooking techniques which influence the:

- colour – myoglobin is the colour pigment which causes the colour of raw meat to be red or purplish. When meat is cooked to above 65°C the colour changes from red to brown.

- texture – proteins in the muscle fibres coagulate and the texture of the meat becomes firmer. Overcooking by dry heat methods can make the meat hard and tough.

- moisture – as the muscle fibres become firm and shrink slightly, meat juices are squeezed out. This adds flavour to cooking liquids and gravy.

- flavour and smell – during cooking the fat melts and helps to add moisture and flavour. Some juices evaporate and leave a coating on grilled, fried and roasted meat, Distinct aromas are created which stimulate digestive juices.

- tenderness – cooking makes meat more tender and digestible. Ways to tenderise meat include:

  - cutting or mincing long muscle fibre meat, e.g. beef stewing steak

  - beating with a meat hammer to separate the fibres

  - scoring across the fibres with a knife

  - marinating in acid-based liquids, e.g. vinegar, lemon juice, to soften the collagen

  - sprinkling with commercial chemical tenderisers which contain enzymes to break down the proteins in the connective tissue

  - using long slow moist cooking methods, e.g. 75°C to 100°C. The collagen is softened in the cooking liquid and converts to gelatine which is soluble.

FISH

Fish can be bought fresh, frozen, canned, smoked or dried. It is caught in the sea or bred on fish farms, e.g. salmon and trout. There are many varieties of fish:

- **white fish:** halibut, haddock, cod, plaice, whiting, coley
- **oily fish:** salmon, trout, herrings, tuna, sardines, pilchards
- **shellfish:** lobster, prawns, shrimps, cockles, mussels, oysters.

Composition

The muscle flesh of fish is made up of bundles of short muscle fibres held together by the connective tissue collagen. Collagen is soluble and, during cooking, converts to gelatine. There is no elastin in fish. Most fish cooks, flakes and tenderises in a short period of time. Overcooking causes the short muscle fibres to fall apart.

Figure 12.8 *Raw fish and shellfish*

Nutritional Components

- protein of high biological value
- calcium and phosphorus
- vitamins A and D in the flesh of oily fish.

Working Characteristics

Fish is used to make many food products. It is made appetising by preservation, preparation and cooking techniques that influence:

- colour – there is very little change in the colour of fish as it cooks
- texture – proteins in the muscle fibre coagulate and the texture of the fish becomes firmer. When cooked the flesh falls into flakes and a creamy liquid oozes out between the flakes. If overcooked, the flesh becomes dry.
- moisture – any juices squeezed out can be used in sauces
- flavour and smell – distinctive aromas develop as fish is cooked or preserved by methods such as smoking
- tenderness – fish flesh is always tender and only requires short cooking times. It can be cooked by a variety of dry or moist methods. Some fish is eaten raw, e.g. Japanese sashimi and sushi, Scandinavian gravad lax. Some preservation methods cook the fish during processing, e.g. canned salmon, tuna, sardines. Marinating fish also adds flavour and tenderises the muscle fibres, e.g. roll mop herrings served in vinegar.

Figure 12.9 *Solid fats and liquid oils*

FATS AND OILS

There are many different types of fats and oils. As a general rule, at room temperature fats are solid and oils are liquid.

Composition

- Fat and oils are formed from glycerol and fatty acids to create triglycerides. The fatty acids are either saturated or unsaturated fats and the proportions and combination produce a solid fat or liquid oil.

  Solid fats are: butter, ghee, lard, suet, margarine made from blended vegetables or fish oils, low-fat spreads and compound white fats, e.g. Trex.

  Oils are: corn oil, olive oil, sunflower oil, groundnut, and distinctive flavoured oils such as walnut. (See Chapter 11 page 80)
- Fat and oil are also visible on some foods, e.g. fat on meat and bacon. They are also present but invisible in foods such as oily fish and processed foods such as cakes, pastry, chocolate, fried foods, crisps, salad dressings.

Nutritional Components

This varies according to the type of fat or oil. For example, butter and margarine contain some saturated fatty acids and vitamins A and D. Lard contains mainly saturated fatty acids, whereas a vegetable oil contains a high proportion of unsaturated fatty acids.

Working Characteristics

There are two main functions of fats and oils in food product development. They are used as an ingredient and as a cooking medium.

1 As ingredients in food products fat and oil are used for:

- shortening – coating flour with fat to prevent gluten formation in shortcrust pastry, rubbed-in cakes. (See Chapter 17 page 131.)
- emulsions – oil forms an emulsion with liquids such as vinegar to make salad dressings and mayonnaise. (See Chapter 13 page 94.)
- aeration – fat creamed with sugar holds air. When heated this acts as a raising agent. (See Chapter 13 page 100.)
- flavouring – fats and oils have distinct flavours which improve or develop the aroma and flavour of food products, e.g. olive oil in salad dressings, butter in cakes and icing.
- plasticity – by combining fats and oils softer fats have been developed which are sold in plastic tubs, e.g. soft margarine. These are useful for all-in-one cake mixtures and spreading straight from the refrigerator
- moisture and keeping quality – fats help to keep food products moist and increase shelf life.
- sealing – sealing foods with melted fat to stop them drying out, e.g. a layer of butter on potted meat, paté, potted shrimps.

2 As a cooking medium fats and oils are used for:

- frying – the fat or oil increases in temperature, e.g. shallow frying of omelette; deep frying of doughnuts
- lubrication – to stop foods sticking to pans and baking trays
- basting – spooning fat over roast, grilled and barbecued meats to stop then drying out and to add flavour and colour

CEREALS

Cereals are cultivated grasses grown for their nutritious edible seeds known as cereal grains. Cereals can be processed from their primary source into a vast range of secondary source ingredients and food products. (See Chapter 11.) They are grown all over the world and transported, stored and used creatively in food product development.

Composition

All cereal grains have the same basic structure but the different types vary in shape, texture, size and colour. Specific uses include:

- **wheat**: several types of flour, e.g. semolina, breakfast cereals, pasta
- **maize (corn)**: cornflour, breakfast cereals, popcorn, sweetcorn, corn oil
- **oats**: rolled oats, oatmeal, breakfast cereals
- **rice**: long grain (patria, basmati rice), medium grain (arborio-risotto rice), short grain (white pudding rice).
  Sold in a variety of forms, e.g. easy cook, pre-cooked, boil-in-the-bag, ground, flaked, as breakfast cereals, instant snacks, canned rice puddings.

Figure 12.10 *Cereal growing*

Figure 12.11 *Different types of rice*

Nutritional Components

- all grains contain a high proportion (10–80%) of carbohydrate in the form of starch
- small amounts of protein, fat and water
- NSP (non-starch polysaccharide), i.e. fibre in the bran layer
- B-group vitamins thiamin, niacin, riboflavin in some cereals

Working Characteristics

Elasticity

The protein content in cereals varies. Wheat contains the highest amount of protein and this makes it a very versatile food ingredient. Two proteins, glutenin and gliadin, combine with water to form gluten. Gluten is elastic and will stretch to hold air and gas produced by raising agents. It is an essential component when creating volume in aerated food products. Strong wheat flour is 12–15% protein; weak wheat flour is 7–10% protein. No other cereal has this characteristic.

Gelatinisation

When milled into wheat flour, cornflour or rice flour cereal grains are insoluble in cold water. When heated the starch grains absorb liquid and swell and soften. Flour granules burst and will then thicken a liquid. Overcooked rice gelatinises and the grains stick together.

VEGETABLES AND FRUIT

Figure 12.12 *A variety of fruits and vegetables*

Vegetables and fruit are edible plants or parts of plants that are eaten raw or cooked. Many different types and varieties are grown worldwide and many countries import a wide range of fruits and vegetables to supplement out of season demand and to add variety to those grown locally.

Composition

- Fruit and vegetables are made up of plant cells containing water, pectin, varying amounts of starch and a cell wall of cellulose. During cooking some softening takes place as a result of absorption of water by the cellulose, starch and pectin. These changes give fruit and vegetables important characteristics which are used in food processing, e.g. gelatinisation and gelling, and also make some fruit and vegetables edible.
- Enzymic browning occurs when some fruits are cut, e.g. apples, pears, bananas. (See Chapter 24, page 167.)
- Fruit and vegetables can be preserved in many different ways.

Nutritional Components

These vary according to the plant or part of the plant used. Fruit and vegetables can contain up to 95% water. They also provide minerals, vitamins, carbohydrate, starch, sugar and protein. Many are important sources of NSP (fibre) and some are major sources of vitamin C.

Working Characteristics

Fruit and vegetables are important food commodities. They are used as:

- colour, flavour and texture, e.g:
  - raw fruit, e.g. fruit salad; decorated fruit gateau; fruit appetisers
  - raw vegetables, e.g. lettuce leaves, coleslaw (cabbage + carrot)
  - cooked fruit, e.g. stewed apples, fruit puddings; fruit sauces
  - cooked vegetables, e.g. stir fried, roasted, casseroled, boiled or microwaved
  - as accompaniments: pineapple with ham, apple sauce with pork
  - processed, e.g. canned peas, chilled potato salad, dried fruit salad, frozen chipped potatoes, crystallised fruit, tubes and cartons of tomato pureé, jars of chopped garlic.

- gels – fruit contains pectin, a gum-like substance which is released from the cells of the fruit during cooking. When mixed with acid and sugar, the pectin helps to set mixtures and forms a gel, e.g. in jams, jellies and marmalades. (See Chapter 13, page 98.)

PULSES

- Pulses are the ripened and dried seeds of legumes (pod plants). There is an enormous variety, e.g. peas, beans, chick peas, lentils and soya beans.

- They provide a good source of vegetable protein and dietary fibre. As you know, soya beans have a high biological value and are used as a meat analogue called TVP. (See Chapter 15, page 114.)

- Most dried pulses require soaking before cooking for a long time at a high temperature, particularly dried red kidney beans.

- Pulses are eaten in place of meat by vegetarians. Pulses absorb flavours well and can be used in a wide range of food products.

Figure 12.13 *Dried kidney beans*

KEY WORDS

These are the key words. Tick them if you think you know what they mean. Otherwise check on them.

aeration	flavouring	characteristic
gelatine	coagulate	gelatinisation
collagen	gliadin	composition
gluten	connective tissue	glutenium
cultivated	muscle tissue	elastin
myoglobin	elasticity	oil
emulsion	plasticity	enzymic browning
shortening	fat	

Check yourself

QUESTIONS

Q1 Name three functions of egg in the making of a lemon meringue pie made with rich (sweet) shortcrust pastry.

Q2 Explain why milk will boil over if heated in a saucepan for too long.

Q3 Two different trays of beef have the following cooking instructions printed on the label.

- Tray 1 – Lean Braising Steak – cook (braise) at 180°C/Gas 4 for 2 hours.
- Tray 2 – Thin Cut Rump Steak – cook under a high grill for 4 minutes turning occasionally.

Explain why the two types of beef need to be cooked in different ways.

Q4 Explain why fish is always tender and requires short cooking times.

Q5 Complete the chart by choosing a fat or oil to use in the following products:

a _____ to cream with sugar in a creamed cake mixture.

b _____ to coat flour in a rubbed-in shortcrust pastry mixture.

c _____ to form an emulsion with vinegar in mayonnaise.

d _____ for easy mixing (plasticity) in an all-in-one cake mixture.

e _____ to deep fry doughnuts or chipped potatoes.

Q6 Explain why the following cereals are used in the food products listed:

a strong wheat flour for breadmaking

b cornflour for custard sauce.

c basmati rice for savoury dishes.

REMEMBER! Cover the answers if you want to.

ANSWERS

A1
i) Rich (sweet) shortcrust pastry base – An egg yolk is added to a 200 g pastry mix. It adds colour and flavour, enriches and helps to bind dry ingredients together.
ii) Lemon filling – 2 egg yolks are added to 250 ml sauce mixture. The egg yolk helps to thicken the liquid because the protein coagulates when added to the hot sauce mixture. Egg yolk also adds colour and flavour.
iii) Meringue topping – 2 egg whites are whisked to make the meringue. The egg white protein albumen stretches to hold air bubbles to make a foam. When baked at 150°C the albumen coagulates to give a solid fine-mesh structure.

A2
- Some water in the milk changes to steam and rises from the surface.
- Fat globules rise to the surface and give a pale creamy colour.
- The proteins lactalbumin and lactoglobulin coagulate and form a skin on the top of the milk.

TUTORIAL

T1 *Eggs are a very useful and versatile ingredient. They have three main working characteristics: coagulation, foam formation and emulsification*

T2 *Protein coagulates on heating. In the case of milk the proteins form a skin on the top of food products such as custard, sauces and milk puddings. Stirring the milk or milk mixture helps to break up the mass of coagulated proteins.*

ANSWERS

- Small bubbles of air rise to the top and collect under the skin.
- As the milk boils the pressure in the bubbles of steam causes them to rise, forcing the skin upwards and the milk boils over!

A3 The differences between the two types of meat are the amount and type of connective tissue present and the length of the muscle fibres.

- Tray 2 – rump steak consists of short, thin muscle fibres with small amounts of collagen (connective tissue). It is also sliced into thin pieces. It will be tender and only require quick cooking to make it palatable. It does not need to be tenderised.
- Tray 1 – braising steak consists of thicker and longer muscle fibres and a larger amount of connective tissue. It needs to be cooked by a long slow moist method to soften the collagen and elastin and make the muscle fibres tender and palatable.

A4 The muscle fibres are short and there is a smaller amount of the connective tissue collagen to hold the fibres together. There is no tough elastin. This flesh structure does not need long cooking methods to tenderise the muscle fibres. The protein coagulates at 60°C and the collagen is converted to soluble gelatine. Cooking times would be: grilled trout 4 minutes each side; baked halibut 20 minutes.

A5 (a) butter or margarine; (b) hard margarine or lard; (c) olive oil; (d) soft margarine; (e) corn oil.

A6 Your answer should include:
a) Wheat is the only cereal that contains the proteins glutenin and gliadin which form gluten when mixed with water. Strong wheat flour has a high gluten content. Gluten stretches to hold air or gas produced by the raising agent, yeast.
b) Cornflour is a starch powder used to thicken a liquid by the process of gelatinisation (i.e. the starch grains absorb liquid, swell, burst and thicken the liquid).
c) Basmati rice is a long-grain rice which has a distinctive smell and flavour. During cooking it softens and cooks to produce light fluffy separate grains.

TUTORIALS

T3 *Meat is muscle tissue made up of long thin muscle fibres held together in bundles by the connective tissue, collagen. Collagen is a water-soluble protein which dissolves during cooking to form gelatine. The connective tissue, elastin, binds the muscles together. Elastin is tougher and less soluble than collagen.*

T4 *Fish is similar in structure and composition to lean meat. The flesh is made up of bundles of short muscle fibres held together by collagen, with no tough elastin. Fish is different to meat in that there is very little colour change in fish during cooking, except in shellfish.*

T5 *You can work out reasons for your choice:*
a) *butter or margarine for colour, flavour and ability to hold air*
b) *solid fat to form a protective layer to prevent gluten forming when water is added*
c) *olive oil to add flavour and form an oil in water emulsion*
d) *soft margarine contains some unsaturated fatty acids to give a solid but softer consistency than butter*
e) *corn oil for heating to a high temperature to seal and cook food for a crisp texture.*

T6 *Cereals are cultivated grasses grown throughout the world for their nutritious edible seeds. They are a staple food in many countries. Cereals are processed to make a vast range of food products.*

HOW ARE FOOD MATERIALS USED?

Most food products are made from food materials combined in ways that determine colour, texture, flavour, shape and volume. The descriptive detail of a particular food product is known as the **product profile**. The combination of food materials in varying amounts and by different methods of preparation and processing enables a vast range of food products to be produced.

You will need to know and understand:

- the working characteristics of ingredients
- the effect of combining different ingredients
- the interaction of different foods during preparation, processing and cooking.

COLLOIDAL STRUCTURES

Processed foods often contain more than one ingredient. When the ingredients are mixed together a structure is formed. This is called a colloidal structure. A colloidal structure consists of two parts which are evenly mixed or dispersed into one another.

The parts may be:

- liquid, e.g. vinegar, oil, water, milk
- solid, e.g. flour – starch grains of cornflour, arrowroot or wheat flour
- gas, e.g. carbon dioxide, air bubbles.

You need to know about the four types of colloidal structures: emulsions, foams (including solid foam), gels and suspensions.

Table 13.1 *Colloidal Structures*

Colloidal Structure	Food Product	Part 1	Dispersed	Part 2
Emulsion	mayonnaise	liquid, e.g. olive oil	in	liquid, e.g. vinegar
Foam	beaten egg white	gas, e.g. air bubbles	in	liquid, e.g. egg white
Solid foam	meringue, pavlova	gas, e.g. air bubbles	in	baked egg white
Gel	jam and jellies	liquid, e.g. water, juice	in	solid, e.g. fruit
Suspension	white sauce	solid, e.g. starch grains	in	liquid, e.g. milk

EMULSIONS

Figure 13.1

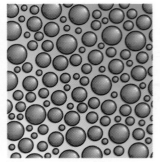

Liquids such as oil and water do not mix. They are said to be 'immiscible', that is they cannot be mixed.

When rigorously shaken with water oil breaks into small droplets which can be seen in the water, i.e. it forms an emulsion of one liquid mixed within another liquid. If left to stand the two parts separate, with the oil floating on top of the water.

— oil

— water

'Oil in water' emulsion   *Two parts separate*

Emulsions can be oil in water or water in oil. For example:

- **oil in water**, e.g. oil beaten into vinegar to make a vinegar dressing;
  - or when if milk is left to stand, the fat in the milk separates into a layer of cream.
- **water in oil** is fat-free milk beaten into a blend of oil to make margarine.

To stop the emulsion from separating an extra substance must be added to attract the two parts together. The 'matchmaker' is called an **emulsifying agent**.

An emulsifying agent is a substance which contains a:

- 'water-loving' group of molecules – **hydrophilic**
- 'water-hating' group of molecules – **hydrophobic**

i.e. one part attracts to water and one part attracts to oil to hold the oil and water emulsion together. The emulsifying agent lowers the surface tension between the two liquids so that they combine and form a stable emulsion.

Examples of emulsifying agents used in food products include:

- **lecithin** in egg yolk. Lecithin stabilises mayonnaise and creamed cake mixtures. Lecithin from soya beans is used in large scale manufacture.
- **glycerol monostearate (GMS)** which is used in large-scale manufacture to stabilise foods such as margarine.

The structure of emulsions is an important characteristic in the manufacture of fats such as butter and margarine. It is also important in the use of fats and oils in food products, e.g. mayonnaise, salad dressings, ice cream, creamed cake mixtures.

Salad Dressings

There are two types of emulsion-based salad dressings.

- unstable emulsion – vinaigrette or French dressing
- stable emulsion – mayonnaise.

Unstable Emulsion – Vinaigrette

Ingredients	Method of Making
6 tablespoons olive oil 1–2 tablespoon wine vinegar 1 level teaspoon salt 1 crushed clove garlic 1 teaspoon mustard fresh milled black pepper	Put all ingredients in a bowl or screw-topped jar and whisk together or shake until thoroughly combined. Adjust seasoning to taste.

Table 13.2

Vinaigrette Variations

Herb: add 2 tbsp chopped herbs such as parsley, thyme, marjoram.
Garlic: add 1–2 crushed cloves, 1 tbsp chopped chives.
Mustard and parsley: add 1 tbsp wholegrain mustard, 2 tbsp chopped parsley.
Blue cheese: add 25 g finely blended Roquefort cheese, 2 tbsp single cream.
Sweet and spicy: add 1 tsp mango chutney, 1 tsp mild curry paste.

Remember

- The emulsion is unstable and will separate out when left to stand. Shake vigorously to suspend the tiny oil droplets in the vinegar.
- The basic dressing mixture will keep for up to a month as long as you don't add perishable ingredients such as herbs.

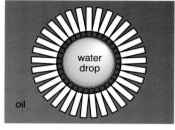

Figure 13.2 *A stable emulsion*

Figure 13.3 *Stable salad dressing, e.g. mayonnaise, and unstable salad dressing, e.g. vinaigrette*

Stable Emulsion – Mayonnaise

Table 13.3

Ingredients	Method of Making
1 egg yolk 125 ml olive oil 1–2 tablespoons wine vinegar half teaspoon salt freshly milled pepper half teaspoon mustard powder	Put egg yolk, mustard, salt, pepper, 1 teaspoon vinegar in bowl and mix thoroughly. Add oil drop by drop, then in a steady stream, whisking constantly until thick and smooth. Add rest of vinegar drop by drop. Season to taste.

The egg yolk contains lecithin. This is an emulsifying agent which helps to hold the olive oil and vinegar (oil and water) together to keep the emulsion stable, i.e. it does not separate out.

Mayonnaise Variations

Tartare sauce: add 5 ml tarragon, 10 ml chopped capers, 10 ml chopped gherkins, 10 ml chopped parsley.

Thousand island: add 30 ml chopped green olives, 30 ml chopped green pepper, 10 ml chopped parsley, 10 ml tomato purée.

Blue cheese: add 75 g crumbled blue cheese, 1 crushed garlic clove, 20 ml sour cream.

Function of Salad Dressing Ingredients

The foundation of a good dressing is the **oil**. A good choice is olive oil which has a rich green colour and distinct fruity flavour. Blending stronger-flavoured oils, such as walnut, hazelnut and almond, with blander oils, such as sunflower or groundnut, also produces well-flavoured dressings.

Vinegar is available in all sorts of flavours, e.g. wine, cider, sherry, balsamic, or fruit vinegar. It can be flavoured with fresh herbs such as tarragon, chillies or garlic. In dressings lemon juice can be used along with vinegar to form an acidic contrast to the oil.

Figure 13.4 *A variety of oils and vinegars*

Other ingredients, such as salt, mustard and pepper are added for flavour. Product development is obtained by adding one or two ingredients such as spices, herbs, cheese, vegetables, yogurt, cream, etc.

Creamed Cake Mixture

Did you know that a creamed cake mixture is an emulsion? (Remember that the recipe for creamed cake is 100 g sugar, 100 g butter/margarine, 2 eggs, 100 g s.r. flour.)

Method of Making	Structure
Beat butter/margarine and sugar together. Egg is added gradually and beaten to a smooth consistency.	Air is beaten into the mixture of fat and sugar to form an *air in fat* foam. Watery egg liquid mixes in tiny droplets throughout the mixture to form a *water in oil* emulsion.

Table 13.4

Note: If the egg is added cold or all at once the emulsion will not form. The fat becomes solid and looks as if it is floating in the egg. This is an oil in water emulsion, i.e. the cake mixture has 'curdled'.

Figure 13.5 *Creamed cake mixture*

FOAMS

A foam is formed when gas is mixed into a liquid, e.g. an egg white foam is gas (air) whisked into liquid (egg white).

When the egg white is whipped, the egg white stretches to hold air bubbles. The large air bubbles break down into very small air bubbles to form a foam. The foam becomes stiffer, white and glossy.
The stability of an egg white foam is measured by the way it keeps its volume. A stabiliser in the egg white foam is the protein **albumen**.

A foam will not become unstable, i.e. lose air and becomes soft or runny, if:

- fat-free equipment is used, i.e. no grease on bowl or beaters
- no egg yolk is mixed into the white
- fresh eggs at room temperature are used
- it is not overbeaten, which causes the protein to overstretch and collapse.

Examples of foams include beaten egg whites, and food products which are whipped, such as whipped cream, ice cream and cold desserts, e.g. mousse. The foam makes these light, aerated products with a smooth texture.

An example of a solid foam is meringue. Here the egg foam has been baked at a low temperature. The air inside the foam expands to increase the volume of the foam and the protein albumen coagulates (sets) to give a solid fine-mesh structure.

Two examples of food products formed from foams are meringue and pavlova. Meringue is made from egg white foam. A variation on meringue, known as pavlova, contains some additional ingredients which change the texture.

Compare the list of ingredients used in each product in Table 13.5.

Figure 13.6 Two food products made from foams: pavlova (top) and meringue nest

Table 13.5

Meringue	**Pavlova**
2 egg whites	2 egg whites
100 gm caster sugar	100 gm caster sugar
	pinch salt
	2 teaspoons cornflour
	1 teaspoon vinegar
	quarter teaspoon vanilla essence

Method of Making Both
Beat egg whites until stiff.
Half sugar added gradually and whisked in.
Remaining sugar folded in.
For pavlova beat in the cornflour, vinegar, vanilla essence, salt.
Bake at 100°C.

Meringue is a solid foam – air is whisked into the egg white foam and baked to form a solid.
Pavlova – cornflour and vinegar (acetic acid) soften the foam to create a soft marshmallow centre. In some recipes cream of tartar (tartaric acid) is used instead of vinegar.

Figure 13.7 *Making marmalade*

Table 13.6

GELS

A gel is formed when a large amount of liquid is set by a small amount of solid, e.g. jam and marmalade. The products are set but are often soft and elastic.

Setting Jam or Marmalade

Jam	Marmalade
1.8 kg raspberries	1.4 kg Seville oranges
1.8 kg sugar	3.4 litres water
(liquid is the juice which	2.7 kg sugar
comes from the raspberries)	juice of 2 lemons

Note the high quantity of liquid compared to the solid parts of the fruit.

The fruit contains pectin, a gum-like substance which is released from the cells of the fruit during cooking. When mixed with acid and sugar the pectin helps to set mixtures and form a gel, e.g:

- pectin in raspberries + sugar + acid in raspberries = raspberry jam
- pectin in Seville oranges + sugar + acid in oranges + lemon juice = orange marmalade.

Gelatine

Gelatine is used to set a variety of cold sweets.

Figure 13.8 *Chocolate mousse*

Table 13.7

Chocolate Mousse	
200 g plain chocolate	zest and juice of 1 large orange
2 whole eggs	50 ml water
2 egg yolks	10 g powdered gelatine
75g caster sugar	75 ml double cream

The gelatine is dissolved in warm water and added to the mixture at room temperature. Air is trapped in the whisked cream and egg whites. These two foams are folded into the egg yolk/chocolate creamy mixture to create a high-volume aerated foam mixture. The gelatine sets the foam into a mousse.

SUSPENSION

A suspension is a solid held in a liquid. The most common example is the starch grains of flour mixed into a liquid to make a sauce or gravy. If left to stand the solids sink to the bottom of the liquid. The mixture has to be stirred to keep the solids evenly mixed in the liquid.

Examples of suspensions include:

- white sauce – plain wheat flour in milk
- gravy – cornflour in vegetable stock
- glaze – arrowroot in water.

Details about making sauce are fully explained in Chapter 17 page 132.

The solids are held in the liquid when the mixture is heated. The starch grains swell, absorb liquid, burst and thicken the liquid. This process is known as gelatinisation (see Chapter 17 page 135). Custard, gravy and sauces are all examples of suspensions. They are usually served hot. If left to cool the suspension forms an elastic solid, e.g. blancmange.

Figure 13.9 *Making white sauce*

Figure 13.10 *Gravy*

PRINCIPAL METHODS OF COMBINING INGREDIENTS

AERATION

Many food products have a light, open, airy texture, e.g. bread, cakes, pastries, meringues and desserts such as soufflés.

Older methods of making bread and cakes produced flat, close-textured products. These **unleavened** products were made by using materials combined in ways that did not aerate the mixture. Today products contain raising agents added in the ingredients or during the production method so that a light, open texture is a characteristic of the final product.

Figure 13.11 *The open texture of bread made with a raising agent*

RAISING AGENTS

Raising agents are gases which are introduced into a food mixture:

- during the mixing process
- in a substance which is added to the mixture.

The gas is incorporated or released when ingredients are combined. On heating (baking) the minute bubbles of gas enclosed in the mixture expand, causing the mixture to rise.

The three most common raising agents are **steam**, **air** and **carbon dioxide**. They are frequently used in combination with each other, e.g. in a creamed cake mixture from:

- steam from liquid (egg/milk/water)
- air beaten in (creaming butter and sugar)
- carbon dioxide from chemical raising agents in baking powder or self-raising flour.

Steam

Some food products have steam as the main raising agent. These products must contain a high proportion of liquid, e.g. choux pastry, batter used to make Yorkshire pudding.

For steam to make mixtures rise, two conditions are needed:

- a large proportion of liquid, e.g. milk/water
- a high baking temperature of 200°C or above.

During baking:

- The liquid content reaches boiling point
- The steam forces its way up through the mixture, stretching the mixture and making it rise.
- The steam escapes and is replaced by air. The mixture bakes and sets into the risen shape.
- Sometimes steam is trapped inside. It condenses on cooling and then the product collapses. This often happens with Yorkshire pudding.

Figure 13.12 *A cross-section of a choux bun*

Figure 13.13 *Sieving flour*

Steam also combines with:

- air in pastry, e.g. shortcrust, flaky pastry
- air and carbon dioxide in bread and cakes.

Air

Mechanical action incorporates air into mixtures. It is the main raising agent in some food products, e.g. whisked sponge cake, soufflé. It is also used in combination with steam and/or carbon dioxide.

Air can be mechanically introduced into mixtures by:

- sieving flour – air is trapped between fine particles, e.g. pastry, cakes, batters
- rubbing fat into flour – air is trapped between 'breadcrumbs', e.g. shortbread, scones, shortcrust pastry
- creaming fat and sugar – air is beaten in to form an air in fat foam, e.g. cakes, biscuits
- whisking egg/sugar or egg white – air is whisked into the egg to form a high-volume foam, e.g. sponge cake, swiss roll, meringue
- beating batter – air is beaten in but steam is the main riser, e.g. choux pastry, batters
- rolling and folding pastry – air is trapped between the layers of pastry, e.g. flaky, puff, rich, yeast pastries, filo, strudel.

Carbon Dioxide

Carbon dioxide is produced in two ways:

- **biologically** from yeast cells during the fermentation process of yeast, i.e. biological raising agents
- **chemically** from the action of bicarbonate of soda with an acid, i.e. chemical raising agents.

Biological Raising Agents

Yeasts are micro-organisms (see Chapter 24 page 165). During the fermentation process the yeast cells feed on sugar and reproduce to produce carbon dioxide.

Figure 13.14 *Folding puff pastry*

Certain factors affect the action of yeast:

Temperature

- The optimum temperature range is 25°C–35°C.
- Above 60°C the fermentation process is destroyed.
- Below 25°C the reaction is slowed down.
- Fresh yeast can be frozen without killing the yeast: on defrosting it becomes active again.

Remember that warm temperatures are crucial! Take care to control the temperature of the liquid and the dough.

Moisture

- This is provided from milk/water/egg added to a mixture.
- Dried yeast needs to soak in a liquid to reactivate it. Remember to control the temperature of the liquid.

Food

- During the complex chain reaction of fermentation yeast cells need to feed on sugar to produce carbon dioxide.
- Sugar is added to yeast mixtures. There is also a very small amount in the flour.

Figure 13.15 *Well-risen sliced bread*

Proportion of Ingredients

- High proportions of fat and sugar slow down the action of yeast, e.g. in rich yeast dough mixtures. A higher proportion of yeast to flour is needed, e.g. rum baba, Chelsea buns.

Salt

- Too much or too little salt prevents the yeast from working well.
- The correct proportion of salt controls the fermentation process and helps to develop the flavour.

Chemical Raising Agents

Carbon dioxide is produced from chemical reactions. This can be made to happen in many recipes for baked products, e.g. cakes and scones, by the addition of chemical raising agents.

Chemical raising agents must be measured accurately. They:

- are used in small quantities
- are easy to use and often already combined, e.g. in self-raising flour
- will produce controlled amounts of carbon dioxide to aerate mixtures evenly.

The three types of chemical raising agents are: **bicarbonate of soda**, known as sodium bicarbonate; **bicarbonate of soda and acid** (alkali and acid); **baking powder**, or baking powder in self raising flour.

Figure 13.16 *Chemical raising agents*

- **Bicarbonate of Soda**
  This is the simplest type of chemical raising agent. When heated in a mixture it produces sodium carbonate (soda), steam and carbon dioxide. The carbon dioxide and steam aerate the mixture. The soda leaves a dark yellow colour (tinge) and gives a sharp alkaline taste to the mixture. It is used successfully in recipes which have other strong-flavoured ingredients to disguise this, e.g. parkin, chocolate cake, gingerbread.

- **Bicarbonate of Soda Plus Acid**
  The bicarbonate of soda reacts with the acid to produce carbon dioxide. The acid helps to neutralise the compound and prevents the taste and colour residue left when bicarbonate of soda is used on its own.

  A traditional source of acid is sour milk, which provides a dilute form of lactic acid. This is still used today in scone mixtures. The level of lactic acid cannot be measured, so it is not an accurate method.

  A more controlled method is to use cream of tartar (tartaric acid). When combined with bicarbonate of soda the reaction releases the carbon dioxide slowly, leaving a tasteless salt behind. It is used in drop scones. The ratio is two parts tartaric acid to one part sodium bicarbonate.

- **Baking Powder**
  This is a commercial mixture of bicarbonate and acid substances ready mixed in the correct proportions. A 'buffer' is added in the form of cornflour or rice flour to absorb any moisture and prevent the reaction taking place in the storage container. Several brands of baking powder are available. Each one will have a specific formula but the amount of carbon dioxide is regulated by law.

  Baking powder is very easy and convenient to use as the raising agent is incorporated as a single ingredient.

  Baking powder is added to plain flour to produce self-raising flour which is an easy and convenient way of incorporating pre-measured raising agents into a mixture.

101

COMMERCIAL BREAD PRODUCTION

Bread is a high-volume, well-risen product. To achieve this characteristic texture three particular methods are used commercially to manufacture dough:

- bulk fermentation process
- activated dough development
- Chorleywood bread process.

Bulk Fermentation Process

(Traditional method)

- Combined dough ingredients are left to ferment for up to three hours.
- During fermentation the dough changes from a dense mass into an elastic dough.
- The time needed for this to happen depends on the amount of yeast and the temperature of the dough.
- Large-scale bakers do not have enough time or space for dough to be left this long.

Activated Dough Development

- A bread improver is added to the dough.
- This speeds up the process so that the dough does not have to be left for long periods of time.

Chorleywood Bread Process

(The most commonly used method for large-scale production.)

- First developed in 1961.
- Flour treatment agents (ascorbic acid – vitamin C) are added.
- The first fermentation stage is replaced by a few minutes of intense mechanical mixing of the dough.
- This rapidly stretches the gluten and produces the elasticity needed to hold the expanding carbon dioxide.
- Yeast is still required to produce the carbon dioxide.

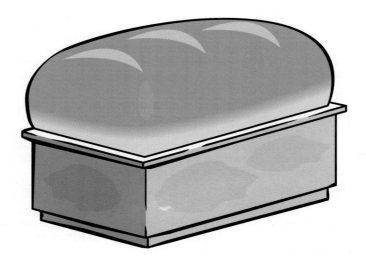

COAGULATION

Figure 13.17 *Heating causes liquid egg yolk and white to coagulate*

In this process protein foods change their soluble structure so that they become insoluble. An example of coagulation occurs when an egg is cooked in boiling water and becomes hard. Coagulation can be caused by heat or strong acids. The structure of the protein is permanently changed. This is called **denaturation**, i.e. the protein coagulates or sets. Examples include:

Heat

High temperatures coagulate:

- eggs in baked cakes, biscuits
- gluten protein in bread dough for loaves
- whisked egg white into solid white hard meringue
- egg yolk into a dry solid for hard boiled egg
- milk proteins to form a 'skin' – lactalbumin and lactoglobulin
- meat proteins (collagen and elastin) firm and shrink slightly when grilled, fried, poached, etc.

Acids coagulate:

- milk by using a lactic acid starter in the cheese making process
- cream/condensed milk by using lemon juice (acetic acid) in cold sweets.

SETTING

Some food products are made by setting a liquid into a semi-solid or a solid, e.g. custard, jelly, mousse. There are several ways to do this, using:

Gelatine

The setting agent is gelatine. This is a protein which is extracted from parts of animals. It is available in powder or sheet form, and when dissolved in a small amount of water it is incorporated into mixtures which then set, e.g. ice cream, jellies, cheesecakes, mousse. It is colourless and almost tasteless. It can also be used in commercially produced yogurts, paté and tinned cold meats, e.g. ham and tongue. For vegetarian products agar is used instead of gelatine. Agar is made from seaweed.

Figure 13.18 *A custard tart is made from a liquid set into a semi-solid or solid*

Pectin

Fruit, sugar and water are boiled to form a mixture that will set and form a gel. Pectin is a complex carbohydrate present in most fruits. The pectin, a gum-like substance, is released from the cell walls by crushing the fruit and cooking it at a high temperature for a short time. To obtain a good, clear, well set jam the fruit should be just ripe and combined with the correct proportion of acid and sugar. The pectin traps the water, sugar and fruit into a gel. The final percentage of sugar is 60%. Fruit which has a low pectin content is often used together with high-pectin-content fruit, e.g. in apple and blackberry jam.

Starch

Starch thickens liquid by the process of gelatinisation. See Chapter 17 pages 132 and 133 for information on:

- starch-based sauces
- methods of making sauces
- thickness and consistency of sauces
- the function of starch and the process of gelatinisation.

Starch is used to:

- thicken sauces, e.g. white sauce, custard
- produce a gel that sets when cooled, e.g. blancmange.

Egg

Egg is a protein which coagulates when heated, e.g. hard boiled egg. Eggs are also used in combination with other ingredients and in some cases the egg is used to coagulate and set a liquid. For example, one medium egg will set 125 ml liquid:

- savoury flan – 1 egg: 125 ml milk/cream
- egg custard tart – 2 eggs: 250 ml milk.

During cooking the egg/milk mixture sets to form a firm, springy filling.

Some factors will affect the coagulation characteristic of eggs, e.g:

- A firmer set is achieved if extra egg is added to the liquid.
- A looser set is achieved if a high proportion of sugar is added.

BINDING

- Loose or dry ingredients are held together by the addition of liquid, fat or egg. The binding ingredient may also have other functions, e.g. water is used to bind fat and flour together in pastry and bread mixtures but the water also helps to develop the gluten in flour required for the elastic stretchy dough in bread making.

- Milk is used to form a suspension when mixed with flour and egg in batters, e.g. pancakes and Yorkshire pudding, but the milk also produces steam which is the essential raising agent in Yorkshire pudding.

- Egg is used to moisten and bind ingredients together in burgers, rissoles, croquettes and savoury loaf, but when these mixtures are cooked the egg protein coagulates, holding the mixture together.

Figure 13.19 *Egg is used to bind the mince in a burger mixture*

BULKING

ometimes ingredients are added to foods to increase the bulk or volume of
he finished product. Some of the most common ingredients are:

- breadcrumbs – used in savoury loaf, nut roast, burgers, stuffing,
  steamed puddings. Breadcrumbs absorb flavours and liquid to
  help bind ingredients together.

- potatoes and other vegetables, e.g. pulses – used in a variety of
  savoury products, e.g. meat pasties, soup, casseroles. The
  potatoes and lentils, etc. help to absorb flavour and liquid and
  add texture and volume.

- textured vegetable protein (TVP) (see Chapter 15 page 114). TVP
  can be reconstituted and added in different ratios to meat-based
  products. TVP needs to be combined with strong-flavoured
  ingredients, e.g. chilli, bolognese sauce, curry, cottage pie.

emember that non-nutritive substances, e.g. non-starch polysaccharides, can
e added to foods designed to aid weight reduction.

FINISHING

is important to make food products look attractive. This can be done by
ecorating the surface of the product with a glaze. Ways of doing this include:

- egg – beaten egg or egg and milk is brushed over the surface of
  savoury products before baking. The surface bakes a shiny golden
  brown as the egg coagulates, e.g. vol-au-vonts, sausage rolls,
  pasties

- milk – brushing the surface of pastry with milk produces a light
  matt brown colour when baked, e.g. mince pies, scones

- sugar – sprinkling sugar or brushing sugar/water over sweet baked
  products produces a shiny, sticky, crystalline surface finish. The
  liquid evaporates and the sugar caramelises to give a very
  attractive appearance, e.g. to Eccles cakes, yeast buns, and some
  cakes where the sugar is combined with lemon juice.

Figure 13.20 *A glazed product*

ther finishes can be obtained by using:

- honey to glaze ham and breakfast cereal
- glaze icing on cakes and biscuits.

THE EFFECT OF ACIDS AND ALKALIS

cids and alkalis are chemical compounds which influence the changes which
ccur when ingredients are combined. Both acids and alkalis have an effect
n the flavour, appearance, texture and nutritional value of food products.
hey are found in many different foods and should be used carefully and
ccurately to gain the desired effect.

cids increase the concentration of hydrogen ions when added to a water
olution (pH 1–6).

lkalis take up the hydrogen ions to produce hydroxyl ions in a solution
H 7–14).

ACIDS

- **Citric acid** (lemon juice) is used to:
    - make jam to help pectin form a gel
    - stop enzymic browning of cut fresh fruit, e.g. dipping sliced banana in lemon juice
    - coagulate the protein caseinogen when cream/condensed milks are used in cold desserts.

Remember that when acids are cooked with a starch mixture they lessen the thickening power of the starch, e.g. adding lemon juice to a cornflour sauce mixture for a lemon meringue pie filling. The lemon juice must be added after the starch has gelatinised (see Chapter 17 page 133).

- **Acetic acid** (vinegar) is used to:
    - preserve a wide variety of foods, e.g. chutney, piccalilli, pickled beetroot, onion, cabbage
    - marinate meat to tenderise it
    - give a sharp acidic flavour to dressings for salad and vegetables.

The most traditional vinegar is malt vinegar but wine vinegar, cider vinegar and vinegar flavoured with herbs are becoming popular.

Ascorbic acid (vitamin C E300) is used to act as a flour treatment agent. It helps to speed up the yeast fermentation process.

Tartaric acid (cream of tartar) is used to neutralise the reaction of bicarbonate of soda used as a raising agent to produce carbon dioxide gas in some sweet baked products, e.g. gingerbread.

Lactic acid starter is used to coagulate milk in cheese making.

Remember that acids are used in commercial food manufacture to help preserve foods. Acidic conditions prevent the growth of micro-organisms.

ALKALIS

Alkalis are used as a raising agent, e.g. bicarbonate of soda which produces carbon dioxide when heated.

KEY WORDS

These are the key words. Tick them if you think you know what they mean. Otherwise check on them.

acid	aeration	alkalis
binding	buffer	bulking
characteristic	chemical reaction	coagulate
colloid	colloidal structure	combination
condenses	curdled	dispersed
droplet	emulsion	emulsifying agent
finish	foam	gas
gel	gelatinisation	glaze
hydrophilic	hydrophobic	immiscible
interaction	lecithin	liquid
mechanical	mixed	molecules
NSP – non-starch carbohydrate	optimum	pectin
perishable	product profile	raising agents
setting	solid	soluble
stable	stabiliser	steam
structure	surface tension	suspension
vigorously		

Check yourself

QUESTIONS

Q1 What is a colloidal structure?

Q2 Describe how an emulsion is made.

Q3 Look at the ingredients list on the label from a bottle of mayonnaise shown in Figure 13.21.

> INGREDIENTS: VEGETABLE OIL, WATER, PASTEURISED EGG & EGG YOLK, SPIRIT VINEGAR, SALT, SUGAR, LEMON JUICE, MUSTARD FLAVOURING , ANTIOXIDANT (CALCUIM DISOFIUM EDTA), PAPRIKA EXTRACT.

Figure 13.21

Egg and egg yolk are included in the list. What is the function of egg yolk in the production of mayonnaise?

Q4 A tray of Yorkshire puddings are made correctly but when brought out of the oven they collapse and are wet inside. Suggest a reason for this.

Q5 Yeast is used to aerate bread products. Why then do large-scale manufacturers use the Chorleywood bread process to make bread? Give three reasons in your answer.

Q6 A cake manufacture is going to use bicarbonate of soda as the raising agent in a range of baked cake products. What advice would you give to him or her on the use of bicarbonate of soda.

Q7 Explain the reason why, when baked in a pastry case, a mixture of 250 ml milk, 2 eggs, 25 g sugar and a pinch of nutmeg sets to form an egg custard tart.

Q8 Meat or vegetable burgers are popular food products for cooking on a barbecue. Why would egg be listed in the ingredients?

REMEMBER! Cover the answers if you want to.

ANSWERS

A1 Processed foods usually contain more than one ingredient. When the ingredients are mixed together a structure is formed. The structure formed in a food product is known as a colloidal structure. A colloidal structure consists of two parts which are evenly mixed or dispersed into one another. The parts may be liquid, e.g. vinegar, oil, water, milk; solid, e.g. flour particles; or gas, e.g. carbon dioxide, air bubbles.

A2 An emulsion is made from two different liquids, e.g. oil and water. But liquids such as oil and water do not mix. They are said to be 'immiscible'. When shaken together the oil breaks into small droplets and mixes into the water, i.e. an emulsion is formed when one liquid mixed into another. If left to stand, the two parts separate, with the oil floating on the water.

TUTORIALS

T1 *There are four colloidal structures: emulsions, suspensions, foams and gels. Make sure you know about each one.*

T2 *The emulsion can be:*
- *oil in water, e.g. oil beaten into vinegar*
- *water in oil, e.g. fat-free milk beaten into oil for margarine.*

ANSWERS

TUTORIALS

A3 To stop the two liquids in an emulsion from separating a third substance is added. This is known as an emulsifying agent. The emulsifying agent has one part which attracts to water and one part which attracts to oil.

T3 *Egg yolk contains lecithin which is a naturally occurring emulsifying agent. It attracts to both the vegetable oil and the spirit vinegar and holds them together. The mayonnaise is then a stable emulsion, i.e. it will not separate out.*

A4 Yorkshire puddings are made from a batter mix of 100 g flour, 1 egg and 250 ml water/milk, salt and pepper. The liquid first helps to form a suspension when mixed with the flour and egg. When the batter mix is cooked at a high temperature of 210°C, the liquid reaches boiling point and creates steam. The steam forces its way up through the mixture, stretching it and making it rise. As the mixture bakes it sets into a risen shape.

T4 *Emulsifying agents lower the surface tension between two liquids so that they combine and form a stable emulsion. Lecithin in egg yolk also stabilises a creamed cake mixture. In large-scale manufacture artificial stabilisers are used. An example is GMS used to stabilise the emulsion formed from milk and oil in margarine.*

Steam is an important raising agent in food products that contain large amounts of liquid, e.g. choux pastry. Two conditions are needed: large amounts of liquid and a high baking temperature to create the steam.

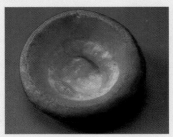

Figure 13.22 *Baked Yorkshire pudding*

Steam can get trapped inside the mixture. The steam condenses on cooling and causes the Yorkshire pudding to collapse. This could be the reason or it may be that the Yorkshire pudding was taken out of the oven before the mixture had set and the shape has collapsed.

A5 The advantages of the Chorleywood bread process are that:
- it is mixed by high-speed mechanical mixers in less than five minutes. This speeds up the time taken to make the bread
- less factory space is needed than for traditional bulk fermentation
- it does not require temperature and humidity control conditions
- less space and less time are required, therefore the production costs are less
- it gives a higher yield of bread per unit of flour
- it enables a higher quality bread product to be made, i.e. keeping qualities, volume, texture, colour and cost.

T5 *The Chorleywood bread process was developed in 1961. Today most bread is made on large-scale automatic manufacturing plant lines. The stages are monitored and controlled by computers. All this helps to produce consistent high quality bread products every time.*

ANSWERS

A6 Bicarbonate of soda is a chemical raising agent. Chemical raising agents produce carbon dioxide in a chemical reaction. Bicarbonate of soda is the simplest form of chemical raising agent. Your advice could include:
- sodium carbonate, steam and carbon dioxide are produced
- the carbon dioxide and steam will aerate the cake mixtures
- the soda leaves a dark yellow colour and a sharp alkaline taste in the mixture
- strong-flavoured ingredients will disguise the yellow tinge and the alkaline taste.

Examples of suitable cake mixtures include parkin and gingerbread. Look at the list of ingredients in this recipe for Cornish ginger biscuits:

Cornish Ginger Biscuits
*1 level teaspoon golden syrup
100 g margarine
100g sugar
1 level teaspoon bicarbonate of soda
125 g plain flour
*1 level teaspoon ground ginger
quarter teaspoon salt

(*flavour masks the use of bicarbonate of soda)

Remember that chemical raising agents must be measured accurately.

A7 Egg is a protein. Proteins coagulate when heated. The soluble structure changes to become insoluble, e.g. when egg is cooked as in hard boiled egg. Eggs can be used in combination with other ingredients, e.g. to coagulate and set a liquid. During the cooking of the egg custard mixture at 170°C for 45 minutes the egg/milk mixture sets to form a firm, springy filling.

A8 Some of the ingredients used to make the burgers would be loose or dry ones. They would need to be held or bound together by liquid or egg. The binding ingredient in burgers would need to moisten and bind the ingredients together but it would also need to stop the burgers crumbling when cooked and turned on the barbecue. The egg will coagulate on heating and bind the burger ingredients firmly together.

TUTORIALS

T6 *There are three types of chemical raising agents:*
- *bicarbonate of soda*
- *bicarbonate of soda plus an acid*
- *baking powder.*

The acid neutralises the chemical reaction with bicarbonate of soda and prevents the taste and colour residual left when bicarbonate of soda is used on its own. One example of a recipe is Singin' Hinny, a traditional scone-type recipe:

Singin' Hinny
200 g plain flour
quarter teaspoon bicarbonate of soda
half teaspoon cream of tartar
quarter teaspoon salt
75 g lard
75 g currants
milk

T7 *Eggs can be used to set milk or cream for a filling in savoury flans or quiche. Other proteins also coagulate on heating, e.g:*
- *gluten protein in bread dough*
- *milk proteins form a skin on heated milk*
- *whisked egg white bakes into a solid white hard meringue.*

T8 *There are three main properties of the proteins in eggs which enable them to be used in many different ways in food products:*
- *egg proteins coagulate on heating*
- *egg proteins stretch when whisked and hold air in the structure to create a foam*
- *egg yolk protein lecithin is a natural emulsifying agent.*

109

SAMPLE STUDENT'S ANSWERS AND EXAMINER'S COMMENTS

1 These are correct answers and it is easy to gain maximum marks with recall questions like these. The vast range of food products available to consumers are made from a smaller number of raw foods. Try and become familiar with some of the main food commodities which are processed for food product diversity.

1 Primary source food materials are processed to make secondary source foods that are used to manufacture a wide range of products.

Complete the chart by naming the Primary source food. (4 marks)

Primary Source	Secondary Source	Manufactured Product
Wheat	Flour	Pasta
Sugar Beet	Sugar	Caramel Toffees
Oats	Oatmeal	Biscuits
Milk	Cheese	Pizza

4/4

2 Parts of this answer are good and show that the student has a sound understanding of alternative proteins to meat. This is particularly true of reasons 1 and 3. Reason 2 gives some accurate information but the answer is not developed to explain the advantage of this when manufacturing vegetarian products. Myco-protein is a substitute for meat and it may be useful to make comparisons to show the advantage points.

2 A manufacturer of vegetarian main meals has decided to use myco-protein (Quorn) in their products. Give three advantages for using myco-protein in vegetarian main meal products. (6 marks)

Reason 1. Myco-protein does not have a strong flavour but it absorbs other flavours. It can be used as a replacement for meat, e.g. in chilli which contains strong spicy flavours.

Reason 2. Good nutrition. High in protein, low in fat.

Reason 3. It has a texture similar to chicken and it can be bought as mince or pieces so it is similar to meat in appearance.

5/6

3 These answers are good and to the point. The term 'enrobing' is used in the food manufacturing industry to describe coating a product with another ingredient, e.g. biscuits, fish, potato. The rest of the question is about the working characteristics of eggs. Eggs are used in many food products and you need to know and understand the main properties of eggs.

3 Fish can be coated with egg and breadcrumbs before it is cooked.

(a) What is the name given to this manufacturing process? (1 mark)

enrobing

1/1

(b) Explain two reasons for coating the fish with egg and breadcrumbs. (4 marks)

Reason 1. Egg holds the breadcrumbs onto the fish. When it is cooked the coating gives a crisp crunchy texture.

Reason 2. When the egg is cooked it sets and stops fat soaking into the fish, e.g. fried fish.

4/4

Question to Answer

The answers to Question 4 can be found on page 241.

4 A food manufacturer decides to develop a range of savoury cheese flans which will be sold from a chill cabinet. The design team have a basic recipe which they will modify to produce two different cheese flans.

Basic Recipe

Pastry Case	**Filling**
200 g plain flour	250 ml milk
100 g fat	2 eggs
quarter tsp salt	75 g cheese
water to mix	salt and pepper

(a) (i) What type of fat would be suitable to make the pastry? (1 mark)
  (ii) Give a reason for your choice. (2 marks)
  (iii) Explain the function of fat in the preparation and cooking of pastry. (3 marks)
  (iv) Explain the function of eggs in the preparation and cooking of the filling. (3 marks)

(b) The test kitchen develops the basic filling recipe to extend the product range. Give details of two fillings that would be suitable for:

  (i) vegetarians
  (ii) a 'value for money' family meal. (12 marks)

Record your answer in the charts below.
Remember to include **all** the ingredients for the filling.

Vegetarian Cheese Flan	Value for Money Family Meal
Filling	Filling
Quantity Ingredients	Quantity Ingredients
Reasons for Choice	Reasons for Choice

(c) Vegetables can be used in several food products which can be served with a cheese flan.

Choose a vegetable that can be used in the following products. Give a reason for your choice.

  (i) The vegetable . . . . used in coleslaw. (1 mark)
    Reason for choice. (2 marks)
  (ii) The vegetable . . . . used in stir-fry vegetables. (1 mark)
    Reason for choice. (2 marks)
  (iii) The vegetable . . . . used in Italian bread. (1 mark)
    Reason for choice. (2 marks)

CHAPTER 15

ALTERNATIVE INGREDIENTS

Figure 15.1 *Soya beans growing as a crop*

Figure 15.2 *A variety of soya products*

Table 15.1 *Types of vegetarianism*

Figure 15.3 *This symbol is used to indicate foods suitable for vegetarians*

WHAT ARE ALTERNATIVE INGREDIENTS?

Food manufacturers need to consider consumer needs when designing new food products. In recent years some consumers have shown an increasing preference for food products which contain an alternative protein food, rather than meat from animal sources.

Manufacturers have developed several meat-like products which are used in commercially manufactured food products as well as being bought by consumers to add to meals made at home. The two terms used to describe this 'new' group of non-meat protein ingredients are:

- **alternative protein foods** – foods used instead of meat to provide necessary protein in the diet
- **meat analogues** – foods which can be used in the same way as meat but which are different in structure.

These meat-like products provide the sensory qualities of meat but they are not produced in the same way. They have some similarities but also some definite differences and you will need to know about meat analogues, how they are made and what they are used for.

During your course or for your coursework project you may have designed and made food products using meat analogues which include:

- soya bean products, such as textured vegetable protein (TVP) or tofu
- mycro-protein product, such as Quorn.

There are a variety of reasons why consumers may prefer to eat a wide range of protein foods and you will consider this again when designing and making main course food products for particular target groups. People's reasons may include:

- the fact that more people are becoming vegetarian, eating a restricted range of animal proteins or no animal protein at all
- the nutritional profile – plant-based protein foods, e.g. soya beans, have a high protein content but are lower in fat than meat
- there is less waste from plant-based protein
- the overall production costs of plant-based protein may be cheaper than the production costs of animal protein.

Vegetarian Groups	Will not eat:	Will eat:
Lacto vegetarian	meat, fish, poultry, eggs	milk or milk products
Lacto ovo vegetarian	meat, fish, poultry	milk or milk products, eggs
Vegan	any animal protein	plant-based protein products

Meat analogues make several other important contributions to the manufacture of food products and they are used in the food industry in both meat-based and no-meat-based products as:

- **meat extenders** – e.g. soya beans can be made into textured vegetable protein (TVP) which is used to replace some of the meat content in meat products to reduce costs
- **bulking agents** – e.g. used to bulk out the meat content and change the product profile of some food products, e.g. to reduce the fat content
- **shelf life extenders** – e.g. added to food products which are stored in a dried or dehydrated state and are then reconstituted with a liquid, such as instant savoury snacks, dried soups.

SOYA BEANS

- The soya bean is a legume vegetable – a pod-bearing plant from the same plant family as beans and peas.

- It has been used as a protein food in Far Eastern countries for hundreds of years.

- The USA grow 70% of the world crop with many varieties also grown in South East Asia.

- Soya beans come in several sizes and colours, such as yellow, green, black and brown.

- There is a high yield per hectare therefore soya beans are cheaper to produce than many other crops.

- Soya beans have a high protein content, a low starch content, and also contain many micronutrients.

- Soya beans were originally grown as an oil seed to produce an important vegetable oil. This is still an important use of the soya bean but it is now also used to make many other food products, such as textured vegetable protein, soya flour, soya milk, bean curd tofu, soya sauce and the fermented soya bean paste known as miso which is used in Japanese cooking.

Raw beans are used to produce fresh bean sprouts for stir fry cooking.

Soya flour

- does not contain gluten so it can be used by people on a gluten-free diet

- is combined with wheat flour in bread and cakes to produce a whiter loaf with improved keeping qualities

- gives a creamy texture to soups and sauces.

Soya milk

- has a high nutritional value but it does not taste like cows' milk

- is used in cooking but may have a slightly bitter flavour unless sugar has been added

- is a useful product for people who suffer from lactose intolerance and who therefore cannot eat dairy products.

Soya oil is a useful, high quality, all-purpose oil with little flavour.

Soya lecithin (protein) is used as an emulsifier in a wide range of products, e.g. low-fat spreads.

Soya concentrates is used in baby foods where the level and type of protein is important.

Figure 15.4 *Soya can be used in bolognese sauce for spaghetti and in soya milk*

113

SOYA TEXTURED VEGETABLE PROTEIN (TVP)

The main stages of production

- Oil is extracted from hard soya beans by large industrial pressing machines.
- The remaining beans are ground into fat-free soya flour with a high protein content.
- Soya flour and water can be mixed to form a dough.
- Any desired colourings and flavourings can be added.
- Soya dough can be heated and extruded through shaped nozzles to produce a variety of shapes, e.g. chunks, flakes, grains.
- Shapes can be dried (dehydrated) and packaged with a shelf life of about a year.

The characteristics of TVP

- A spongy-textured mass which can be extruded to resemble the shape and texture of pieces of meat.
- The flavour is bland but flavourings can be added to give a taste of meat. A wide variety of flavoured TVP products are available.
- TVP is best cooked with distinctive-flavoured foods such as tomatoes, curry spices, garlic and herbs.

The nutritional content of TVP

- It is high in biological protein, containing all the essential amino acids. Methionine and tryptophan are sometimes added during production.
- It is fortified with vitamin B and iron.
- It is low in fat.
- It is low in cholesterol.
- It is high in dietary fibre.

TVP is used in:

- the food industry to add bulk, i.e. as a 'meat' extender in very many types of food products, e.g. sausages, burgers, pies and mince-based products such as lasagne, chilli, cottage pie
- canned, dried (dehydrated), frozen, chilled ready meals and snack meals
- food products made at home. TVP is sold as an individual ingredient. It can be used along with meat, e.g. in a percentage of 50/50 TVP/minced beef, or to replace meat totally in a recipe. Well-flavoured stock flavours the TVP. It requires a shorter cooking time than meat.

Figure 15.5 *TVP burger*

TOFU

Tofu is also known as soya bean curd. It is an important food in East Asia, China and Japan where is has been used for thousands of years.

Production

- Soya beans are washed and then soaked in water at a temperature of 25°C for 5–6 hours.
- The beans are ground to a paste and sieved, to produce a milk.
- The milk is boiled then cooled to 50°C and calcium sulphate is added to set (coagulate) the milk.
- The solids (curds) are separated (precipitated) out.
- The curds are pressed to remove extra liquid and to form blocks of tofu.

The characteristics of tofu

- Tofu is a soft, smooth-textured, semi-solid food.
- It is available in original flavour, smoked or marinated forms.
- It is high in protein and low in fat.
- It has very little flavour of its own but it does absorb the flavour of the ingredients it is mixed with, e.g. marinated in dressings.

Figure 15.6 *Tofu curd and tofu pieces used in a sauce*

Tofu is used in:

- a wide variety of food products, e.g:
  - cut into chunks for oriental dishes, stir fry, casseroles, savoury flans, soups, salads
  - grated or chopped to make burgers and roasts.
- Silken tofu is soft and creamy and can be used in dressings, cheesecakes, sauces and dips.

MYCO-PROTEIN, E.G. QUORN

Myco-protein is a tiny fungus which is processed in a similar way to yogurt or cheese. It is a relatively new product but is already a popular replacement for meat.

Production

- Myco-protein is produced commercially by fermentation in large vats.
- It is a fungus-like organism which grows rapidly under carefully controlled conditions, e.g. temperature, food and pH.
- Oxygen, nitrogen, glucose and vitamins are added.
- The myco-protein is grown as fine fibres of different lengths depending on the texture required in the final meat analogue.
- It is heat-treated to stop further growth.
- The mycro-protein is separated from its liquid in a centrifuge.
- Egg white is added to bind the micro-protein fibres together and to develop the texture.
- Flavours and colours are mixed into the mycro-protein.
- It is then processed into shapes, i.e. cubed, sliced, shredded or minced to produce a meat analogue.

Figure 15.7 *Quorn used in vegetarian moussaka*

Characteristics

- After processing the texture is similar to chicken.
- It is high in protein, low in cholesterol, low in fat.
- It contains a small amount of fibre but is higher in fibre than some meats.
- It can be processed to taste like chicken, veal or ham.
- It lacks flavour but absorbs surrounding flavours well.
- It benefits from being marinated before cooking.
- It is available as mince or pieces which have the appearance and texture of lean meat.
- It is sold fresh and stored in a chill cabinet.
- It can be frozen for up to three months and used straight from the freezer.
- It is unsuitable for vegans because it contains egg albumen.

Myco-protein is used in:

- ready meals, e.g. nuggets, fillets, sausages, burgers, grill steaks
- meals made at home as an alternative to meat, e.g. kebabs, pies, sauces.

KEY WORDS

These are the key words. Tick them if you think you know what they mean. Otherwise check on them.

alternative	analogue	bulking
characteristic	coagulate	dehydrate
emulsifier	extrusion	fermentation
gluten free	legume	marinate
meat extender	myco-protein	precipitate
protein	rehydrate	replicate
tofu	TVP	vegan
vegetarian	Quorn	

Check yourself

QUESTIONS

Q1 A selection of milk chocolates filled with soft, flavoured mallow are made from the following ingredients which are listed on the label.

INGREDIENTS
SUGAR · DRIED WHOLE MILK · COCOA BUTTER · COCOA MASS · GLUCOSE SYRUP · PECAN NUTS · BUTTEROIL · WALNUTS · DRIED EGG WHITE · DRIED SKIMMED MILK · EMULSIFIER: SOYA LECITHIN FLAVOURINGS · COFFEE · DRIED ORANGE JUICE · COLOURS: E100, E120, E150(a), E153. E160(c) · ACIDITY REGULATOR: CITRIC ACID.

Figure 15.8 *List of ingredients for milk chocolates filled with mallow*

Soya lecithin is included in the list. Give a reason for this.

Q2 A bag of six soft white bread rolls are made from the following ingredients which are listed on the cellophane packet.

INGREDIENTS: Unbleached wheat flour, water, yeast, soya flour, salt, wheat protein, emulsifiers: E471, E472(e), E481; preservative: calcium propionate; flavourings, flour treatment agents: ascorbic acid (vitamin C).

Figure 15.9 *List of ingredients for bread rolls*

Soya flour is included in the list. Give reasons for this.

Q3 A snack meal for one consists of dehydrated pasta noodles, vegetables and small cubes of flavoured 'beef'. The list of ingredients displayed on the packet includes textured vegetable protein.

NO ARTIFICIAL COLOURS OR PRESERVATIVES
NOODLES IN A BEEF & TOMATO FLAVOUR SAUCE MIX WITH TEXTURISED SOYA PIECES, DRIED VEGETABLES AND A SACHET OF TOMATO SAUCE.

Ingredients: Noodles (Wheatflour, Vegetable Oil, Salt), Wheatflour, Beef & Tomato Flavour [Flavourings, Colour (Paprika Extract)], Maltodextrin, Texturised Soya Pieces (produced from genetically modified soya flour), Vegetables (Tomatoes, Carrots, Peas). Sachet: Tomato Sauce.

Figure 15.10 *List of ingredients for a snack meal*

Give two reasons why textured vegetable protein has been used in this product.

Q4 Which meat analogue would not be suitable for a vegan to eat?

Q5 What is meant by the term 'meat-extender'?

Q6 Packets of dried soya mince can be bought to use in food products made at home. Before use the dried soya mince must be rehydrated by adding one and a half cups of water to one cup of soya mince and simmered for two to three minutes. A tablespoon of oil may be added to the water to enhance the flavour. The rehydrated soya mince can then be used in the following recipe for rissoles.

RISSOLES
4½ ozs Soya Mince
½ pint water
1 medium onion chopped
1 oz vegetable fat
2 tsp Marmite
Pepper
1 tbs Tomato Ketchup
1-2 level tsp mixed herbs
1 egg, beaten
2 tsp Holbrooks Worcester Sauce

Hydrate Soya Mince with water, seasoning and herbs. Cook onion in the fat until soft and just colouring. Add Soya Mince and brown over the heat until the mixture is firm. Cool a little, and bind with beaten egg. Form into rounds and coat in seasoned flour. Fry in hot oil until browned, turning once.

Figure 15.11 *A recipe for rissoles using TVP, dried soya mince*

Give reasons for adding Marmite, tomato ketchup, herbs and Worcestershire sauce to the recipe.

What is the function of the egg?

Q7 Tofu is available in original, smoked or marinated forms. Look at the label from a packet of marinated tofu pieces.

MARINATED TOFU PIECES
Ingredients: Tofu (water, soya beans, calcium sulphate - natural coagulant), marinade (water, soya sauce, salt, fructose, citric acid, spice extracts), vegetable oil.
FREE FROM ARTIFICIAL ADDITIVES

Figure 15.12 *List of ingredients for marinated tofu*

What are the advantages of buying ready-marinated tofu pieces?

ANSWERS

A1
Soya lecithin is a protein which is used as an emulsifier to stabilise and improve the consistency of the mallow filling during processing and storage.

A2
White bread is a popular choice for many consumers. Wheat flour often produces a light yellow colouring and therefore bleaching agents used to be added to the bread to make it whiter. However, many people do not like the idea of artificial additives such as bleaching agents being added to bread. So bread manufacturers looked for another way of making white bread. Soya flour bakes white and is a alternative natural bleaching agent. It is combined with wheat flour to produce whiter bread and cakes.

A3
Your answer could include the following points:
- TVP is made from soya beans which are processed to resemble the shape and texture of meat.
- Soya beans give a high yield per hectare so they are cheaper to produce than meat. This saving in cost will be reflected in the price of the snack meal.
- TVP can be dried and packaged with a shelf life of about a year. This makes the snack meal a convenient product to store.

A4
Myco-protein is not a suitable meat analogue for vegans. This is because during the final stages of production the myco-protein fibres are bound together with egg white. This binding agent also helps to develop the texture. The myco-protein is then processed into shapes, i.e. cubes, sliced, shredded or minced to produce meat analogues.

TUTORIALS

T1
Emulsions are substances such as oil and water mixed together. If left to stand, these two liquids would not stay mixed. A third substance is added to hold the two parts together. The 'match maker' is called an emulsifying agent. Other examples of emulsifying agents include:
- *lecithin, found naturally in egg yolk, which stabilises mayonnaise and creamed cake mixtures*
- *glycerol monosterate (GMS) which is used to stabilise a wide range of processed food including margarine. (Refer to Chapter 13 page 94.)*

T2
Soya flour helps to improve the overall qualities of bread products by producing a moister, softer crumb, an improvement in crumb colour and more flavour. It also increases the amount of dough and improves the keeping qualities of the finished product.

T3
You could have included different reasons, e.g. some consumers are vegetarian. This means that they eat a restricted range of animal proteins, i.e. no meat. A plant-based substitute such as TVP would be an acceptable form of protein for a vegetarian.

T4
Vegans are a specific group of vegetarians who do not eat any animal product such as meat, eggs or milk.

ANSWERS

A5 A meat extender is a meat analogue which is used to 'bulk out' or extend food products. TVP could be used to reduce the cost of a minced beef product, e.g. shepherd's pie, lasagne, minced beef pie. The meat analogue would not totally replace the minced beef. It would be used in a ratio which did not change the characteristic of the food product. TVP has little flavour but it absorbs the flavour of the ingredients it is cooked with, e.g. in this case beef stock, garlic, herbs.

A6 Your reasons could include:
- TVP has a bland flavour and the soya mince and onions would not provide an interesting flavour or any colour for the rissoles.
- TVP is best cooked with distinctive-flavoured foods and in this recipe these are Marmite, tomato ketchup, herbs and Worcestershire sauce. These add a distinct savoury flavour to the TVP.
- These ingredients also add a deeper colour to the soya rissole mixture.
- The egg is used to bind the ingredients together. Egg coagulates on heating so the egg will coagulate when the rissoles are cooked by frying in hot oil.

A7 Marinated tofu pieces are:
- time-saving – marinating food, i.e. soaking food in flavoured liquid, requires time for the flavour to be absorbed into the product
- pre-cooked and convenient to use as they simply need adding to a recipe and heating through
- easy to use in a range of food products, i.e. stir-fry, casseroles, soup, as an alternative to meat
- a variation on the original plain soya bean curd which has been used for many years in East Asia, China and Japan.

TUTORIALS

T5 If TVP *has been added to a food product, the information on the label must not mislead the consumer, i.e:*
- *The name of the product must clearly tell consumers what the product is. For example, beef lasagne must contain minced beef. It could not be made just from TVP. If it was it would need to be called beef-flavoured lasagne.*
- *The list of ingredients would indicate the proportion of beef to TVP as ingredients are listed in descending order of weight. Whichever of these two ingredients (beef or TVP) was there in the larger quantity would be put first in the list. (Refer to Chapter 28 page 198.)*

T6 *Soya mince is made from defatted soya flour which has been extruded to resemble the shape and texture of pieces of meat.*

T7 *Tofu is a vegetable protein, made from soya beans that are ground to a paste and sieved to produce soya milk. The milk is boiled and cooled to 50°C. Calcium sulphate is added to coagulate the milk. The solid curd is pressed and formed into tofu blocks.*
Look back at the list of ingredients. Note the ingredient calcium sulphate, which is a natural coagulant.

CHAPTER 16

MANUFACTURING IN QUANTITY

HOW DO MANUFACTURERS PLAN THEIR PRODUCTION?

Food manufacturers need to ensure that all the products they make are of a quality that will be acceptable to the consumer. Manufacturers carefully plan how the different parts of a product can be produced and put together to meet the design specification. The design specification includes details about the size, weight, appearance and cost of the product and the number to be made.

The manufacturer needs to decide:

- how quickly the product needs to be made
- how each part of the product can be made
- how much each part or process will cost
- how each product will turn out exactly the same.

Manufacturers often find it quicker, cheaper or simpler to 'buy in' ready-prepared ingredients or parts to make their food product. These are called standard components.

Figure 16.1 *Stock cubes can be used in many different recipes*

STANDARD COMPONENTS

You should be aware of following facts about standard components:

1   A standard component is a pre-manufactured or ready-made ingredient.

    For example:

- A manufacturer of novelty cakes may choose to 'buy in' marzipan, ready to roll icing and cake decorations from another supplier.

Figure 16.2 *A decorated novelty cake may use 'bought in' marzipan*

- A manufacturer of cook-chill spaghetti bolognese may choose to 'buy in' ready-grated parmesan cheese and ready-chopped herbs from other suppliers.

Figure 16.3 *A cook chill ready meal may use ready-made ingredients*

2 Standard components are used to maintain consistency of outcome in:
- size, e.g. pizza base, sponge flan case, meringue nest
- weight, e.g. sachet of gelatine, canned pie filling
- shape, e.g. cake decoration, pastry case
- flavour, e.g. chopped herbs, stock cubes, dried vegetables
- ratio/proportion, e.g. cake mix, ready-made filo pastry.

3 Using standard components helps to:
- save time by reducing the number of manufacturing processes
- keep the assembly process as simple as possible
- achieve consistent outcomes, i.e. each product is of the same quality
- reduce the production costs as little or no skill is required to use them
- maintain stock control because some components have a relatively long shelf life.

4 When manufacturers buy in standard components from another supplier they need to check to make sure the standard components will not change the product profile.

For example, do the standard components:
- contain additives such as flavour enhancers or artificial colours?
- contain additional amounts of fat, salt or sugar?

Or will the standard components:
- reduce the quality as the flavour, texture and colour may not be as good?
- increase the overall cost of the product because they are expensive to buy in?

KEY WORDS

These are the key words. Tick them if you know what they mean. Otherwise check on them.

component	**consistency**	**flavour**
pre-manufactured	**proportion**	**ratio**
ready made	**ready prepared**	**shape**
size	**standard component**	**stock control**
weight		

Check yourself

QUESTIONS

Q1 A manufacturer of novelty celebration cakes buys in ready-made marzipan from two different suppliers. Give reasons for this.

Q2 A pie manufacturer decides to develop a new savoury product by adapting a sausage and apple roll. At first the company chooses to buy in ready-made frozen pastry because they are unable to make the necessary quantity of pastry themselves. Give three advantages and three disadvantages of buying in ready-made pastry.

Q3 A pizza manufacturer wins a contract to supply a supermarket with a range of 'traditional Italian pizzas'. To produce the order on a weekly basis the manufacturer decides to buy in some standard components. This will speed up production. List three standard components that the manufacture could buy in. Give reasons for your choice.

Q4 A cafe prepares, cooks and serves 60 lunches every day. The menu is changed each week. Name two standard components that could be kept in stock to use in a variety of food products on the cafe menu.

Q5 An independent baker makes individual fruit pies in tin foil dishes. Canned pie filling is used instead of fresh fruit. Give reasons for this.

REMEMBER! Cover the answers if you want to.

ANSWERS

A1 The cake manufacturer uses two suppliers to make sure that they have a constant supply. If one supplier had difficulties, e.g. with obtaining raw ingredients, such as the ground almonds, or with the processing machinery which makes the marzipan, this supplier would not be able to supply the cake manufacturer. But marzipan would still be available from the second supplier.

A2 (i) Three advantages could include:
- It saves the time needed to buy and store the raw ingredients for the pastry, e.g. flour, fat.
- It saves preparation time, i.e. no weighing or mixing of the ingredients is necessary.
- It guarantees a consistent result.

(ii) Three disadvantages could include:
- Frozen foods need to be stored at a specific temperature (−18°C). This needs to be planned into the manufacturing schedule.
- Special storage conditions are needed, e.g. a freezer room.
- Frozen pastry takes time to thaw.
- It could be expensive if only bought in small quantities.

TUTORIALS

T1 *It is quite common for standard components to be bought from more than one supplier. This follows the traditional saying: 'Don't put all your eggs in one basket.' A constant supply of a standard component must be guaranteed.*

T2 *Manufacturers need to consider both the advantages and the disadvantages when using standard components. Points to consider include cost, time of storage, ease of use and the quality of the product. Balance the points for with the points against to reach a decision.*

ANSWERS

A3 Any three from:
- ready-made pizza bases
- ready-grated mozzarella cheese
- ready-chopped vegetables for the toppings
- ready-made tomato and herb sauce.

Reasons should include a reference to savings in time, cost and labour costs, consistency of result and quality, and storage

A4 Standard components kept in stock could include:
- stock cubes: chicken, beef, fish, vegetable flavours. To use in lasagne, chilli, meat or fish pie, etc.
- canned vegetables: tomatoes, kidney beans, sweetcorn. To use in hot main-course meals, salads, etc.
- dried foods: chocolate strands or shapes, chopped nuts, wafer biscuits, sugar strands or shapes. To use to decorate puddings, cakes, ice cream sundaes, etc.

A5 Several varieties are available, e.g. blackberry and apple, cherry, strawberry, gooseberry. Reasons for use could include:
- Some fruits are only available at certain times of the year, e.g. cherries, strawberries.
- Some fruit takes time to prepare, e.g. stoning cherries, hulling strawberries, peeling apples.
- Consistency of the quality of the filling is guaranteed between different batches.

TUTORIALS

T3 Buying in standard components helps manufacturers to increase production without major investment in:
- equipment for extra production lines
- extra staffing costs
- storage of raw ingredients.

T4 These standard components can be used directly in recipes whenever they are needed. They can be used in a variety of products on different menus. They:
- have a long shelf life
- add variety, colour, flavour and interest to a product
- give consistency of results.

T5 Canned pie fillings have several advantages. Before choosing the supplier of the pie filling it would be necessary to do a quality check on the pie filling. Check the ratio of solid fruit pieces to fruit sauce. The cheaper pie fillings will contain more fruit sauce. In this context the baker would need to decide how much he or she could afford to pay and what quality he or she wants the individual fruit pies to have.

CHAPTER 17

MEASUREMENT, RATIO AND PROPORTION

WHY DO YOU NEED TO MEASURE INGREDIENTS?

It is important to be accurate when:

- weighing and measuring raw materials (ingredients) and/or components
- working out the ratios and proportions of raw materials and/or components
- selecting and maintaining the correct temperature for cooking or cooling food products.

During your course you will have used recipes which are made up of a collection of ingredients, each with a specified weight. Some recipes are known as **traditional** recipes because they can be found written out in early recipe books. These recipes are often referred to as **basic** or **foundation** recipes. These include recipes for biscuits, cakes, pastry, sauces and bread. Today these foundation recipes form the basis of **recipe development** or **product formulation**. They can be adapted or amended to make food products which meet particular consumer needs or preferences, e.g. low-sugar biscuits, fruit-flavoured cakes, enriched bread dough.

DESIGNATED TOLERANCES

Recipe development has to be done skilfully because ingredients can only be added or altered to a certain degree before the recipe will no longer produce the desired outcome. For example:

- A creamed cake mixture containing a large amount of sugar will probably have a crisp top and will sink in the middle.
- A savoury scone mixture with too much extra cheese will not rise but will spread out and become flatter.

These are examples of **exceeding designated tolerances**, i.e. not working within limits which have been proved to lead to a successful outcome.

To produce good quality food products you need to:

- understand the importance of combining materials and components in appropriate ratios and proportions to make and shape particular types of food products
- demonstrate accuracy in weighing and measuring to obtain the desired outcome
- understand that any changes you make to the quantities of an individual ingredient or any addition of one or more different ingredients can affect the structure, shape or texture of the finished product.

WEIGHT OR VOLUME

Food ingredients can be measured by weight or volume.

Weight

- Weighing is accurate if reliable scales are used.
- Scales may be: spring balance, digital electronic, or balances with loose weights.
- Most foods are sold and weighed in metric measurements, i.e. grams and kilos.

Volume

- Liquid and some solid (granules or powder) ingredients can be measured by volume.
- Volume measuring equipment includes: measuring jugs, funnels, spoons or American cups.
- The units or measurement are fluid ounces or millilitres and litres.

Figure 17.1 *Different types of weighing machines*

Calibration

Calibration is the term used in the food industry for any activities which involve weighing and measuring. It includes any regular checks that are made to make sure that weighing scales are providing accurate readings. Think what would happen in the manufacture of rich tea biscuits (e.g. when 4 tonnes of rich tea mixture are made every hour for 24 hours a day) if inaccurate weights of ingredients were used. There would be a lot of wasted biscuit mixture!

Figure 17.2 *Spoons used to measure volumes*

COMBINING INGREDIENTS

Proportion

Each ingredient has a specific function in a recipe and all ingredients need to be combined in specified amounts, i.e. in the correct proportions, to produce a successful result. Ingredients combined in the same proportion each time should produce the same result over and over again.

For example, the proportions of a foundation recipe for a cake made by the creaming method are:

Proportion:
100 *g self raising flour*
100 *g caster sugar*
100 *g butter/margarine*
2 *eggs*

Figure 17.3 *Large-scale weighing of spices in the commercial food industry*

Ratio

The amount of one ingredient in a recipe in relationship to another ingredient in the same recipe can often be expressed as a number. This is known as the **ratio of ingredients**.

Shortbread recipe

Proportion:
150 *g flour*
100 *g butter*   **Ratio:** 3:2:1 (*3 parts flour to 2 parts fat to 1 part sugar*)
50 *g sugar*

125

SMALL-SCALE PROTOTYPES

In the test kitchen of a commercial food manufacturer basic or foundation recipes will be studied and changes will be made to meet a general design specification. The following information will be needed:

- the function of each ingredient
- the exact ratio and proportion of ingredients
- accurate weights and measures of ingredients
- an accurate method of mixing and combining ingredients
- accurate temperatures for heating or cooking.

Sample or test recipes are made and the results recorded. Sensory tests are carried out to tell the manufacturer what changes are needed.

THE PRODUCTION SPECIFICATION

The production specification contains essential information about a product:

- types of ingredients
- ratio and proportion of ingredients
- finished weight or volume
- manufacturing processes
- specific time schedules and temperatures
- quality control procedures

as well as information relating to packaging, labelling, shelf life, storage requirements and distribution.

SCALING UP

Figure 17.4 *Large-scale production of sauce*

- The small-scale recipe has to be scaled up for mass production.
- Scaled-up quantities must be in the same proportion as the prototype. This can be worked out by computer.

Table 17.1 *Moving from a small-scale prototype to a large-scale manufactured product*

Small-scale/prototype	Large scale
Egg Custard	**Egg Custard**
Pastry	
200 g flour	100 kg flour
50 g vegetable fat/lard	25 kg shortening
50 g margarine/butter	25 kg margarine
2–3 tablespoons water	15 kg caster sugar
pinch of salt	14 kg whole egg
	dextrose
	salt
Egg Custard Filling	
2 small eggs	10 kg whole egg
50 g caster sugar	7 kg caster sugar
500 ml milk	32 kg whole milk
2–3 drops vanilla essence	vanilla flavour
grated nutmeg	colouring
	grated nutmeg

AMENDMENTS REQUIRED FOR LARGE-SCALE PRODUCTION

To enable ingredients to be combined and processed successfully by large-scale production lines some adjustments may need to be made, such as:

- the use of oil instead of solid fat to increase the **plasticity** of a pastry mixture
- adding glycerine to increase the moisture of a cake mixture
- adding water to create steam as an additional raising agent
- adding dextrose to pastry to give a light brown colour when baked
- the use of additives such as emulsifiers to stabilise a mixture
- adding preservatives to increase shelf life.

To carry out recipe development and product formulation successfully you will need to understand:

- foundation recipes
- the function of ingredients
- ratio and proportion.

BISCUITS

There are many types of biscuit, made from a variety of ingredients. The

Table 17.2 *Two methods of making biscuits*

	Proportion of Ingredients	Ratio	Method	Outcome (Designated Criteria)
Rubbed in biscuit mixture e.g. shortbread	150 g plain flour 100 g butter 50 g caster sugar	3:2:1 Air trapped during rubbing in	Mix flour and sugar ↓ Rub in butter ↓ Knead well to form smooth paste (Sometimes the sugar is added after rubbing in)	Sweet, short, crumb texture  *Figure 17.5 Shortbread*
Creamed biscuit mixture e.g. Viennese fingers	150 g self raising flour 150 g butter/margarine 50 g caster sugar Few drops of vanilla essence	6:6:2 Air trapped during creaming	Cream fat and sugar ↓ Stir in flour and essence	Sweet, rich short texture 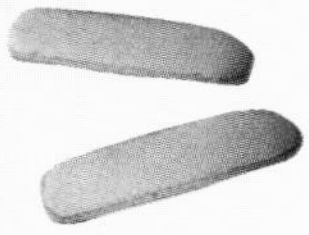 *Figure 17.6 Viennese fingers*

ingredients are combined using the same methods as for cake making. Two examples are given in Table 17.2.

CAKES

- The main ingredients in cake making are fat, sugar, eggs, flour, a raising agent and often a liquid such as milk or water.
- All ingredients, especially the raising agent if added separately, need to be measured accurately.
- Each ingredient has a specific function in the recipe.
- Additional ingredients e.g flavourings, essences, chocolate, coffee, spices, dried fruit, may be added.

There are four basic cake recipes. Using these four basic recipes, ingredients are added or combined in different ratios to produce different textures and finishes.

THE FUNCTION OF CAKE INGREDIENTS

Figure 17.7 *Cake ingredients*

Flour

- forms the main structure of cakes
- soft flour with a lower gluten content produces a soft, even texture

Raising agent

- aerates the mixture to increase the volume.

Fat

- gives colour and flavour if butter or margarine is used
- holds air bubbles produced from mixing or the raising agent to create texture and volume
- creates texture according to the ratios used, e.g.
  – short crumb from the rubbed in method
  – soft even texture from the creamed method
- helps to extend shelf life.

Sugar

- sweetens cake mixtures
- develops flavour, e.g. soft brown sugar, or treacle in the melted method
- increases the bulk of the mixture
- when creamed with fat, sugar helps to hold air as an additional raising agent.

Eggs

- adds colour and flavour to all cakes
- egg **protein-albumen** holds air when whisked into a foam – this is used as a raising agent in the whisked method
- forms an emulsion when mixed into fat, e.g. egg beaten into creamed sugar/fat
- egg yolk contains **lecithin** which helps to keep the emulsion stable

Liquid

Detail	Proportion of Ingredients	Ratio	Method	Outcome (Designated Criteria)
Creamed cake e.g. Victoria sandwich, small buns, Madeira cake	100 g self-raising flour 100 g caster sugar 100 g soft margarine or butter 2 eggs	Equal quantities Raising agent – self raising flour (chemical)	Fat + sugar creamed together → Beaten egg added gradually → Fold in flour	Light brown sponge with fine even texture
All in one method	Plus 5 ml baking powder All ingredients mixed together for 2 minutes by hand, mixer or food processor.			 *Figure 17.8 Victoria sandwich cake*
Whisked cake e.g. swiss roll, sponge buns, cake, gateaux, flan case	50 g caster sugar 50 g plain flour 2 eggs (100 g) No fat May go stale quickly	1:1:2 Raising agent – Air Steam from water in eggs	Whisk eggs and sugar until thick and creamy → Fold in flour	Very light sponge Even, soft moist texture *Figure 17.9 Whisked sponge product*
Rubbed-in cake e.g. fruit loaf, cake, rock buns, raspberry buns, scones	200 g plain flour 10 ml baking powder 100 g margarine 100 g caster sugar 2 eggs 30 ml milk Flavouring ingredients 175 g dried fruit or 75 g cherries (half or less fat to flour)	8:4:4:2 cake mixture or 8:4:2:1 scone mixture Raising agent baking powder or self raising flour (chemical)	Fat rubbed into flour → Add additional ingredients → Bind together with liquid	Well-risen product Rougher surface Open crumb texture *Figure 17.10 Rubbed-in product*
Melted cake e.g. flap jack, parkin, gingerbread cake or biscuits	200 g plain flour 50 g soft brown sugar 100 g margarine 150 g black treacle 50 g golden syrup 125 ml milk 2 eggs 5 ml bicarbonate of soda 100 ml ground ginger 5 ml mixed spice 50 g sultanas (optional) Proportion of syrup/treacle	8:4:2:8 (sugar content is 50 g sugar + 150 g black treacle) Raising agent bicarbonate of soda – chemical Spice masks the flavour and yellow tinge caused from raising agent	Melt fat, treacle, syrup, sugar → Stir into rest of dried ingredients → Add egg/milk	Moist and sticky Soft even texture *Figure 17.11 Melted method product*

Table 17.3 *Basic cake making*

- liquids such as milk or water produce steam which acts as a raising agent
- gluten is formed when liquid mixes with protein in the flour.

PASTRY

- main ingredients are flour, fat, water and a little salt
- richer pastries may include eggs, cheese, sugar, herbs, spices
- There are several types of pastry, e.g. filo, strudel, hot water crust, suet, shortcrust, choux and flaky.

Similar ingredients are combined in different ratios by different methods to produce a variety of textures and finishes. (See Table 17.4.)

THE FUNCTION OF INGREDIENTS

Table 17.4 *The function of ingredients in shortcrust and flaky pastry*

Ingredient	Shortcrust	Flaky
Type of flour	Soft plain flour Low gluten content for short crumb texture	Strong plain flour High gluten content for crisp flaky layers Stretchy dough needed to roll and fold
Fat	Mixture of white fat and butter or margarine Coats the flour granules with fat to reduce the water mixing with gluten	Mixture of white fat and butter/margarine blended together Place in small pieces on the dough to trap air between the layers of dough
Water	Binds rubbed in fat/flour mixture together Ease of rolling out	Combines with gluten to form stretchy elastic dough Lemon juice (citric acid) added to strengthen the gluten
Salt	Helps develop flavour	Helps develop flavour and strengthen gluten

IN PASTRY

Table 17.5 *The function of ingredients in choux pastry*

- **Shortcrust and flaky pastry** contain some similar ingredients, i.e.

Ingredient	Function
Water – boiled to 100°C	Mixes with strong flour to develop gluten Heat causes starch to gelatinise
Flour – strong, plain	Starch cooks in the boiling water, i.e. gelatinisation takes place Contains high gluten content Gluten is strengthened by beating in the eggs Gluten stretches to hold the expanding steam and air Coagulates when baked at high temperature
Fat – butter/margarine	Flavour
Egg	Helps to hold air in the starch mixture Gives a smooth glossy finish to aid piping through a tube or nozzle

	Proportion of Ingredients	Ratio Flour to Fat	Method	Outcome (Designated Criteria)
Shortcrust Pastry e.g. pies, pasties, tartlets	200 g plain flour 100 g margarine/white fat pinch of salt 2 tablespoons cold water to mix **Wholemeal pastry** 100 g wholewheat flour 100 g white flour	2:1 Air trapped during rubbing-in process	Rub fat into flour to look like breadcrumbs → Mix together with cold water	Short crumb, light, crisp texture  Figure 17.12 *Products made with shortcrust pastry*
Rich shortcrust pastry e.g. fruit flans and tartlets	200 g plain flour 100 g margarine or butter 50 g caster sugar pinch of salt 1 egg yolk about 1 tablespoon cold water to mix **Cheese pastry** exchange sugar for 150 g dry grated cheese + pinch of cayenne pepper	2:1 Air trapped during rubbing-in process	Rub fat into flour to look like breadcrumbs → Stir in sugar → Mix together with egg and water	Short crumb, sweet, light crisp texture  Figure 17.13 *Rich shortcrust pastry product*
Choux pastry e.g. eclairs, profiteroles, cream buns	75 g plain flour 25 g butter or margarine 2 eggs 125 ml water	3:1 Raising agent steam from high water content Air from beating in eggs	Heat water and melt fat in pan → Add flour → Beat in eggs	Light, well risen Crisp texture Hollow inside 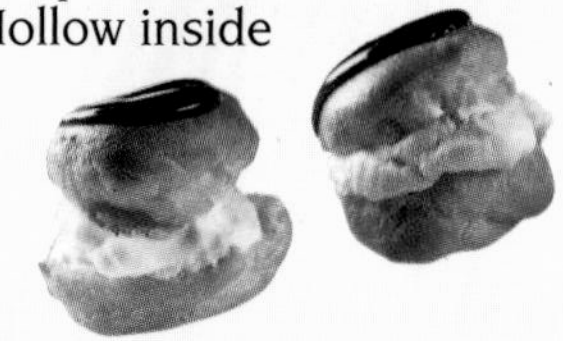 Figure 17.14 *Choux pastry products*
Flaky pastry e.g. Eccles cakes, sausage rolls, vol-au-vents	200 g plain flour 150 g fat mixture – white fat with butter or margarine pinch of salt 2 teaspoons lemon juice 100 ml cold water (approx.)	4:3 Air trapped between many layers	Rub quarter of fat into flour → Mix together with liquids → Roll and fold adding a quarter of the fat each time	Many layers of crisp flakes  Figure 17.15 *Flaky pastry forms many layers in cooking*

Table 17.6 *Pastry chart*

flour, fat, water and salt. The functions of each of these ingredients is explained in Table 17.4.

- **Choux pastry** contains egg and is made in a very different way. Check yourself if the function of the ingredients is the same in chou pasty. Look at Table 17.5. Cover the right-hand side of the page, gi your answer and then check your answer against the table.

SAUCES

Figure 17.16 *A variety of sauces*

There are several types of sauces, based on different ways of thickening mixtures. Some of the main ones are listed below.

- **Egg-based sauces** – egg coagulates on heating and thickens a liquid. For example, 1 egg will thicken 125 ml milk to be used to make egg custard.

- **Oil/water emulsion sauces** – used for oil and vinegar dressing. Egg yolk stabilises the emulsion used to make mayonnaise.

- **Fruit or vegetable sauces** – fruit or vegetables are cooked and puréed to make and thicken sauces, e.g. raspberry coulis, tomato sauce.

- **Starch-based sauces** – starch from wheatflour, cornflour or arrowroot is used to thicken liquids such as water and stock:
  - wheatflour is used in white sauce and flavoured to make parsley sauce
  - cornflour is used in custard and gravy
  - arrowroot is used in a glaze for fruit flans and gateaux

STARCH-BASED SAUCES

Thickening a liquid with starch is a traditional method of making sauces. The ingredients are combined by three different ways:

- **roux** method – flour is stirred into melted fat. Liquid is then carefully added. This is the best way of making sauces when the liquid is hot

- **all-in-one** method – uses the same ingredients and proportions a the roux method but all ingredients and cold liquid are mixed together in a pan and then brought to the boil

- **blended** method – starch is blended with the liquid. No fat is added.

The proportion of flour/fat to the amount of liquid used determines the consistency (thickness) of the sauce. Traditionally, three thicknesses can be achieved, to pour over, coat or bind ingredients together:

	Proportion of Ingredients	Ratio	Method	Outcome (Designated Criteria)
Pouring white sauce	15 g plain flour 15 g fat 250 ml milk	1:1:16	Roux or all in one method	Smooth well-flavoured sauce Pours freely in thin flow
Coating white sauce	25 g plain flour 25 g fat 250 ml milk	1:1:10	Roux or all in one method	Smooth, well-flavoured sauce Thick enough to coat the back of a spoon and not run off. It is served on cauliflower/fish etc.
Binding white sauce	50 g plain flour 50 g fat 250 ml milk	1:1:5	Roux or all in one method	Smooth well-flavoured sauce Very thick to hold other ingredients or bind them together, e.g. egg white in soufflé, dried ingredients in meat loaf

Table 17.7 *Types of sauces*

- **pouring sauce** – white sauce flavoured, e.g. with vanilla or chocolate and poured over sponge pudding
- **coating sauce** – white sauce flavoured, e.g. with cheese or parsley and used to coat fish
- **binding sauce** – white sauce used as a base, e.g. for cheese soufflé.

Gelatinisation occurs in the following way:

- Starch grains are mixed into a liquid. Because the starch grains do not dissolve, they are suspended in the liquid. This is called a **suspension**.
- Stirring helps to keep the starch grains suspended.
- If the liquid is not stirred, the starch grains will join together and form lumps of starch which may not cook correctly.
- The mixture is heated and at approximately 60°C the starch grains will absorb the liquid and swell.
- As heating continues the starch grains swell even more then break open and release starch which forms a gel with the liquid. This is known as gelatinisation. The process of gelatinisation is completed at boiling point (100°C).
- If the gelatinised starch mixture is cooled, the gel becomes stiffer and will set to form a mould, e.g. in blancmange. This is the same for all starch-based sauces but do remember that cornflour and arrowroot are pure starch while wheatflour contains a high proportion of starch and also some protein.

FUNCTION OF STARCH-BASED SAUCE INGREDIENTS

When mixed with a liquid and heated, starch thickens the liquid. This is called **gelatinisation**.
When you are designing and making products which require or contain a sauce you must consider anything which may affect the consistency e.g:

- For a sweet sauce you may add sugar, but large amounts of sugar will soften the starch gel.
- For a sauce made from cornflour, e.g. for a lemon meringue pie, you need to add lemon juice, but too much acid will reduce the

Figure 17.17 *A range of bread products*

thickening ability of the starch.

- To extend the shelf life of a main course pasta dish with a sauce, e.g. vegetable lasagne, you may store the lasagne in a chill cabinet or freezer cabinet but the change in temperature may affect the consistency of the sauce when reheated. An adaptation may need to be made at the recipe development stage.

White Bread – Proportion of Ingredients	Designated Criteria
450 g white strong flour 15 g fresh yeast 25 g fat 5 ml salt 5 ml caster sugar 150 ml warm water	Increased volume Well risen and golden brown Firm outside structure Maybe crisp crust Soft even open texture inside Distinct smell and taste

Table 17.8 *The ingredients of bread*

BREAD

- The main ingredients of bread are flour, yeast, liquid and salt.
- Additional ingredients can be added, such as sugar, fat, eggs.

- In large-scale bread production flour treatment agents, such as soya flour, ascorbic acid (vitamin C) and emulsifiers, are added.

THE FUNCTION OF BREAD INGREDIENTS

Flour

- Use strong wheat flour with a high gluten content.
- Gluten is a protein which, when mixed with a liquid, forms an elastic stretchy dough.
- Gluten stretches to hold the carbon dioxide bubbles produced by yeast.
- During cooking at high temperatures the gluten coagulates (sets) to form the structure of the bread.
- Wholemeal flour contains bran and wheatgerm. It absorbs more water than strong white flour and the gluten is often weaker. For best results use half wholemeal flour to half white strong flour in a standard recipe.

Flour Treatment Agents

- These agents include soya flour, emulsifiers, ascorbic acid and preservatives.
- They are added to improve the keeping quality of the bread and qualities such as texture.

Yeast

- Yeast is the raising agent used in bread making.
- Three types of yeast are available for use: fresh yeast, dried yeast, easy blend yeast with vitamin C added.

Salt

- Salt is a very important ingredient, used in the ratio of 2% to the weight of the flour.
- Salt provides three functions:
  - It strengthens gluten.
  - It controls the action of yeast.
  - It develops flavour in the dough.

Liquid

- Usually water is used but in an enriched dough milk, or milk and water, are added for a soft texture.
- Liquid must be lukewarm (25°C–35°C) to provide warm conditions for yeast fermentation.
- Correct temperature is vital. If the temperature is too hot, it destroys the yeast. If too cold, it slows the action of the yeast.

Sugar

- Small amounts of sugar are added to aid the fermentation process of the yeast.
- Larger amounts of sugar are added to rich yeast doughs, e.g. for

---

KEY WORDS

These are the key words. Tick them if you think you know what they mean. Otherwise check on them.

accuracy	calibration	coagulate
components	design specification	designated criteria
designated tolerance	emulsion	function
gluten	ingredient	large scale
manufacturing specification	measurement	production run
proportion	prototype	ratio
raw materials	small-scale sample	volume
weight		

Check yourself

QUESTIONS

Q1 What type of measuring equipment would a manufacturer choose to install on a new large-scale production line to weigh the filling for fruit pies which are being assembled on the line? Give reasons for the method the manufacturer would choose?

Q2 One recipe for curry sauce contains the following spices: ground coriander, fenugreek seeds, ground cumin, turmeric. These are fried together for two minutes. An experienced chef may guess the right amounts of the spices to add to one small batch of curry sauce. Would a manufacturer who is mass producing hundreds of cartons of cook-chill curry sauce be able to guess the amounts equally as well?

Q3 A cake manufacturing company produces chocolate sponge cakes in three factory units situated in different parts of the country. How would the cake manufacturer know that all the cakes produced were made to the same standard and that consumers would not be able to tell which factory the cakes were made in.

Q4 Work has started in a test kitchen to improve and promote a 'meal for one' pasta and cheese sauce product which has recently become less popular than it used to be. Suggest three recipe developments which could make the pasta and cheese sauce more popular. The prototypes would be assessed by consumers carrying out sensory analysis.

Q5 A small bakery business makes a batch of white bread dough every day and uses the dough to produce loaves and bread rolls. Fresh yeast, bought in 1-kg blocks, is the amount required in each batch of bread dough. Give three reasons why the baker uses fresh yeast.

REMEMBER! Cover the answers if you want to.

ANSWERS

A1 The manufacturer would probably choose an electronic weighing machine. Some of these record in grams, whilst others record to the decimal point of a gram. The sensor in the electric circuit sends a signal to a digital display unit each time a portion of fruit filling is weighed. The digital display can be situated in a position where it can be easily read.

The reading can also be connected to:
- an alarm system which sounds if incorrect amounts of fruit filling are being deposited
- a computer to monitor the weighing process as part of the quality control procedures.

TUTORIALS

T1 *Accurate weighing of ingredients is vital to the production of consistent and successful results. In the example of the fruit filling going into fruit pies, the weight of the filling is a crucial factor. Too much fruit filling will boil over during cooking. Too little filling causes the finished weight of the pies to be too low. Consumers would complain and the manufacturer would not be complying with the Weights and Measures Regulations 1985.*

ANSWERS

A2

No, certainly not. Even though the spices are added in small amounts, i.e. in a much lower ratio to the main ingredients of stock, onion and yogurt, they each have an intense and distinct flavour. Adding too much, too little or the incorrect combination could ruin the overall quality of the curry sauce. The spices would have to be weighed out accurately and in the correct ratio.

A3

After the prototype for the chocolate cake had been developed in the test kitchen a manufacturing specification would be compiled. This would be very detailed and contain all the information about the manufacture of the chocolate cake, e.g. ingredients, ratio and proportion of ingredients, finished weight, processes, specific times and temperature schedules, quality control procedures. This gives clear guidance to the production manager who will make sure that the product matches the manufacturing specification.

A4

Three modifications or adaptations could include:
- using a mixture of interesting cheeses to flavour the sauce, e.g. Italian three-cheese sauce
- adding a vegetable such as dried porcine, mushroom, asparagus or leek
- using low-fat ingredients, e.g. skimmed milk, low-fat cheese.

The new products could be promoted as a new product range to reflect the changes made, e.g. 'Italian Fare', 'Vegetarian Selection', 'Low-fat Option'.

A5

Three reasons may include:
i) The yeast is bought in in pre-weighed units of 1 kg. This ensures that an accurate amount of yeast is used in each batch. Pre-weighed ingredients are referred to as standard components.
ii) Fresh yeast is blended with warm liquid just before adding to the flour. It can be used immediately and reduces any waiting time.
iii) Yeast is the raising agent in bread. During the fermentation process yeast produces carbon dioxide. If an incorrect amount of yeast is used in a batch of dough the final bread products would not be satisfactory, i.e:
- too much yeast – over-risen dough with a large, uneven texture
- too little yeast – unrisen dough with a close, heavy texture.

TUTORIALS

T2

In a small-scale sample, using 450 ml of vegetable stock, the spices are added in the following quantities: 10 ml ground coriander, 5 ml fenugreek seeds, 5 ml ground cumin, 10 ml turmeric. A 5-ml measuring spoon could be used to measure them out. An additional point to watch would be to make sure the measure is level and not heaped. In a large-scale manufacturing situation large quantities of the spices would be used. These may be weighed by an electronic weighing machine or, because the spices are dry and powdery, they could be measured by volume in a measuring container. Whichever method is chosen, it must be accurate.

T3

The manufacturing specification must be strictly adhered to if the final products are going to be of a consistent quality.

T4

Changing individual ingredients or putting in additional ingredients will affect the flavour and the texture of the pasta and sauce product. Sample or test recipes need to be made and the results recorded. Only one variation should be made each time to enable the impact of the change to be assessed. This is known as 'fair testing'.

T5

The selection, combination and specific quantity of ingredients are very important. Foundation recipes have a designated tolerance and qualities of ingredients above or below this tolerance will affect the quality of the final product. Successful recipe development could include:
- accurately weighing and measuring each ingredient
- combining ingredients in appropriate ratios and proportions
- carrying out fair tests to monitor the affect of recipe amendments.

SAMPLE STUDENT'S ANSWERS AND EXAMINER'S COMMENTS

EXAMINER'S COMMENTS

1   *These are good answers to each part of the question. They show that the student has a sound understanding of the materials that are being used as standard components. You should be able to think around the issues and apply knowledge gained from practical lessons when you have made these or similar food products.*

All these processed tomato products give authentic Italian flavours, colours and textures. Some of the main advantages are that they save the manufacturer time and labour costs as they are ready prepared and give a consistent quality. They also have a longer shelf life than fresh tomatoes.

---

1   A manufacturer of Italian foods buys in processed tomato products to use as standard components. Explain why the manufacturer would use the following processed tomato products in each of the Italian foods.

(a)   Tinned Italian chopped tomatoes to use for making minestrone soup.   **(3 marks)**

> Saves time preparing the tomatoes because they are washed, skinned and chopped before they go in the tin. The chopped pieces are in tomato juice. Also they add colour, flavour and liquid to the soup. Sometimes they have herbs added.

3/3

(b)   Sundried tomatoes to use for making Italian focaccia bread.   **(3 marks)**

> These can be bought in packets or in jars of oil. They have a highly concentrated flavour and a rough texture. They are interesting ingredients in the soft bread.

3/3

(c)   Tomato pureé to use for making pizza toppings.   **(3 marks)**

> This can be bought in tubes or tins. It is thick and concentrated with no solid bits of tomatoes in it. It is a dark red colour. It can be spread on a flat pizza base and no juice will run off.

3/3

EXAMINER'S COMMENTS

2   *These are correct answers to the question, which is testing your ability to plan before making a product. Think about the things you need to know before you carry out your own project work and then think about what you would need to know if you were to make large quantities on a regular basis.*

Point 2 (b) is not fully explained. It refers to the recipe and the ingredients but it does not explain what the manufacturer would need to be aware of, e.g. do they already use the ingredients? Have they got the correct storage conditions? Is the recipe part of a manufacturing specification?

---

2   A cake manufacturer is planning to make a new range of 'Tray Bake' style cakes.

Explain **four** pieces of information that would be needed in order to plan for production.   **(8 marks)**

(a)   The manufacturer will need to know how many tray bake cakes have to be made, and when they need to be made to meet the orders from shops.

(b)   The recipe and the type of ingredients.

(c)   What equipment has the manufacturer got to make the cakes and how many workers are available to operate the equipment.

(d)   What is the final product to be like. Is it to be sold in a tin foil tray? Or cut and wrapped to be sold as individual pieces.

7/8

3 Give two advantages of each of these two types of manufacturing systems:

(a) Batch production
(4 marks)

Advantage 1 – This is used to make more than one product in small quantities e.g. a bakery business makes a batch of bread buns. Advantage 2 – The equipment can be used for more than one product, e.g. a baker may make a batch of bread dough in the large mixer and then make a batch of pastry using the same mixer.

3/4

(b) Continuous flow production
(4 marks)

Advantage 1 – This produces one specific product all the time. It means that a large quantity of a product can be made to a consistent standard to meet consumer demands. Advantage 2 – The production line is usually controlled by computers CAM which saves time because the same task e.g. cutting out pastry lids can be done at the same time and quickly.

4/4

EXAMINER'S COMMENTS

3 Different manufacturing systems are an important aspect of industrial practice. Explaining what they are and the reasons for choosing a particular system are usually straight forward questions to answer.

This answer contains some good points but you need to be careful to direct your answer to what the question is asking for. In this case the question was asking for the advantages of each system, not just a description of what they are.

Question to Answer

The answers to Question 4 can be found on page 242.

4 Popular biscuits for children are large gingerbread shapes. A biscuit manufacturer uses the following recipe for the gingerbread mixture.

Recipe: 350 g plain flour
5 ml (1 tsp) bicarbonate of soda
10 ml (2 tsp) ground ginger
100 g butter/margarine
175 g light brown sugar
60 ml (4 tbsp) golden syrup
1 egg beaten

(a) (i) Name a method for combining the ingredients to make the biscuits. (1 mark)
(ii) Give a reason for your choice. (1 mark)

(b) Explain the function of the bicarbonate of soda in this recipe. (2 marks)

(c) Explain how the manufacturer could get the maximum number of biscuits from the rolled out biscuit mixture and avoid wastage. (2 marks)

(d) The biscuit manufacturer has asked you to design two ideas for a large shaped gingerbread biscuit to celebrate the Olympic Games. Show how your shaped biscuit would be decorated. The manufacturer has asked you to use no more than three standard components for decoration.

(i) Use notes and sketches to describe your ideas in the spaces below. (6 marks)

Design Idea 1   Design Idea 2

(ii) Explain in detail the reasons for your choice of three standard components used to decorate your biscuit designs. (6 marks)

DIFFERENT SCALES OF PRODUCTION

It is important for you to identify different types of manufacturing processes and the characteristics of different scales of production.

INDIVIDUAL ONE-OFF CRAFTED PRODUCTION

This production system is sometimes known as **job production**. It is used when one product is made. It occurs when:

1   The product meets the design specification drawn up from a request or order from an individual customer, e.g. a novelty birthday cake, celebration cake, extra-large pizza. It will involve:

- an individual recipe, method or components being used
- more processes being carried out by hand than by equipment
- special skills from experienced staff
- an individual or unique finished product
- more time to make and finish the product
- the production of high quality goods.

2   The product is a prototype made in a test kitchen to meet a design specification from a client such as a major retail supermarket. It will involve:

- a prototype being presented to the client to see if it meets their requirements
- modifications being made to finalise the design
- the prototype being used as the reference product for the manufacturing specification.

BATCH PRODUCTION

This production system is used when more than one production is required. Small numbers of identical or similar products are made. For example, each day a small bakery may make batches of Chelsea buns, teacakes, white loaves and wholemeal bread rolls. Each day a butcher may make 20 kg of sausages.

Some of the reasons and advantages of this system include:

- Raw materials and components may be purchased in bulk.
- Only a small number of people are involved.
- Equipment can be used for more than one product, which reduces the 'down time' of machines.
- Production costs are reduced as more products can be made in the same time it takes to make a 'one-off' product.
- Slight adaptations can be made to different batches to meet consumer demand or to create consumer interest. For example:
  - Different flavours can be added to batches of pork sausages to make pork and leek, pork and apple, etc.
  - Different colours and decorations can be used for icing small cakes.
  - Different flavours can be added to a sponge cake recipe, e.g. coffee, chocolate, lemon, vanilla, etc.

Figure 19.1 *A batch production system*

MASS PRODUCTION

This production system is used when large numbers of one product are required, e.g. white sliced loaves, digestive biscuits, potato crisps, tea bags. Some of the advantages of this system include:

- The manufacturing processes are split into tasks which are sequenced into a production line.
- At each stage, specialised equipment or line operators carry out the tasks.
- Large-scale, specialist equipment is used for processes such as cutting, mixing, moulding, wrapping and packaging. Sometimes special equipment is developed to do a particular process, e.g. to cut lattice pastry tops for pies; to cut and shape chicken for chicken Kiev.

- As it passes from one stage to the next the food product is assembled by means of a series of moving sections, e.g. conveyor belt, rollers.
- Food products are produced quickly and efficiently.
- Raw materials and components are purchased in bulk.
- There is a lower ratio of workers to the number of products produced.
- The workers do not have to be highly skilled.
- Parts or all of the production line can be automated.
- Maintenance routines and checks must be very thorough and regular to avoid a breakdown which would be very expensive to the company in terms of lost production, i.e. 'down time'.
- The large numbers of food products produced keeps the unit cost per item low because the production costs are spread over a large volume output.
- After a large run is finished the production line may be adjusted to make another product.

Figure 19.2 *A mass production assembly line*

CONTINUOUS-FLOW PRODUCTION

This production system extends mass production by producing one specific product continuously, e.g. 24 hours a day, seven days a week, every year.

It will involve:

- the production of a product which is sold in large quantities regularly
- high investment in equipment and machinery that is used constantly to produce high-volume food products with a low unit cost
- wasting time if the process is stopped and started several times a day.

AUTOMATED MANUFACTURE

Production process systems are becoming increasingly automated. The whole production line may be fully automated or large sections of the line may be involved.

Automated manufacture and the use of computers to control individual machines and the overall system are part of many commercial food industries. You will be expected to know the reasons for automating production and to be able to quote examples of how it is used in the food industry.

Automated manufacture is often referred to as **CAM (computer-aided manufacture)**. Reasons and examples for using CAM include:

- It saves time – 'multi-tasks' can be carried out simultaneously, e.g. cutting out several pastry pie tops at one time rather than one by one.

- It increases speed – tasks can be repeated rapidly and continuously without any variations in quality or level of effort, e.g. cutting and weighing pieces of bread dough, rolling and forming biscuit shapes.

- It standardises production – the process time can be repeated time after time with accuracy and precision, e.g. spraying flavouring onto potato crisps or sugar coating onto breakfast cereal.

- It monitors the production system – by the continual surveillance of critical control points, e.g. designated tolerances for temperature, pH, moisture content, weight, thickness, etc.

- It increases the reliability of the finished product – all stages of production are controlled which reduces the need to 'end test' and reject substandard products, e.g. it ensures evenly baked bread products, an even coating on chocolate biscuits, etc.

- It increases productivity – there are more products to divide into the overall cost of production. More products mean a lower unit cost, e.g. popular, high-demand products cost less, such as white sliced bread, biscuits, etc.

- It reduces the need for storage – manufacturers are able to work on the 'just in time' system, i.e. nothing is made in advance and put into store. Food products are made only as an order is received. This saves floor space in ambient, chilled or frozen storage facilities. It is used, for example, in batch production of specialist bread products, certain flavours of potato crisps, etc.

- It increases safety by reducing the need for workers to carry out hazardous tasks, e.g. cutting, mixing processes, etc. (None the less, risk assessment and all health and safety procedures still need to be observed.)

- Data handling can deal with the large amount of information required to set up and monitor complex production schedules, e.g. HACCP schedule, stock control, etc.

Figure. 19.3 *Computer-aided manufacture*

When you study a commercial food industry to find out about production process systems you will find that certain key words or terminology are used to describe tasks, systems or processes. Some of the terms you may need to know about are listed below:

- **assembly** – fitting/putting together the parts of a food product, e.g. base with topping for pizza pastry case, lemon sauce with meringue for lemon meringue pie

- **combining** – joining together different raw materials or components to produce food products with specific qualities, e.g. the ingredients for cakes can be combined by the melting, rubbing-in, creaming or whisking method, each producing a different type of cake

- **enrobing** – coating a product with another ingredient to give it an outer layer, e.g. putting chocolate round a biscuit to make a chocolate bar, breadcrumbs on fish fingers or fillets, etc. Dry coatings, e.g. breadcrumbs, chopped potato skin, are put on after the product has been dipped or sprayed with a liquid

- **extrusion** – a process which forms or shapes food. A soft mixture is extruded (squeezed) under pressure through a specially shaped die into three-dimensional continuous strips. A wire cutter or blade cuts the product into smaller, even-sized pieces which are either dried or cooked, e.g. snacks, pasta, confectionery, breakfast cereals, etc.

- **filling** – (i) putting a measured amount of a sweet or savoury mixture into a case, e.g. fruit in a pastry case with a lid to make a pie, or a quiche-egg mixture into a pastry case

    (ii) injecting mixture into the centre of a food product, e.g. jam in a doughnut, cream in a choux bun

- **forming** – shaping foods by methods which make sure that all products are the same, e.g. cutters for biscuits, gauge rollers for dough, drum moulds for pattern markings on biscuits, moulds for chocolates

- **mixing** – combining materials which interact to produce a desired texture, volume, flavour, etc.

Try to find examples of food products which have been made by these methods.

Even though many production processes are automated today there is still a need for these systems to be managed and co-ordinated. The food industry offers career opportunities in a wide range of management, technical and operational fields. You will need to acquire some information about the management structure of a food company and about the type of work involved in each job role.

KEY WORDS

These are the key words. Tick them if you think you know what they mean.
Otherwise check on them.

accuracy	automated	batch
bulk	CAM	client
continuous	conveyor belt	data handling
designated tolerance	individual	large scale
maintenance	mass production	'one-off'
precision	'prototype'	simultaneous
small scale	surveillance	test kitchen
unit cost	variation	

Check yourself

QUESTIONS

Q1 Food products can be manufactured by different types of production systems. What points should a food manufacturer consider when selecting the best method of production?

Q2 A cake shop sells approximately 120 cream cakes each day. Choux pastry is used as the base for some of the cakes. Describe a product range of cakes that could be developed from a batch of choux pastry made in the bakery each day.

Q3 A biscuit manufacturer uses the mass production system to manufacture chocolate-coated digestive biscuits. The manufacturer links the mass production system to a 'just in time' method of production. What is meant by 'just in time' production? Give some reasons why the biscuit manufacturer uses this method?

Q4 'Enrobed' products have become increasingly popular. What does the term 'enrobing' mean? Give some reasons for the increased use of this production method. Include examples in your answer.

Q5 What does CAM mean and how is CAM used in the food industry?

REMEMBER! Cover the answers if you want to.

ANSWERS

A1 Your answer would need to include some of the following points:
- The number of food products to be made
- how often, e.g. every day, weekly?
- type of equipment available
- cost of the final product
- number of workers available
- level of skill of the workers
- money available for investment in new equipment/machinery.

TUTORIALS

T1 *There are several types of production process systems. They include one-off, batch, mass and continuous-flow production systems. Some of the main points which influence the choice of production method include:*
- *the number of products to be made, e.g. one hundred, several thousand*
- *the cost of making the product and the selling price of the product, e.g. an expensive celebration cake or a packet of economy digestive biscuits*
- *the equipment or money available to set up a production system.*

Remember to draw a conclusion from the points you have listed and to give your choice of the most appropriate method of production system.

ANSWERS

A2 Choux-based products could include eclairs, profiteroles, buns.
Variations could be developed by using different toppings, filling and flavours:
- toppings – melted chocolate, coffee icing, dusting with icing sugar
- fillings – fresh cream, fresh cream with fruit filling, e.g. strawberries, fresh cream with vanilla custard, flavoured fresh cream, e.g. vanilla, coffee.

A3 The 'just in time' system is when food products are made only to order. Nothing is made in advance. The biscuit manufacturer will only manufacture the chocolate digestive biscuits to meet regular orders, i.e. a supermarket may have a regular order every week, or to meet special orders they receive. Reasons for 'just in time' systems include:
- No finished products are put into storage.
- This saves floor space.
- There is no waste because products do not get damaged in storage nor do they pass their 'date marks'.
- Raw materials do not have to be bought in in advance for food products that may never be made.

A4 Enrobing is coating a food product with another ingredient to give it an outer layer. Reasons for the use of enrobing include:
- To increase a product range, e.g. plain digestive biscuit, milk chocolate-coated digestive biscuit, plain chocolate-coated digestive biscuit.
- To give a contrasting texture, e.g. fish coated with breadcrumbs (soft fish – crispy coating).
- To give contrasting flavours, e.g. chicken coated with batter (e.g. chicken dippers).
- To increase the range of cooking methods which may add texture and flavour, e.g. shallow-fry fish fingers (the crispy, crunchy texture and flavour are changed by frying).
- To allow food to be hand held, e.g. fish or chicken goujons (cut into strips and coated with breadcrumbs) for a buffet party (may be served with selections of dips).

A5 CAM stands for computer-aided manufacture. Your answer would need to show how CAM is used in the food industry by explaining when CAM is used and giving reasons, e.g. for standardising production. Here equipment can be programmed or set to repeat a process time after time with accuracy and precision, e.g. cutting pastry circles, spraying flavourings. Any changes in size or rate of spray are made on the computer and this makes for an accurate and speedy adaptation of the production line.

TUTORIALS

T2 *The production system used for the choux pastry is batch production. A small number of similar products are required. Slight adaptations would be made to the base product to meet consumer demand or to create consumer interest. To extend your revision on batch production you could think about:*
- *some of the other features of batch production systems*
- *what other base products could be made to complete the range of cream cakes sold in the cake shop each day.*

T3 *The 'just in time' system is one of the main features of modern automated manufacture. Manufacturing processes can be organised very quickly in response to orders received. 'Just in time' is also used in other industries, especially the electronics industry, where goods can be damaged and can become outdated if stored for long periods. In the food industry the shelf life of a product is always well defined by 'date marks'.*

T4 *Food manufacturers are always looking for new products to develop. Enrobing foods in different coatings is one way of creating new foods or extending an existing product range. You may like to make a list of all the enrobed products you have seen, used or eaten yourself.*

T5 *You will need to explain fully each of the examples of the use of CAM that you give. Some production lines may use CAM in individual pieces of equipment, or, alternatively, only parts of the production line may involve CAM. Other production lines, particularly continuous-flow systems, will be fully automated, with a central computer unit.*

CHAPTER 20

QUALITY ASSURANCE AND QUALITY CONTROL

WHAT DO THESE TERMS MEAN?

It is important that all food products produced by manufacturers are safe to eat. Consumers expect a consistent standard each time they purchase the same food product so food manufacturers must aim to meet the demands and expectations of consumers if they are to remain in business and make a profit.

Quality assurance and quality control procedures are used in the food industry to set standards which meet consumer demands and expectations. You will need to understand these two systems, how they relate to each other and how they are applied in the food industry.

QUALITY

If you look 'quality' up in a dictionary, you will find it defined as 'a degree of excellence or character'. It can be used to describe a food product or the level of service a consumer receives. For example, a lamb rogan josh with pilau rice could be described as 'good quality' because:

- It may have been designed and made so that it is very authentic to Indian cuisine.
- There is a consistent standard of the lamb rogan josh each time a batch is made so consumers feel that they receive good quality service from that food company.

The level of excellence is determined by the expectations of the consumer. For example, the lamb rogan josh may be described as good quality because it accurately represents the combination of spices expected in an Indian curry. On the other hand, some consumers may think that it is good quality because it has a large number of lamb pieces in the sauce.

From this you can see that it is important for the food manufacturer to find out what consumers expect of the products they buy and then to use this information to set quality standards for the food company.

QUALITY ASSURANCE

The word 'assurance' means 'a level of guarantee' or 'positive declaration'. Food manufacturers use the term 'quality assurance' to describe and guarantee the total standard of the food products they design, make and sell. The food manufacturer sets criteria or specifications for all the stages involved in designing and manufacturing a food product. This makes sure that the food product is manufactured to agreed standards, with consistent outcomes guaranteed.

The **quality assurance system** will be a series of planned criteria or specifications to cover:

- sourcing of suppliers to provide good quality raw materials or components
- consistent and reliable supplies of raw ingredients and components
- recipe formulation and development to satisfy consumer preference
- manufacturing processes and equipment

- methods and types of production
- process control and feedback systems
- suitable food packaging
- accurate food labelling and instructions for the consumer
- storage, temperature and environment control
- distribution and retail (sales)
- consumer aftersales service.

By making sure that standards are met in these areas, the manufacturer knows that the consumer will be supplied with food products that are safe to eat and of a reliable standard every time.

Figure 20.1 *Quality control includes temperature checks*

QUALITY CONTROL

You will recall that quality is defined as 'a degree of excellence'. The term 'control' means a check or restraint.

In the food industry quality control is part of the quality assurance system. It involves checking the standards of a food product as it is being designed and made. Quality control checks make sure that the product meets both the design specification and the manufacturing specification. If you refer to Chapter 22, page 158, you will learn about the control checks that are identified and monitored using the HACCP system of risk assessment. You will learn that if things go wrong at certain stages of production, the food product may not be safe to eat. These stages are known as critical control points. At these points extreme care must be taken to control the standards of production, i.e. they are critical if a safe, reliable outcome is to be achieved.

Quality control checks may include:

- measurement checks of weight or volume
- temperature checks of tolerance limits, e.g. 0°C–5°C for a chill cabinet
- sensor detectors for finding metal or foreign bodies
- random sampling for microbacterial checks.

TOTAL QUALITY MANAGEMENT (TQM)

Figure 20.2 *A process model for quality assurance*

This is an extension of quality assurance. It is used by manufacturers who aim for, or pledge to make, continuous improvement in their working practice, i.e. they are always trying to make things better.

Some food industries now follow established **guidelines** and **standards** for delivering quality products and services. These guidelines are set out in British Standard Number BS5750 and also as a European Standard ISO9000 for quality management systems.

A food company can gain the BS5750 accreditation certificate by drawing up a policy document which outlines procedures such as:

- contracts and transactions with all suppliers
- contracts and transactions with all clients
- purchase and maintenance routines for equipment and large-scale machinery
- risk assessment documentation to include HACCP
- customer relations and a complaints procedure
- the appraisal and training of the workforce.

KEY WORDS

These are the key words. Tick them if you think you know what they mean. Otherwise check on them.

consistent
criteria
guarantee
procedure
quality assurance
specification
total quality management

consumer
expectation
preference
quality
quality control
standard

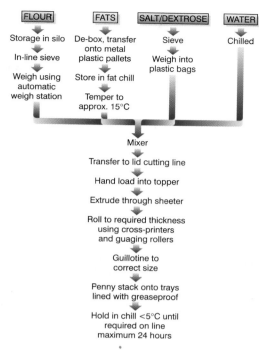

Figure 20.3 *Production stages in making pastry pie lids*

Check yourself

QUESTIONS

Q1 What could a food manufacturer do within a quality assurance system to make sure that only the best and freshest raw materials and components are used?

Q2 How would a research and development team apply quality assurance procedures to the development and formulation of a new food product?

Q3 Why do some food companies use systems such as TQM (total quality management) or British Standard 5750?

Q4 What is meant by the terms quality assurance and quality control?

ANSWERS

A1

Your answer could include:
- concise specification for each raw ingredient and component – this may include weight, size, shape, moisture content, nutritional content, colour, etc.
- sourcing from more than one country if seasonal ingredients are required all year round
- using more than one supplier to make sure that ingredients are always available
- keeping raw materials free from contamination during delivery
- using correct contamination-free storage equipment and areas, e.g. strict control of debagging, deboxing, and environment control conditions
- using supplies in strict rotation.

A2

At this stage the quality of design would be guaranteed or assured if the research and development team linked the development of the new product to the needs and preferences of consumers. Your answer could include:
- research and analysis of consumer needs and preferences
- defining a target group of consumers who will buy the product
- writing general design criteria to guide the research and generation of ideas
- writing a design specification to develop critical ideas through to prototypes
- evaluation of the prototypes against the design specification.

A3

These systems set out guidelines and standards which help companies to achieve the level of quality they require in their food products. The company has to state their plans and actions clearly in manuals or policy documents. These systems involve everyone in the company as being responsible for their part in the production system.

A4

Quality assurance is all the procedures that cover the total design and manufacture of a food product. Quality control examines the production of the food product.

TUTORIAL

T1

Remember that quality assurance is applied before, during and after production.

The selection, purchase, delivery and storage of raw ingredients and components are an important part of quality assurance procedures.

T2

It is important to build in quality assurance procedures at the design stage. This makes sure that time, effort and money are not wasted by taking a badly thought out product through to the manufacturing stage. A company could not afford to set up large-scale production lines, buy in bulk ingredients and manufacture large quantities of a product that no one wanted to buy. Quality of design is essential.

T3

Some food companies try very hard to improve the quality of their food products and to build up a good relationship with consumers.

T4

Remember that quality control is part of a food manufacturer's quality assurance procedure.

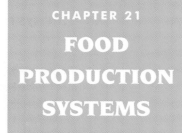
WHAT IS A PRODUCTION SYSTEM?

Food manufacturers plan carefully the way food products are manufactured in large quantities. This is known as a production system. It is a series of interconnected events which work together to manufacture food products efficiently, safely and consistently. To understand industrial food production you will need to know what a system is and to understand how systems are set up and work.

A system is a sequence of activities which work together to make a food product.

A system has three parts: input; process; output.

INPUT	PROCESS	OUTPUT
All materials, ingredients, components and energy that go into the system.	All manufacturing processes and activities which transform the input into output.	The finished product and any waste materials which can be sold as by-products

Figure 21.1 *A food production system*

A system must be monitored closely if the processes are to run efficiently and continuously. This is known as **process control.** Process control monitors the system and information is fed back to the controllers of the system to make sure that all processes are being carried out correctly. This is called **feedback**. Process control is sometimes referred to as a **closed loop system**.

Continuous monitoring provides feedback on the performance of all the stages of production. Monitoring, receiving feedback and acting on the information received all increase the efficiency of production.

For example, this system will prevent:

- raw materials and components from being wasted
- time being wasted while production lines are temporarily closed down to find and fix manufacturing faults
- faults occurring which cause inconsistency of results in the final product.

See also Chapter 7 pages 41 and 42.

A systems approach is a useful way of managing the complex production of a food product. To set up a new system or to review an existing system a **systems analysis** needs to be undertaken. This involves looking at each part or process and identifying the sequence and connection between them. A **logical order of events** can then be established.

An analysis of complex situations may lead to the system being broken down into a series of smaller **sub-systems**. The sub-systems then operate alongside the main system, linking in at the appropriate stage of production.

The total system needs to be carefully monitored and controlled so that information from one part of the complex system is received as feedback in another part. This makes sure that the system runs smoothly.

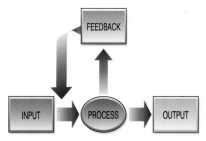

Figure 21.2 *A closed loop system*

Figure 21.3 The use of three sub-systems to make a quiche

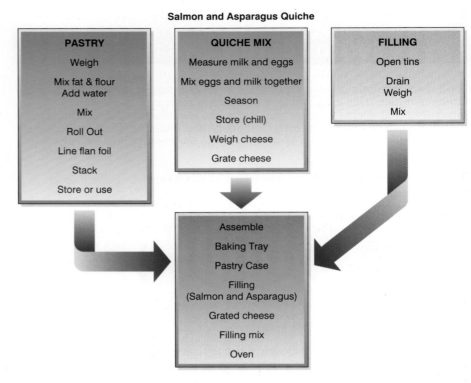

Salmon and Asparagus Quiche

A flow diagram is often used to represent the many stages of a food production system and the interconnection of sub-systems. The flow diagram must indicate clearly:

- the different stages of production in correct sequence
- a logical order which makes economical use of energy and labour
- connections with sub-systems
- control points and feedback systems.

PROCESS CONTROL METHODS

You can now understand that control and feedback are important in food production systems. Many manufacturers use computers to operate a control and feedback system. **Data logging systems**, which you may have used in developing your own food products, are part of this control and feedback system process.

Computers monitor aspects such as:

- weight, e.g. of an individual ingredient, component or finished product
- temperature at various stages, e.g. storage, mixing, baking, chilling, freezing
- moisture content, e.g. during storage of dry ingredients, mixing, heat processing, etc.
- the pH level – the pH condition of ingredients (i.e. acid, neutral or alkaline) is important to the shelf life and processing of some products

- flow rates, e.g. the speed at which ingredients are added to the product, such as chocolate coating on biscuits, flavourings sprayed onto potato crisps, etc.

- the metal detection of pieces of metal that may enter the food product, such as nuts or bolts from pieces of equipment

- the rate of production, e.g. the speed of a biscuit production line through a tunnel oven or bread through a proving oven

- the quantity of products, e.g. the total number of products produced in a specified time counting the number of products into a packaging system.

This is known as **computer-integrated manufacture** (CIM).

The information in the computerised control system is collected by electronic sensors and relayed to the main computer system. Appropriate action is taken in response to the feedback received. Electronic devices include:

- moisture sensors

- mechanical switches

- transducers

- temperature sensors in temperature probes

- thermostats

- weight/volume sensors.

In the last few years the use of computerised control systems has become more and more sophisticated, with recent developments assisting in the control and monitoring of:

- the sorting and grading of raw materials, e.g. potatoes for potato crisps

- units of weight for a product that is to be packaged

- colour and shades, e.g. of baked products, breakfast cereals, etc.

- shapes and decorations, e.g. the position of toppings on cakes and pizzas through the use of digitised visual images stored in the computer

- the bacterial content of products

- seals on food packaging, e.g. packets of crisps.

You may find other examples of computerised control systems in the particular commercial food system that you study. You must remember, however, that in some instances control checks are made by the workers operating the production line. They may carry out processes which have not yet been automated, e.g. a visual check of peeled potatoes for blemishes before they are sliced to make potato crisps. The workers may also carry out spot checks at a variety of stages along the production line.

KEY WORDS

These are the key words. Tick them if you think you know what they mean. Otherwise check on them.

closed loop system	**complex**	**continuous monitoring**
feedback	**flow diagram**	**input**
integrated	**monitor**	**output**
process	**process control**	**sequence**
sub-system	**system**	

Check yourself

QUESTIONS

Q1 (i) Temperature control is a critical measurement in food production. With reference to a product flow diagram or to the production system for a product you have designed and made yourself, give three different examples of production stages with a temperature control point.

(ii) Describe how the temperature would be monitored.

Q2 Computer-integrated systems can be used for monitoring the amount of raw materials, components or finished products a company has in stock. This is often called stock control. List some of the advantages of stock control.

Q3 The stages in a food production system can be divided into input, process and output. Explain these three stages by referring to the production of a fruit pie.

Q4 During manufacture a food product moves along a conveyor belt. Products that are overcooked or undercooked are diverted to a waste bin by a control gate.

(i) Draw a flow diagram to describe the system, using the six stages listed below in the correct order:
- chill unit
- packaging unit
- waste bin
- weighing/forming unit
- tunnel oven
- control gate.

(ii) Show how feedback will be used to form a closed loop system.

REMEMBER! Cover the answers if you want to.

ANSWERS

A1 (i) Your answer would need to include three stages with temperature controls from production systems you have studied. The following are examples of the type of things you might include:
- ready made pastry for pies and pastries stored at 12°C–15°C
- raw meat and fish stored below 4°C
- cook chill products stored at 0°C–5°C
- bread proved at 40°C and baked at 300°C
- frozen foods stored at –20°C to –25°C
- meat in tomato sauce cooked at 90°C–100°C
- fresh vegetables stored below 8°C.

(ii) Different methods can be used to record, monitor and control temperature e.g:
- a temperature sensor or thermometer used to record the temperature of a freezer chill cabinet or an oven
- a thermostat to keep temperature at a set point or within a range

TUTORIALS

T1 *Temperature is critical to food safety. You will find that reference is made to this vital aspect of food production in several areas of study into food technology.*
Temperature is critical to:
- *the control of the growth of micro-organisms, e.g. during storage*
- *the prevention and destruction of micro-organisms during preparation, cooking and preservation, e.g. heating food to high temperatures*
- *the quality of food products, such as texture and palatability, e.g. a starch-based sauce will have an incorrect texture and bland flavour if not heated to 100°C for two minutes to allow gelatinisation of the starch to take place;*
and fried foods e.g. potato crisps/chips, will not have a crisp texture if the oil or fat has not been heated to a high enough temperature.

ANSWERS

- a temperature probe to monitor temperature, e.g. throughout a product; at the centre of bread during baking
- a continuous digital display of temperature levels
- connection to a central computer system which will activate an alarm system if the temperature moves out of range
- regular checks by food handlers/ workers, e.g. every hour.

A2 Your answer could include:
- Computers can be programmed to hold very detailed records of each ingredient, e.g. original source, supplier, amount delivered, delivery date and characteristics such as moisture content.
- Electronic sensors can signal the need for ordering more stock.
- This can ensure the automatic use of materials in correct rotation.
- It can control the delivery or flow of ingredients to the production area.
- It provides data for stock taking.
- It allows the storage and retrieval of codes which are allocated to each delivery of raw materials. In the event of problems with a finished product, the raw materials can be traced back. This is known as traceability.

A3 Your answer could be in the form of a diagram to show input → process → output.

A4 Your answer needs to include a flow diagram and a feedback loop.

Figure 21.4 *How a weighing/forming unit works*

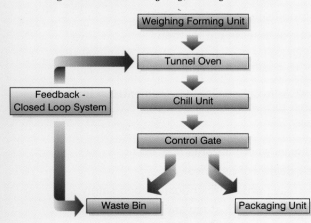

TUTORIALS

T2 *You can now see that computers can be used extensively for the control of stock. Computers are also used for recording and tracking in retail outlets. Bar codes are printed on the packaging of all food products. When products are purchased the bar codes are scanned at the check out. Computers record which products have been sold and how many were sold each day and each week. The information is analysed to find out:*
- *consumer needs and preferences*
- *market trends, e.g. seasonal requirements, dietary groups, age groups*
- *popular and unpopular selling lines.*

The computer system can also be used for automatic ordering of new stock which, in the case of large supermarkets, is delivered on a 24-hour schedule.

T3 *Remember that a system is a sequence of activities which work together to make a food product. A system has three parts: input, process, output. Try to identify the stages of production in a food product that you have designed and made. Put them in a logical order and show the links between each part or particular process.*

T4 *Don't forget that control and feedback are important in food production systems. Process control monitors the system and information is fed back to make sure all processes are being carried out correctly. This is called feedback. In this example the feedback information would indicate that either:*

(i) *The oven temperature is incorrect or working at varying levels because some products are undercooked and some are overcooked.*

(ii) *The conveyor belt is not moving at the correct rate or at a regular rate. A consistent flow rate through the tunnel oven is necessary to make sure that all the products are baked evenly.*

CHAPTER 22

RISK ASSESSMENT

WHAT IS RISK ASSESSMENT?

There are many regulations for the food industry, which set out basic requirements to make sure that our food is safe to eat. One of the new requirements of the new Food Safety (General Food Hygiene) Regulations 1995 establishes **risk assessment** as the starting point of food manufacturing management's responsibility for food hygiene and safety standards.

Risk assessment means making an assessment of any risk to a food product during its production. This involves working out what chances there are of a food product being damaged or made incorrectly.

Useful definitions include:

- **risk** – the likelihood of occurrence, i.e. what could happen and when it could happen
- **assessment** – to form an estimate of something.

Remember that risk assessment is:

- thinking about what could happen
- planning how to prevent it from happening.

HAZARD ANALYSIS AND CRITICAL CONTROL POINTS

The system of risk assessment in the food industry is referred to as the **hazard analysis and critical control point system (HACCP)**.

This approach is used to analyse what *could* go wrong in the production of food and to set up procedures and controls to *avoid* any potential problems. HACCP replaced earlier systems which relied heavily on 'end testing', i.e. inspecting the finished product and rejecting any faulty or damaged ones. Although 'end testing' is a form of control method, it does waste a lot of money, time and ingredients if manufacturers have made food products that they can't sell. It could also mean complaints from customers or local health inspectors if faulty goods slip through the net.

WHAT IS HACCP?

HACCP is:

- a method of food safety management
- an important risk assessment method
- a procedure whereby the whole food company makes a commitment to quality production.

HACCP may be part of TQM (total quality management), an important management system used by some companies.

HACCP involves:

- identifying stages where hazards may occur
- assessing the degree of risk involved
- deciding on stages which are critical to food safety
- setting standards for each stage and maintaining them

- checking the critical points
- taking action to maintain safe limits.

Some important terms to understand include:

- **hazard** – anything that can cause harm to the consumer
- **critical control point (CCP)** – a stage where a food safety hazard can be prevented, eliminated or reduced to an acceptable level
- **control** – setting standards for a system and maintaining them.

See also Chapter 7 page 42.

WHY DO WE NEED HACCP?

Hazards may be:

- **microbiological**, e.g. salmonella in chicken, listeria in soft cheese. (To discover the conditions for the growth of pathogenic micro-organisms which can cause food poisoning, refer to Chapter 22.)
- **physical**, e.g:
  - glass from bottles, jars, light fixtures
  - metal from machinery, equipment, packaging
  - wood from pallets, boxes
  - insects from plants, open windows
  - personal items, e.g. jewellery, hair, cigarettes
  - packaging faults, e.g. bags not sealed.
- **chemical**, e.g. agricultural chemicals, cleaning chemicals, paint, oil.

Hazards can occur at any stage in the food production chain from field to factory to shop to table.

HOW IS HACCP APPLIED IN THE FOOD INDUSTRY?

A team of people is needed to organise the HACCP system. They will collect and collate data and then act on the information they have gathered. The team needs to:

- understand food processing
- be trained in food hygiene
- have knowledge of microbiology.

Such a team would usually involve:

- up to six people
- a range of staff, i.e.

  - quality assurance staff
  - an engineer
  - a microbiologist
  - production staff
  - and maybe an external consultant on HACCP.

To understand fully how HACCP is applied in the food industry you will need to know the various stages involved in HACCP

Figure 22.1 The HACCP team

THE STAGES OF HACCP

There are seven basic principles in the HACCP system.

1 Hazard Analysis

- Draw up a flow chart of the food production process, from raw materials, processing and storage to consumer use.
- Identify any potential hazards.
- Describe ways and options for control of the hazards.

2 Critical Control Points (CCPs)

- Identify the critical control points using a decision tree (see Figure 22.2).
- At critical control points hazards must be prevented by the manufacturer taking special care to set up preventive measures.

Figure 22.2 *Critical control point decision tree*

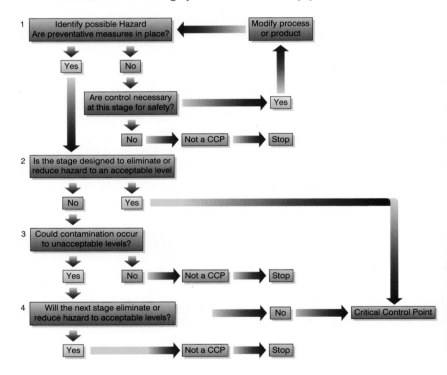

CCPs could involve:

- Control of temperature during storing, processing or the storage of the final product to prevent growth of micro-organisms.
- Control of temperature during cooking to give even cooked results.
- Control of time at specific stages, e.g. the proving of bread, the cooking time of products or the setting of chilled desserts.
- Control of weights to give consistent quantities, e.g. raw ingredients, or of portion control to give even-sized products.
- Safety from contamination by unwanted materials, e.g. metal, wood, glass, jewellery.

3 Critical Limits

- To control each CCP target levels need to be set, e.g. the correct temperature range for a cook-chill cabinet is 0°C–5°C.
- These targets or tolerance levels are called **critical limits**.

4 Monitoring

A monitoring system must be set up for each CCP. This involves:

- measuring or observing stages of the production process
- making sure that the critical limits of each CCP are being met, i.e. everything is under control.

Examples of monitoring activities could include:

- digital temperature displays on refrigerator cabinets
- metal detectors on production lines
- pest control units
- wiping temperature probes before and after use
- regular checks by staff, e.g. taking temperature readings every hour.

Figure 22.3 *Using a temperature probe*

Some information or data is monitored all the time, e.g. temperature or weight. This is known as **continuous monitoring**. All checks must be carefully recorded: time, date, results and the name of the checker.

5 Corrective Action

If a problem occurs and critical limits are exceeded, e.g. the temperature of a refrigerator rises to 22°C, all staff must know what action to take.

Solving the problem is known as **corrective action**. It could include:

- repairing a refrigerator
- training staff in food hygiene
- replacing a machinery part
- sieving an ingredient to detect any unwanted bits.

6 Record Keeping

Full details of the raw materials, components, the processing and the final product are required. Additional details could include:

- the HACCP plan
- staff training
- audit details
- temperature logs of cold storage
- cleaning schedules
- maintenance records
- delivery schedules.

Records must be made and kept. Computerised record keeping is often used.

7 Verification

- Set up a system, tests or procedures to check if the HACCP plan is working effectively.
- Review or modify the HACCP plan according to the findings.

APPLYING HACCP IN THE FOOD INDUSTRY

At first the HACCP procedure seems quite complex but it is a straightforward series of events which eliminate health risks.

Some points to remember about HACCP include:

- HACCP can be used by any food industry.
- HACCP can be applied to the total production process or to one part of the process.
- The HACCP team will draw a flow chart to show the whole process.
- During the identification of hazards the team may identify all hazards or only one category, e.g. physical, microbiological or chemical.
- If too many hazards are identified, the total production process needs to be redesigned.
- All staff must know and understand the HACCP system which has been put in place.
- Training is essential for all staff.

KEY WORDS

These are the key words. Tick them if you think you know what they mean. Otherwise check on them.

analysis	continuous monitoring	control
corrective action	critical control point	critical limits
decision tree	end testing	flow diagram
HACCP	hazard	microbiological
monitoring	preventive measure	procedure
record keeping	risk	risk assessment
step or stage	system	tolerance
TQM (total quality management)		verification

Check yourself

QUESTIONS

Q1 Critical control points can occur at any stage in the food production process.
(i) What potential hazards could there be in the purchase, delivery and storage of raw materials?
(ii) What control checks would need to be put in place to ensure that raw materials are safe?

Q2 The manufacture of cook-chill chicken curry has the following instructions printed on the label.
Conventional Oven: Remove packaging and pierce film lid. Place directly onto oven shelf in a preheated oven at 190°C, 375°F, Gas Mark 5 for 25 minutes.
Why does the consumer need this information?

Q3 A bread manufacturer receives a complaint from a customer who has found a piece of metal in a loaf of bread. What could be the cause of this?

Q4 HACCP analysis is carried out by a small team. Which personnel would make up the team? Give a reason for your answer.

Q5 One hazard may be contamination of food products caused by the poor personal hygiene standards of food handlers. What control measures could be applied to ensure and maintain high standards of personnel hygiene.

REMEMBER! Cover the answers if you want to.

ANSWERS

A1
(i) Potential hazards include:
- raw materials being delivered to the factory
- micro-bacterial growth during storage
- contamination from foreign bodies
- cross-contamination from components, e.g. nuts.

(ii) Control measures include:
- detailed specifications given to suppliers of raw materials
- checking goods on delivery, i.e. as to temperature, condition of food, date marks
- sorting food by debagging and putting into containers
- storing all raw materials covered and off the floor
- separating raw and cooked foods
- sieving some foods to check for foreign bodies
- storing at safe temperatures
- strict stock rotation using foods in order of purchase.

TUTORIALS

T1 *You will find that the aim of all the procedures is to identify hazards and prevent them from happening. The first checks involve making sure that the raw materials are not contaminated on arrival. Then methods of handling and storing the foods must be organised to prevent the food becoming contaminated at the factory. Monitoring may involve:*
- *regular quality control checks of suppliers*
- *continuous monitoring of temperatures*
- *record keeping and recording of suppliers' codes, date marking and stock rotation*
- *hygiene standards of storage containers and food handlers*
- *segregation of packaging materials from food materials by use of designated areas or colour coding to prevent cross-contamination*
- *computer-controlled equipment to display temperatures, atmospheric control, etc.*
- *sensors – to measure acidity, pH conditions, metal detection, etc.*

ANSWERS

A2 Chicken is a high-risk food. The manufacturer will have made sure that the chicken was thoroughly cooked during production of the curry. To eliminate a hazard at the later stage of reheating the curry by the consumer, the manufacturer needs to give clear instructions. All of the curry needs to be heated to above 70°C. To make sure this happens the manufacture gives two critical limits:
- temperature: 190°C, 375°F or Gas Mark 5
- time: 25 minutes.

A3 The bread is contaminated by a piece of metal. This could have entered the product at these stages:
- delivery of the raw material, i.e. flour
- by dropping off the packaging
- by dropping off a piece of machinery or equipment during processing
- by dropping off a piece of jewellery worn by a food handler.

A4 The team has to collect, collate and act on the data. The team would usually involve six people representing a range of responsibilities, e.g. quality assurance, engineering, microbiology, production, hygiene. These people need to have a wide knowledge and sound understanding of food processing and food hygiene. Technical data about microbiology, engineering and food processing will be needed to identify hazards accurately and plan preventive and corrective measures.

A5 Your answer could include these details:
- induction training in personal hygiene is required for new personnel
- all food handlers must meet the personal/hygiene standards set out in regulations on:
  – jewellery
  – gloves
  – handwashing procedure
  – hair and facial hair policy
  – protective clothing
  – changing procedure
- personnel are not permitted to enter the food production plant if suffering from any infection or illness. A 'return to work' policy must be followed when such a person returns to work
- all staff undergo initial training and training updates in personnel hygiene.

TUTORIALS

T2 *HACCP is a safety system which applies throughout the entire production of a food product, from raw ingredients to serving. All hazards have to be identified and procedures put in place to eliminate them. Instructions on the label inform the consumer of the final process needed to make sure the food product is presented, served and eaten to the standard intended by the manufacturer.*

T3 *There are three categories of hazard: microbiological, physical and chemical. Physical hazards include contamination by other materials, such as wood, metal, plastic, etc. The presence of metal in any of the food products can be identified by fitting sensors on the production line.*

T4 *The HACCP team play an important role in drawing up the arrangements for food safety. A small team of people with different roles and responsibilities has worked well in many food industries applying HACCP. An example of team membership in a food company preparing ready meals is:*
- *Product Development Manager*
- *Senior Development Chef*
- *Technologist*
- *Process Development Manager*
- *Process Development Technologist*
- *Microbiologist.*

T5 *The points about personnel hygiene apply to all staff including production workers, management, engineers and visitors and contractors entering or working in the production areas. Checks are made to monitor personnel hygiene standards. This may include visual inspection, hand swabs and factory audits.*

SAMPLE STUDENT'S ANSWERS AND EXAMINER'S COMMENTS

1 In food production there are usually three stages in the system.

What do the following refer to in the production of a bread product?
(6 marks)

Give an example in your answer.

INPUT	PROCESS	OUTPUT
These are the raw ingredients that are needed including the wheat grain that has to be turned into flour.	This is the step when the input is turned into the output. It normally includes a mechanical process.	This is the finished product so it will be the actual bread product.
Example	Example	Example
Flour, yeast	Mixing and kneading dough	Sliced bread, bread buns

6/6

1 The student has gained full marks for this question. The question was obviously read carefully because the student has given examples in the answer she was asked to do. Some students do not read the question fully and begin to write their answer after merely skim reading the question.

The box which asks for information about process could have had more information in it, e.g. 'In bread production the process could be milling the wheat, mixing the ingredients together or kneading the dough'. However, the student included this information in the example box and therefore was still given credit.

2 During the setting up of a food production system it is vital for the manufacturer to test the product at different stages to ensure and maintain quality.

(a) Explain the terms:
    (i) quality assurance
    (ii) quality control
    (4 marks)

    Quality assurance is when the quality of a food product is assured by the manufacturer by looking at the quality of all the steps in the production process.
    Quality control is the testing of a product as it is made.

    3/4

(b) Giving examples, explain the term quality control in relation to a lasagne product.
    (5 marks)

    In the case of a lasagne several things would have been checked. These are the quality of the ingredients, the weighing out, the size of the pieces of vegetables, the type and thickness of the sheets of lasagne and the consistency of the sauce. There would be sensory evaluation of the different parts of the product and the final lasagne.

    5/5

2 (a) In part (a) the student has shown an understanding of both quality control and assurance but has not given a clear explanation. Better revision and learning of these terms would have helped. The student would have gained 3 marks out of 4.

(b) In part (b) the answer about the quality control in a lasagne product is good and the student has given at least five different points which would have gained full marks.

163

Questions to Answer

The answers to Questions 3 and 4 can be found on pages 243 and 244.

3 HACCP is a standard procedure used in the food industry.

(a) (i) What does HACCP stand for? (2 marks)
   (ii) How is it used in the food industry? (2 marks)

4 The flow chart below shows the system which a manufacturer might use to produce a frozen chicken pie.

On the chart show:

(a) Possible hazards that might occur during the production of the pie.

(b) The controls which can be used to prevent these.

(c) Quality control checks which will be carried out during production.
(10 marks)

One example is already shown in bold type.

Stages in the production of a frozen chicken pie	Possible Hazards	Controls Used	Quality Control Checks
Collect raw ingredients	Cross contamination Temperature control	Separate storage areas for dry and perishable goods	Reputed supplier, visits to supplier, quality standards
Weigh ingredients			
Mix ingredients for pastry			
Cook chicken			
Make white sauce for chicken filling			
Combine sauce with chicken and cool			
Roll out pastry			
Add filling			
Bake			
Freeze			
Store			

WHAT CAUSES FOODS TO GO BAD?

Fresh foods cannot be stored for very long before changes occur which affect the texture, flavour or colour of the food. For example, it is easy to see the changes in the colour of a banana as it ripens from green to yellow. Eventually it will turn black. Some changes in foods are not as noticeable as this but within short periods of time foods can often undergo changes which make them unfit to eat. This is known as **food spoilage**. It is important for you to know the causes of these changes.

CHANGES CAUSED BY MICRO-ORGANISMS

Many of the changes in food are caused by **micro-organisms** and **enzymes** and you will need to know about their characteristics.

There are three types of micro-organisms:

- yeasts
- bacteria
- moulds.

Micro-organisms can perform useful functions in the production of food products such as cheese, yogurt, bread, beer and Quorn, but they can also be harmful and cause food spoilage. Foods which are unfit to eat are described as **contaminated** which means that they are infected with micro-organisms and therefore are not safe to eat. Some micro-organisms, known as **pathogenic bacteria**, can cause food poisoning, resulting in serious illness or even death.

Micro-organisms are usually only visible under a microscope. They are found in water, soil, air and rubbish and on animals, humans and equipment. They can be transferred to food by poor hygienic practices, e.g. by humans, flies and rodents. Some foods may already contain micro-organisms, e.g. salmonella in chicken.

YEASTS

Yeasts are:

- found in the air, in soil and on the skin of some fruits, e.g. grapes
- microscopic single-celled fungi which reproduce by budding, i.e. the yeast cell divides into two cells
- anaerobic, i.e. the cells do not need oxygen to reproduce
- active in warm, moist conditions with food for growth and reproduction. The optimum temperature is 25°C–30°C
- inactive in very cold conditions, i.e. the yeast cells are dormant and will not grow or reproduce
- destroyed at high temperatures of 100°C or over
- able to break down sugars to produce alcohol (ethanol) and carbon dioxide gas. This process is known as fermentation

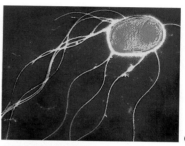
(a)

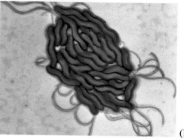
(b)

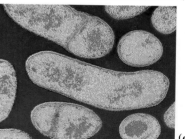
(c)

Figure 24.1 *Bacteria (a), moulds (b) and yeasts (c)*

- used for fermentation, a process used to make bread, alcoholic drinks and yeast extract spreads
- responsible for food spoilage in high-sugar foods such as fruit, jam and fruit yogurts.

MOULDS

Figure 24.2 *Mould on a slice of bread*

Moulds are:

- fungi which grow as thread-like filaments in food. They can be black, white or blue
- visible as minute plants which grow on many types of food. The food may be dry, moist, acid, alkaline, or have salt or sugar concentrations
- able to reproduce by producing spores which travel in the air. The spores settle, germinate and multiply into new growths
- very productive in moist conditions at temperatures between 20°C–30°C. They grow slowly in dry, cold conditions
- able to produce heat-resistant spores, e.g. clostriclium botulism. Very high temperatures are required to destroy these spores, e.g. above 100°C
- harmful when they produce **mycotoxins** which are poisonous substances
- used in food manufacture to produce specific flavours and textures, e.g. the manufacture of blue-veined cheeses such as Danish Blue, Gorgonzola, Stilton. The moulds are injected into the cheese and left to ripen during the maturing stage of cheese production. These moulds are considered harmless.

BACTERIA

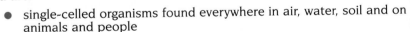

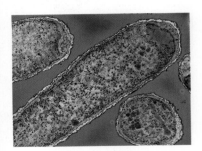

Figure 24.3 *E. coli bacteria seen under a microscope*

Bacteria are:

- single-celled organisms found everywhere in air, water, soil and on animals and people
- microscopic, i.e. they are extremely small and can only be seen under a microscope
- classified, and those which cause food poisoning are known as **pathogenic bacteria**, e.g. E*scherichia coli* (E. *coli*) which is infectious and very harmful
- able to reproduce very rapidly by dividing in two and again in two in minutes – often as quickly as between 10–20 minutes. From one bacterium a whole colony of bacteria can develop within 12 hours
- active in optimum conditions of warmth, moisture, food and oxygen
- able to grow rapidly in neutral pH conditions (6.8–7.2) Most pathogenic bacteria are unable to grow in acid or alkaline conditions, e.g. beetroot preserved in vinegar
- able to form spores that can lie dormant but will germinate when the right conditions occur
- often undetected because the food looks, tastes and smells as it should but the presence of bacteria makes it potentially very dangerous to eat

- most active in the wide temperature range of 5°C–65°C. The optimum temperature is 37°C, i.e. the human body temperature. During storage, preparation and cooking processes it is very important that food is not kept in this temperature zone for longer than necessary
- used in food manufacture, e.g. in making cheese and yogurt. The lactic acid bacteria cultures used in these products are not harmful.

> Some key terminology you may come across includes:
> **aerobic** – requires oxygen to grow
> **anaerobic** – does not require oxygen to grow
> **binary fission** – reproduces by means of a cell dividing in two again and again.

CHANGES CAUSED BY ENZYMES

Enzymes also cause changes in food. Enzymes are:

- protein molecules that control chemical reactions in food
- active at the optimum temperature of 35°C–50°C
- inactive at high temperatures
- most active in neutral conditions around pH7
- sometimes inactive in acid conditions.

Enzymes are used in a wide range of manufacturing processes, e.g:

- bread and brewing, where enzymes that are present in yeast are active in the fermentation process
- cheese, where enzymes speed up the ripening stage.

Enzymes can cause undesirable changes in foods which make them unsightly. This is called 'browning' and is caused by the action of an enzyme called polyphenol oxide in the presence of oxygen. Enzymatic browning can be reduced by:

- high temperatures, e.g. blanching cut vegetables in boiling water
- acidic conditions, e.g. dipping cut fruit into lemon juice
- other methods which are used in commercial food processing.

FOOD RISK CATEGORIES

Food can be infected with micro-organisms at any stage of its production, from the source of the raw ingredients through to when being served and eaten by the consumer. Everyone involved in the food chain, e.g. farmer, manufacturer, retailer and consumer, must make sure that the food is safe to eat.

You have learnt that micro-organisms multiply rapidly in conditions which, when combined, offer:

- warmth
- moisture
- food
- time.

Foods can be put into three categories of risk against micro-organism growth. These three categories are:

Figure 24.4 *Enzymic reaction – the surface of cut fruit goes brown*

Figure 24.5 *Raw meat is a high-risk food*

Figure 24.6 *Sandwiches are a medium-risk food*

Figure 24.7 *Chutney is a low-risk food*

1 High-risk Foods

These are foods which have a high protein and moisture content. They provide ideal conditions for micro-organic growth, e.g:

- raw meat, fish
- dairy products
- cooked meat and poultry
- shellfish and seafood
- gravies, sauces, stocks, soups and stews
- egg products, e.g. raw egg in chilled desserts and mayonnaise
- cooked rice
- protein-based baby foods.

2 Medium-risk Foods

These include:

- dried or frozen products containing fish, meat, eggs, vegetables, cereals or dairy ingredients
- fresh sandwiches and meat pies
- fat-based products.

3 Low-risk Foods

These include:

- high acid-content foods, e.g. pickles and chutney, fruit juice
- high sugar-content foods, e.g. marmalades, jams, fruit packed in syrup
- sugar-based confectionery, e.g. sweets, icing
- unprocessed raw vegetables, e.g. potatoes, carrot
- edible oils and fats.

FOOD POISONING

Food poisoning is an illness caused by eating contaminated food or water. Thousands of cases of food poisoning occur each year. Food poisoning occurs if food is contaminated by:

- harmful bacteria or other micro-organisms
- toxic chemical contamination.

It can also develop following an adverse reaction to certain **proteins** or other naturally occurring **constituents** in the food.

However, most food poisoning is caused by bacterial contamination which occurs because of some of the following reasons:

- storage of high-risk foods at room temperature
- poor hygiene routine at any stage of production and serving
- cross-contamination between raw foods and cooked foods, e.g. raw meat to cooked ham
- poor personal hygiene standards of food handlers

- poor preparation and cooking routines, such as:
  - not thawing foods thoroughly
  - not re-heating foods to the correct temperature for a long enough time
  - not allowing foods to cool before putting them in chill cabinets or freezers
  - keeping 'hot' foods below 63°C
  - under-cooking 'high-risk' foods, e.g. shellfish
  - preparing food too far in advance
  - leaving food on display at room temperature for longer than the maximum safe period of four hours.

Some people are more susceptible to food poisoning than others. And extra care must be taken with food products manufactured for babies, pregnant women, elderly people or anyone else with a low resistance to infection.

Many types of bacteria cause food poisoning and the incubation periods, symptoms and methods of control vary accordingly. Some of the most common types of food poisoning are listed in Table 24.1.

CROSS-CONTAMINATION

During food processing micro-organisms can transfer from raw to cooked foods, causing infection. This is known as cross-contamination.

To prevent cross-contamination you must avoid:

- allowing raw and cooked foods to touch each other, e.g. raw chicken and boiled ham
- allowing the blood and juices of raw foods to drip onto cooked foods, e.g. during storage in refrigerators
- allowing bacteria to be transferred during handling or preparation, e.g. from hands, work surfaces, equipment.

FOOD SAFETY LEGISLATION

Several laws cover the regulations for the preparation, storage and sale of food. You will find it useful if you can identify and understand the main pieces of legislation.

Bacteria	Symptoms	Period of Incubation and Illness	Found in	Control
Salmonella • Most common form of food poisoning in UK • Optimum temperature for growth 7°–45°C. • Does not form spores	• High fever, diarrhoea, vomiting headache, abdominal pains • Frequent but rarely proves fatal	Incubation – 12–36 hours Duration of illness – 1–7 days	• The gut of most animals and birds particularly chicken • Raw meat, poultry, eggs and raw egg products, sea food, dairy products e.g. cream • Cross contamination from infected food handlers and pets	• Destroyed by heating to temperatures above 70°C • Make sure food is cooked through to high temperature in the centre e.g. food which have been frozen • Avoid cross contamination • Government warning to avoid the risk of infection from raw egg or uncooked egg products.
Listeria monocytogenes • Common form of food poisoning • At risk – pregnant women, new-born babies, elderly and sick. • Does not form spores.	Ranges from • Mild flu like illness to meningitis, septicemia, pneumonia • Can cause miscarriage, premature labour or birth of an infected baby	Incubation – no specific time may be few days to several weeks Duration of illness – no specific time e.g. 1–70 days	• Unpasteurised sheep and cattle milk, soft cheese, meat based pate, meat, cooked poultry • Cook chill ready meals may be a source if they are not heated to the correct temperature for long enough	• Store products below 5°C • Use with date marked on label • Accurate stock rotation • Heat food to be cooked to 100°C e.g. poultry • Make sure food is heated through to the centre
Camploybacter • Most frequent cause of food poisoning in milk. • Often known as gastroenteritis • Optimum temperature for growth 30°–40°C	• Diarrhoea is the most common symptoms. • Headache, fever and abdominal pain	Incubation – 1–11 days Duration of illness – 2–7 days but may recur over several weeks	• Meat, poultry, milk, shellfish • Untreated water • Cross contamination from animals • Easily transmitted between humans	• Destroy by heating above 60°C • Avoid cross contamination of raw to cooked foods • Avoid infection from animals or pests
Staphylococcus aureus • Bacteria creates toxins which cause toxic food poisoning. • Present in nose, throat and skin of humans	• Mild to severe vomiting • Abdominal pain • Diarrhoea • Low temperature	Incubation – 1–6 hours Duration of illness – 6–24 hours	• High risk foods e.g. meat, meat products, poultry and poultry products, egg, filling for sandwiches, baked potatoes, salads • Food handlers by infected nose, throat, skin etc.	• High standards personal hygiene • Storage of food below 5°C • Handle food as little as possible • Spores germinate in warm slow cooking methods but do not multiply at high temperatures
Escherichia coli (E-Coli) 0157 • Several types which cause gastroenteritis in humans • Causes toxic food poisoning which can be fatal i.e. results in death	• Diarrhoea, abdominal pain, vomiting • Bloody diarrhoea • Kidney failure in serious cases	Incubation – 12–24 hours Duration of illness – 1–5 days	• Raw meat and poultry. • Unpasteurised milk and dairy products • Untreated water in some countries	• Cook foods thoroughly at a high temperature • Avoid cross contamination from raw to cooked meats • Drink bottled water rather than untreated water • Avoid foods with high water content
Clostridium perfringers • Common form of food poisoning • Optimum temperature 15°C–50°C • Forms spores which cause toxic food poisoning.	• Nausea and diarrhoea • Abdominal pain • Vomiting rare	Incubation – 8–22 hours Duration of illness – 12–24 hours	• Raw meat, poultry • Cooked meat, meat products, gravy	• Bacteria grow fast in optimum temperature range so heat food rapidly and cook at high temperature • Cool food rapidly and store below 5°C • Spores are not normally killed by high temperatures but will multiply in warm conditions
Colstridium botulimium • Rare type of food poisoning • Spores from toxic bacteria which are very poisonous • Majority of cases are fatal	• Difficult in breathing and swallowing. • Double vision, headaches, nausea, vomiting • Paralysis very slow recovery	Incubation – 12–48 hours Duration of illness rapid decline, death within a week or	• Incorrect processing of food or food too low temperature. e.g. faulty canning, vacuum packed foods • Packaged and canned meat, fish, vegetables	• Quality control procedures in processing of canned or packaged foods • Does not multiply in high acid foods. Take care with low acid canned foods • Spores are not destroyed by high temperatures but toxins are
Bacillus cereus • Two forms of food poisoning with the most common caused by toxic bacteria • Forms spores	• Nausea, vomiting, diarrhoea	Incubation – 1–6 hours Duration of illness 6–24 hours	• Cooked rice products • Cereal products • Starchy foods such as potatoes • Grows in soil and can survive milling and processing techniques	• Avoid cooking rice and pasta well in advance and keeping warm – better to cook when required • Cook thoroughly and cool rapidly

Table 24.1 *Common types of food poisoning*

THE FOOD SAFETY ACT 1990

This Act was introduced to ensure that all food produced in the food industry is safe to eat. The Food Act covers the whole spectrum of food production, manufacture and retail. The Food Safety Act is very detailed and some of the details you need to know about it include:

Aims

- To ensure that all food produced or prepared is safe to eat.
- To prevent the sale of food which may be harmful to health by causing food poisoning.
- To prevent the sale of food which is contaminated by pieces of metal, pests, chemicals, antibiotics, etc.
- To make sure that food products actually match the descriptions or claims made about them, i.e. 'the nature, substance or quality' expected by the consumer.

Foods included:

- all materials used as a food ingredient, either in or on a food product, e.g. ingredients, additives, water
- liquids and ingredients used in drinks
- nutrient supplements and slimming aids
- food sources, e.g. farms and the growing areas of animals, plants, cereals.

The Act covers:

- all stages of food production, from farm to factory to retail outlet. A retail outlet may be:
  – any type of shop, from a vending machine to a large supermarket
  – eating places such as restaurants, cafes, takeaway outlets, railway buffets, hotels, fast food outlets
- everything that comes into contact with the food, e.g. equipment, machinery, storage and transport equipment
- all people who handle the food at each stage of the food industry.

Enforcement

The Food Safety Act is enforced by local government officers, i.e:

- trading standards officers
- environmental health officers.

They have the authority to:

- enter food premises to investigate a possible offence
- inspect food to see if it is safe
- take suspect food or food samples away for testing
- condemn unsafe food to stop it from being sold
- give instructions for improvements to unsatisfactory food premises
- close down unfit food premises.

Food Safety Act
1990

CHAPTER 16

First Published 1990
Reprinted 1998
£7.95

Figure 24.8 *The Food Safety Act 1990 (Reproduced under the terms of Crown Copyright Policy Guidance issued by HMSO)*

FOOD SAFETY (GENERAL FOOD HYGIENE) REGULATIONS 1995

These regulations give specific instructions about food hygiene standards in the UK and across the European Union, as set out in the European Food Hygiene Directive (93/94/EEC). Some of the important details include:

Aims

- To ensure high standards of hygiene in the food industry.
- To ensure that all food and food products are prepared, supplied or sold under hygienic conditions.

The stages covered by the regulations include:

- preparation
- processing
- manufacturing and packaging
- transportation
- distribution
- serving in a commercial eating place or selling in a shop.

In addition, the regulations also require the food industry to assess the risks involved in food production. This means that there is a requirement to **identify** and **control** food safety risks at each stage of production and the selling of food.

This is done by:

- identifying food safety hazards
- knowing which stages in a food production system are critical to food safety
- setting up and monitoring safety checks and procedures.

An example of a risk assessment procedure is HACCP (hazard analysis and critical control points).

This ensures that an analysis of the system is made and all potential hazards identified. A set of safety rules is then made for each CCP (critical control point) (see Chapter 21 pages 156 and 158).

Some of the other important legal requirements for the food industry are set out in the:

- Health and Safety at Work Act
- Sale of Goods Act
- Food Safety (Temperature Control) Regulations 1995
- Food Labelling Regulations 1984
- Protective Workwear Act

Figure 24.9 *The Food Safety (Temperature Control) Regulations 1995 (Reproduced under the terms of Crown Copyright Policy Guidance issued by HMSO)*

FOOD HYGIENE TRAINING

An important factor in food safety is developing the knowledge and understanding of all staff involved in food production and serving. These people are known as food handlers and they must all be trained in food hygiene and food safety risks. The first level of qualification is the Basic Food Hygiene Certificate. This certificate is awarded by the Chartered Institute of Environmental Health (CIEH).

The Basic Food Hygiene course covers topics such as:

- hygienic food preparation
- causes of food poisoning
- prevention of food poisoning
- food preparation areas
- personal hygiene
- food storage
- waste and pest control.

PERSONAL HYGIENE

Personal hygiene is vital and all food handlers are expected to:

- wear clean, protective clothing, e.g. overall, apron, hat, shoes
- remove all jewellery, e.g. rings, watches, bracelets, earrings and necklaces
- cover over all cuts and skin grazes with a waterproof dressing, e.g. blue waterproof plaster, often incorporating a metal strip to aid detection along the production line
- tie back and/or cover their hair with a net, e.g. hat net or beard net
- take special care with their hands before touching food ingredients, e.g:
  - wash with bacterial soap and hot water
  - keep fingernails short and scrubbed, with all nail varnish removed
  - dry their hands with a hot air drier or disposable paper towels
  - wear disposable gloves whenever possible for handling food (these gloves are often blue in colour).
- report any illness to a supervisor, e.g. sickness, diarrhoea, cold, flu
  - this is a legal requirement
- follow clean handling rules, such as:
  - do not cough, sneeze or spit over food
  - do not eat, chew or smoke near food
  - do not transfer bacteria by touching nose, hair or ears when handling food
  - do not taste food with fingers or lick equipment, e.g. spoons.

Figure 24.10 *Food handlers wearing protective clothing*

Figure 24.11 *A commercial food preparation area*

FOOD PREPARATION

Food preparation equipment can become infected with micro-organisms and soiled with contaminated food during preparation.

Arrangements for keeping food preparation areas and equipment clean and hygienic include:

- well-designed food preparation areas that give good lighting, ventilation, efficient cleaning and adequate washing facilities
- regular maintenance of the fixtures and fittings to avoid cracked surfaces, flaking paint, etc. by organising routine repair and painting programmes
- keeping different work areas for designated tasks, e.g. the separation of preparation areas for high-risk foods, medium-risk foods, low-risks foods and waste products to prevent cross-contamination. These areas are often colour coded:
  – **red** for raw meat
  – **blue** for raw fish
  – **green** for fruit and vegetables
  – **yellow** for cooked meat
- the equipment can also be colour coded and often the food handlers wear coloured neck ties to distinguish their area and the type of food they work with. All of this helps to prevent cross-contamination
- good facilities for washing and cleaning, e.g. hot water, stainless steel sinks, drainage
- equipment kept in good condition and appropriately designed for the intended task, e.g. no cracks or chipped or porous surfaces
- specific equipment used for raw and cooked foods, e.g. chopping boards, bowls and knives may be colour coded
- efficient waste disposal units and systems, e.g. clean bins, colour-coded bin liners, regular removal of rubbish and waste
- methods for preventing insect contamination, e.g. food covers, ultra-violet light insect traps, fly screens on windows, control of rodents, etc.
- separate facilities for staff from each area, e.g. changing areas with washing facilities.

Food must continue to be protected during distribution to retail outlets and storage.

Figure 24.12 *A refrigerated food delivery lorry*

STORAGE AND DISTRIBUTION

Storage and distribution arrangements for keeping food safe from contamination include:

- keeping food at a temperature which will prevent the growth of micro-organisms, i.e. well below 5°C in refrigerated delivery vans and lorries, point of sale display cabinets, etc.
- temperature control checks of equipment such as refrigerators, chill cabinets and freezers

- protective packaging for products during transportation and storage. The choice of packaging material is important as it needs to:
  - prevent contamination from micro-organisms, pests, dust, dirt and fumes
  - prevent contamination from the packaging materials, e.g. splinters from wooden pallets, metal staples used to seal boxes, etc. Suitable packaging materials include plastic trays or pallets, shrink-wrap plastic, plastic adhesive tape and first-grade cardboard, i.e. not recycled materials which could be contaminated with toxins or chemicals

- clear labelling with date marking, e.g. 'use-by', 'best before', 'display by'

- well-monitored stock rotation

- clear instructions and symbols for stacking and handling containers to prevent drainage of the contents, e.g. 'store this way up'.

KEY WORDS

These are the key words. Tick them if you think you know what they mean. Otherwise check on them.

aerobic	anaerobic	bacteria
binary fission	contaminate	cross-contamination
enzymes	fermentation	food spoilage
micro-organisms	moulds	pathogenic
risk categories	toxic	yeast

Check yourself

QUESTIONS

Q1 Yeast is an ingredient used in the food industry. Name a food product that has yeast as an ingredient. Explain the function of yeast in your chosen product.

Q2 A simple approach within food safety is to describe foods as belonging to a risk category. What is meant by the risk category of foods? Give reasons for this approach.

Q3 The local environmental health officer announces that there has been an increasing number of reported cases of salmonella food poisoning. What factors could have led to this increase in salmonella food poisoning?

Q4 Many people are employed in the food industry, preparing or serving food products. These people are often referred to as food handlers. What has been done to make sure that food handlers understand food hygiene and food safety risks?

Q5 Bananas, apples and pears are sometimes dipped in lemon juice (citric acid) when being prepared for fruit salad. What is the reason for this process?

ANSWERS

A1 Yeast is used as the raising agent in bread products. Yeast is a living organism which, in the optimum conditions of warm temperatures (25°C–30°C), moisture and food, undergoes a process known as fermentation. The yeast breaks down sugars to produce alcohol and carbon dioxide. In breadmaking the carbon dioxide expands when heated and aerates the dough.

A2 Foods can be grouped into three categories of risk: high, medium and low. Foods that have a high protein and moisture content provide ideal conditions for micro-organisms to grow and multiply. Foods considered to be of high risk are raw meat, fish, dairy products, cooked meat and poultry, shellfish, sauces, soups, egg products, cooked rice.

A3 Salmonella bacteria are found in the gut of most animals and birds, particularly chicken, and in raw meat, eggs, seafood and dairy products. If the foods have been prepared or kept in the temperature range of 7°C–45°C, the salmonella bacteria will have multiplied to a level likely to cause food poisoning. The bacteria can be destroyed by high temperatures but if frozen foods are not thawed completely before cooking, the foods may not be cooked thoroughly in the middle. There is also the risk of cross-contamination from infected food handlers or from raw to cooked foods.

A4 Recent legislation, i.e. the Food Safety Act 1990 and Food Safety (General Food Hygiene) Regulations 1995, have set out specific guidelines to reduce the risks of cross-contamination of food by food handlers. Two examples are:
- food hygiene training. On successful completion of the Food Hygiene Training course, food handlers are awarded the Basic Food Hygiene Certificate.
- personal hygiene standards – food handlers are expected to wear protective workwear and follow guidelines related to all aspects which may cause food to become infected.

A5 When the fruit is cut an enzyme called polyphenol reacts in the presence of oxygen to cause a browning reaction. Enzymes are inactivated in acidic conditions and therefore dipping the fruit in the acidic lemon juice reduces the rate of browning.

TUTORIALS

T1 *When you make bread you will find that the yeast can be bought in three forms: fresh yeast, dried yeast and easy-blend yeast. Some interesting bread products can be made with yeast, e.g. teacakes, Chelsea buns, bread rolls, croissants, ciabatta, bara brith. However, you must remember that yeast can also cause food spoilage in some foods. This can occur in high-sugar foods, e.g. jam, fruit yogurts.*

T2 *Remember that micro-organisms can cause microbial spoilage which makes foods unfit to eat. Foods can be infected by moulds, yeasts or bacteria. Each type grows in specific conditions. Some bacteria are pathogenic and it is pathogenic bacteria which cause food poisoning. If left unrefrigerated, high-risk category foods provide optimum conditions for the growth of pathogenic bacteria, e.g. food (high protein), moisture and warmth.*

T3 *Don't forget that bacteria are microscopic organisms which reproduce by binary fission (cells divide over and over again). They are most active in the optimum conditions of warmth, moisture and oxygen. Several types of bacteria cause food poisoning. Some bacteria are toxic which means that they produce a poisonous substance . These toxins can be harmful and can cause severe symptoms or death, e.g. Clostrichium botulinium.*

T4 *Read through the main points of the existing legislation to make sure that all food is safe to eat. When you visit supermarkets or buy food from restaurants, cafes or takeaway snack bars, look to see how the staff who handle or serve the food meet the requirements for personal hygiene as covered by the food legislation.*

T5 *Remember that enzymes bring about both desirable and undesirable changes in food. Enzyme reactions are beneficial in bread, brewing and cheese manufacture.*

WHY DOES TEMPERATURE MATTER?

Temperature control is critical in food production systems, risk assessment, food safety and food spoilage.

Temperature can:

- change the working characteristics of a raw food ingredient
- change the physical properties of individual foods and combination of foods
- change the nutritional profile of some foods
- destroy micro-organisms and enzymes to preserve or extend shelf life.

HEAT TRANSFER

The characteristics of certain foods can be altered by the transfer of heat to or from the food.

When applied to foods **warm**, **high** or **hot temperatures** have the following effects:

- Food is made more digestible, e.g. heat softens the cell structure of potatoes.
- Heating improves the appearance, flavour, texture and smell of a wide range of foods, e.g. meat, fish.
- Heating prevents food spoilage as very high temperatures destroy micro-organisms.
- Heating preserves or extends shelf life.
- Heating increases the availability of some nutrients.

Figure 25.1 *High temperatures*

When applied to foods **low temperatures** have the following effects:

- They prevent food spoilage by retarding the growth of micro-organisms.
- They extend shelf life, e.g. chilling between −1°C to 4°C.
- They introduce a greater variety of textures and flavours, e.g. ice-cream, chilled desserts.

Milk is a good example of how both high and low temperatures can change the characteristics of a primary source food to create a wide range of different products.

Figure 25.2 *Low temperatures*

Figure 25.3 *The temperatures used to produce different milk products*

MILK

132°C	ultra heat treated (UHT)	shelf life in airtight cartons 6 months
115°C	evaporated	canned
113°C	sterilised	bottled with a shelf life of a few weeks
80°C	condensed	sugar added and canned
72°C	pasteurised	with a cream line and bottled
	semi-skimmed	half the fat is removed, bottled
	skimmed	all fat removed and bottled
	homogenised	fine sieving breaks up the fat into fine droplets. No cream line
43°C	yogurt	lactic acid culture sets the milk.
30°C	cheese, creme fraiche, fromage frais	lactic acid starter and enzyme cause milk to clot and form curds and whey
5°C		
4°C		legal storage temperature for chilled foods
−1°C		
−30°C	ice cream	stirred, frozen and stored
−30°C	frozen yogurt	skimmed milk with yogurt culture

Figure 25.4 *Long life milk products*

METHODS OF HEAT TRANSFER

Heat can be transferred in three ways: **conduction**, **convection** and **radiation**. One or more methods may be used together depending on the food concerned and the time and equipment available.

EFFECTS OF HEAT ON THE PROPERTIES OF FOOD

An increase in temperature can cause foods to change. For example, fat softens or melts, protein sets, sugar caramelises, starch thickens liquids, baked products turn brown.

MACRO NUTRIENTS

Fat

Solid fats soften at room temperature. This is important for:

- spreading butter or margarine on bread, etc.
- creaming butter or margarine with sugar to incorporate air for a creamed cake mixture.

Solid fat or foods which contain a high percentage of fat, such as chocolate, melt to a liquid at high temperatures. This is useful for:

- melted cake or biscuit mixtures, e.g. gingerbread, flapjack
- melted chocolate for chocolate mousse or cake decoration.

When heated fat or oil can be used for cooking, e.g. shallow frying or deep fat frying. Each fat or oil has an optimum temperature, e.g. butter 140°C; corn oil/lard 220°C. Above this temperature the fat/oil begins to break up. It will produce an acrid smoke with a flash point occurring when flames appear.

Protein

Protein changes when heated. The main change is that protein coagulates. The changes that occur are known as the **denaturation** of protein. (See Chapter 13 page 103.)

Carbohydrates

Starch

- When mixed with a liquid and heated starch grains (flour) undergo the process of gelatinisation (see Chapter 17, pages 132 and 133).
- When baked or toasted the starch in bread, cakes, pastry and biscuits changes to dextrin and turns a light golden brown. This is known as **dextrinisation**.

Sugar

- Sugar dissolves in liquids. A syrup is formed which, when heated, gradually gets thicker, producing various degrees of hardness on cooling, e.g. fudge 116°C; caramel 138°C. The colour changes to shades of brown and the whole process is known as **caramelisation**.
- When heated sugar dry melts and caramelises. It is used to give texture and colour to some cakes and desserts such as creme brulee.

Colour and flavour

Heating foods which contain a combination of protein and carbohydrate causes reactions which produce brown colours and flavourings. This is characteristic of roasted vegetables and nuts, baked bread and cakes and toasted breakfast cereals. It is often referred to as non-enzymatic browning or the Maillard reaction. This reaction can also produce unpleasant flavours, e.g. in overcooked crisps or chipped potatoes.

Heat causes other foods to change colour, e.g:

- green vegetables such as broccoli and cabbage change from bright green to dark green.
- red meat changes to brown as the protein coagulates.

Heat can change or intensify the flavour of some foods and often produces distinctive smells (aroma) as food cooks, e.g. baked bread, roasted coffee beans.

Figure 25.5 *Bread is heated to make toast*

MICRO NUTRIENTS

- Minerals, e.g. iron and calcium, and fat-soluble vitamins, e.g. A, D, E and K, remain unchanged by cooking temperatures.
- Water-soluble vitamins, e.g. B and C, are usually destroyed by heat and high cooking temperatures.

PRESERVATION AND SHELF LIFE

All around the world various methods of storing food have been developed. Some methods, e.g. smoking and salting, have been used for centuries to preserve locally produced food, while modern methods, e.g. freezing and chilling, are used to preserve vast quantities of raw and ready prepared foods for worldwide distribution.

Many techniques use the principle of temperature to preserve or extend shelf life. High temperatures, low temperatures or temperature in combination with high concentrations of sugar can be used to preserve a wide variety of foods.

HIGH TEMPERATURE METHODS

Pasteurisation

- Pasteurisation is a method of heat treatment.
- Heat, i.e. high temperatures, destroys pathogenic micro-organisms.
- It extends the storage time of foods for a limited time.
- It is used mainly to heat-treat milk.
- The process of pasteurisation destroys all the pathogenic bacteria by passing the milk through a plate heat exchanger, which heats it to 71°C, holds it at that temperature for 15 seconds then cools it rapidly to 10°C.

Sterilisation

- Sterilisation is a method of heat treatment for a longer period of time at higher temperatures.
- Heat destroys nearly all micro-organisms and enzymes.
- It extends the storage period.
- It is a process used for milk and fruit juice.
- The process of sterilisation destroys pathogenic bacteria and heat-resistant spores by heating the milk to 104°C for 40 minutes or 113°C for 15 minutes.
- The combination of high temperatures and time change the flavour and colour of milk to a creamy flavour with a slight caramelisation of the milk sugar content.
- Sterilised food products can be packaged before or after the heat treatment process.

Ultra Heat Treatment (UHT)

- Very high temperatures are used to destroy all bacteria.
- This process is used to extend the storage period for milk.
- Milk is heated to 130°C–140°C for 1–5 seconds.
- The advantages of this process over the traditional sterilisation process is that there is:
    - little colour change
    - only slight change in taste
    - little loss of nutrient content.
- UHT milk is sold in airtight cartons and will keep for up to six months.

Irradiation

- Irradiation is a relatively new technology introduced into Great Britain in 1991.

- It is a method of preservation which is strictly controlled.

- In irradiation X-rays from a radioactive or electron beam are passed through the food. This means that the food has been treated with ionising radiation.

- This process helps to:

  - stop vegetables sprouting, e.g. potatoes and onions

  - delay fruits from ripening

  - destroy insects and pests which may damage foods, e.g. rice, wheat, spices

  - destroy micro-organisms which may cause food spoilage.

- All foods preserved by irradiation must be clearly labelled.

Figure 25.6 *Irradiated strawberries (right) last longer*

Some people are concerned are about the process of irradiation. Consumers have asked the following types of questions:

Question   Will the food be radioactive?

Answer   No there is no evidence to suggest that the food is unsafe.

Question   Are the food factory workers safe?

Answer   Yes, strict safety regulations control the processing of the irradiated food and risk assessment is undertaken.

Question   Is the nutrient content of the food changed during the irradiation process?

Answer   There is no major change to the macro nutrients – carbohydrates, proteins, and fats – or to the mineral content. However, the micro nutrient content of vitamins A, C, E K may be affected.

Canning

- Canning is one of the most widely used methods of preserving a huge range of foods, e.g. fruit, vegetables, meat, fish, soup, sauces.

- High temperatures, i.e. heat sterilisation, destroy the micro-organisms and enzymes which cause food spoilage.

- Foods are prepared for canning:

  - fruit and vegetables may be washed, peeled, sliced, chopped

  - meat and fish may be boned, cut, chopped, diced.

- Foods are often packed into the cans together with a liquid, e.g. water, brine, fruit juice, sugar syrup or a sauce. A space is left at the top of the cans to prevent them destorting in shape during cooking due to an expansion of the liquid.

Figure 25.7 *A range of canned foods*

- Cans are sealed with a double seam to prevent leakage or the re-entry of bacteria.

- The filled, sealed cans are placed in a retort (a large pressure cooker). They are heat-treated to 121°C. The time span is adjusted according to the filling, e.g:

  - fruit and vegetables in liquid approximately 10 minutes

  - meat packed solid approximately 15 minutes.

- The type of packaging includes tin plate cans and aluminium cans (see Chapter 29 page 207).

- Acid foods, e.g. fruit and vegetables such as rhubarb and grapefruit, are often canned in plastic-lined cans to prevent corrosion caused by the reaction of acid with metal.

- Cooked ready meals are often packed in plastic trays or containers. These are known as plastic cans. They are used for ready meals stored at ambient temperatures.

- Accuracy with regard to time and temperature is essential so that:

  – the sterilisation process is complete and harmful spore-forming bacteria will not germinate after processing

  – the food retains its structure and texture, e.g. too high a temperature would overcook and soften fruit.

- After sterilising the cans are sprayed with water or passed through a cooling tank to prevent the contents overcooking.

LOW TEMPERATURES

Two familiar but different methods of storing food products at low temperatures are freezing and chilling.

- Freezing is a method of preservation. It preserves food for between one week to one year. The food often needs to be thawed fully before being cooked.

- Chilling does not preserve food. It merely extends shelf life by a few days. The foods do not need to be defrosted.

Remember that a key safety point for both of these methods is that food must be kept in the recommended temperature zone. This temperature must not rise during transportation or storage.

Figure 25.8 *A deep freeze in a supermarket*

FREEZING

- Over the past 50 years freezing has become the most popular domestic method of food preservation.

- Freezing involves preserving foods at very low temperatures. Recommended temperatures are:

  – minus 18°C for domestic freezers.

  – minus 18°C to minus 29°C for commercial freezers.

- At these temperatures the following principles apply:

  – The growth of micro-organisms stops at very low temperatures.

  – Enzyme activity is slowed down.

  – Water in the food changes to ice crystals and is not available to promote the growth of micro-organisms.

- Food must be frozen very quickly so that small ice crystals form in the cells and no damage is caused to the structure of the food. A slow freezing process allows large uneven ice crystals to form which will later rupture the cells and cause the flavour, texture and nutritional value to change when the food is thawed.

- Overall there are no changes to the food during storage. The nutritional value of the food is mainly unaffected. In some cases flavours may become weaker or stronger. However you must remember that:

  - cell damage can occur in soft fruits e.g. strawberries

  - the colloidal structure of some food products, e.g. sauces, can collapse when frozen.

Frozen food products must have instructions for storage printed on the packaging to inform consumers on the correct ways of keeping the product in good condition after purchase. A system of star ratings is used on all commercially prepared foods (see Chapter 28 page 119).

CHILLING

This is a method of extending shelf life for a short period of time.

- This method of extending shelf life has become very popular during the last fifteen years.

- Chilled foods are perishable foods, e.g. prepared salads, fresh pasta, sandwiches, pâtés, pies, which are kept in prime condition for a limited amount of time by storing them at a low temperature between −1°C to 8°C.

- The low temperature inhibits the growth of micro-organisms. Bacteria are not killed but they will remain dormant.

- The low temperatures also slow down enzyme activity.

- The bacteria *Listeria monocytogenes* has become a common form of food poisoning. The main sources of this bacteria are high-risk foods. Because of this it is required by law that chilled foods are stored below 4°C, i.e. in the temperature range of −1°C to 4°C.

- A cook-chill system is when foods are prepared, cooked and chilled rapidly. This system is used for retail sales and in the catering industry.

- Chilled foods are always sold from chill cabinets. At home chilled foods and those prepared by the cook-chill process must be kept in a refrigerator.

Some advantages of chilling as a method of extending shelf life include:

- Single or a mixture of fresh foods can be kept in prime condition for a longer time, e.g.

  - single raw foods such as meat, fish, salad, vegetables

  - a mixture of fresh foods such as coleslaw, stir fry vegetables.

- A large range of ready prepared foods are available. These require little or no preparation and are convenient for consumers to use.

- Some food products are a mixture of cooked and raw ingredients, e.g. potato salad.

- There is very little change to the flavour, colour, texture or shape if best quality foods are used.

- There is no change to the nutritional content.

- Manufacturers must provide storage instructions including temperature. Consumers should check the temperature of their refrigerator.

OTHER METHODS OF LOW TEMPERATURE STORAGE

Cold Storage

Some foods are held in cold storage in an atmosphere of carbon dioxide gas. This method is often referred to as **controlled atmosphere (CA)** storage. In these conditions the growth of micro-organisms is slowed down. CA is used for storing eggs, apples, pears, root vegetables and meat.

Figure 25.9 *A variety of dried fruits*

DRYING

- Drying is the removal of moisture by warm or hot temperature. It is often referred to as **dehydration**. Micro-organisms need moisture to grow and reproduce so without moisture they cannot thrive.

- **Sunlight** – Drying foods in direct sunlight is a very old and traditional method of preserving foods, e.g. fruit and vegetables such as tomatoes, raisins. The moisture evaporates slowly but the foods can become contaminated by bacteria in the air or by the re-entry of bacteria.

- **Oven drying** – Warm ovens are used for this type of preservation which is suitable for vegetables, herbs, tea and coffee.

- Removing water from food may cause:

  – a concentration of flavours, e.g. in juices, syrups and tomato puree

  – an increase in the concentration of salt and sugar

  – a reduction in the bulk and weight of the food which often means it is cheaper to handle and transport

- Dried food must be stored in a cool dry place.

- **Rehydration** is when liquid is added to reconstitute the foods. When the foods have absorbed liquid they must be treated in the same way as fresh food because micro-organisms will be able to grow and reproduce again.

- The effects of dehydration may include changes in:

  – colour, e.g. green grapes to brown sultanas

  – texture, e.g. crumbly coffee granules, brittle herbs or peas

  – a shrunken and wrinkly skin, e.g. prunes

  – flavour, e.g. sweeter or saltier fruit and vegetables

  – nutritional profile, e.g. vitamin C or thiamin may be destroyed

  – additives, e.g. anti-caking agents are added to salt and icing sugar to help them flow freely.

In industry, mechanical drying methods are used. These methods include:

Spray Drying

- This method is suitable for foods which may be damaged by excessive heating, e.g. milk, coffee, potato.

Fluidised Bed Drying

- This can be used to clump-dry particles into granules which dissolve more easily in water, e.g. potato, coffee.

Roller Drying

- Used for instant breakfast cereal, mashed potato and baby foods.

Accelerated Freeze Drying (AFD)

- This is the most modern method of commercial drying. It produces an excellent quality dried product.
- The food is frozen and then the temperature is increased to vaporise the ice which turns to steam as it dries out the food.
- Advantages of AFD are:
  - the colour, texture and most of the flavour are kept
  - the food does not shrink as much as in other methods
  - the nutritional profile is retained
  - it preserves the food longer than other drying methods
  - it can be used for coffee and complete meals which include meat and fish. Products have an open texture which rehydrates well.
- Disadvantages of AFD include:
  - It is a more costly method of drying.
  - AFD foods need to be handled with care as they crumble easily.

Preservation techniques also include drying, smoking and adding chemicals such as salt, vinegar or sugar.

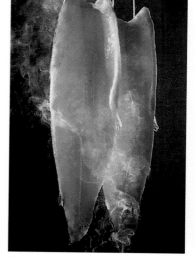

Figure 25.10 *Smoked fish*

Chemicals

Micro-organisms are unable to grow in strong solutions of vinegar, salt or sugar. For example:

- **Vinegar** is acetic acid with a low pH of 3.5. The strong acid solution preserves foods such as pickled onions and cabbage because the bacteria cannot survive below pH4.5.
- **Salt** is used to coat foods such as ham, bacon and fish or it is also used in a solution of salt and water (brine). It reduces the moisture content of the food by **osmosis**. Some foods are canned in brine.
- **Sugar** in high concentrations prevents bacteria from growing. It is used in jams, marmalade and jellies where the sugar content is 60% of the final product. A strong sugar solution is also used for coating candied and crystallised fruit which dry out by the process of osmosis.

Modern methods of extending shelf life and preservation include:

- additives – preservatives are added to foods to extend their shelf life (see Chapter 27)
- packaging – **modified atmosphere packaging (MAP)**; **controlled atmosphere packaging (CAP)**; **vacuum packaging** (see Chapter 29).

Figure 25.11 *Pickled onions*

FOOD SAFETY AND RISK ASSESSMENT

Temperature control is a critical measurement in food production. In a food production system the temperature for a particular process will be a **critical control point (CCP)** and vital to the food safety.

Look at the temperature control points in the production of a meat-filled pastry product.

Table 25.1 *The production process for a meat-filled pastry product*

- **The critical temperature control points must be strictly kept.**
- Pastry ingredients mixed and kept below 20°C
- Cutting and shaping pie lids and bases below 10°C
- Meat-based filling mixed and stored below 10°C
- Baked in a rotary oven at 195°C
- Very quickly cooled to ambient temperature of approx. 20°C
- Blast chilled in chilling unit at −10°C
- Transported by chilled delivery vans below 5°C
- Stored in chilled cabinets between −1 to 4°C
- Stock used in strict 'use-by-date' order
- To prepare for eating, reheat in centre to 70–75°C

KEY WORDS

These are the key words. Tick them if you think you know what they mean. Otherwise check on them.

accelerated Freeze drying	irradiation	acrid
microwaves	canning	molecules
caramelisation	non-enzymic browning	characteristics
pasteurisation	chilling	perishable
conduction	poor conductor	convection
preserves	convection currents	preservation
dehydration	radiation	denaturation
rehydration	dextrinisation	sous-vide
digestible	sterilisation	drying
temperature	extending shelf life	transfer
freezing	ultra heat treatment	good conductor
vibrate	infra-red rays	insulation

Check yourself

QUESTIONS

Q1 Why is 'Refrigerate after opening' printed on the product labels of mayonnaise and salad cream?

Q2 Why is it important to monitor the temperature of chill cabinets and freezers?

Q3 Complete a chart to show that foods can be preserved in a number of ways. Use the following headings to show ways of preserving raspberries, tomatoes, fish.

Food   Preservation Method   Principle

Q4 Explain three changes which happen to solid fats stored in a refrigerator at 5°C when there is an increase in temperature. Give examples to qualify your answer.

Q5 Irradiation is a new technology used to preserve foods. What are the advantages of irradiation as a method of preservation?

Q6 Chilling is a method of extending the shelf life of certain food products. It has become a very popular method over the last fifteen years. Give three reasons why chilling has increased in popularity.

REMEMBER! Cover the answers if you want to.

ANSWERS

A1 Mayonnaise and salad cream contain high-risk ingredients, e.g. egg and dairy products. They provide ideal conditions for the growth of micro-organisms. They are packaged into sterile jars or bottles and sealed to prevent re-entry of bacteria. When the seal is broken there is a chance that micro-organisms will grow because of the air and warm conditions. Between −1°C to 4°C is the recommended temperature zone for high-risk foods.

A2 Food manufacturers are required by the Food Safety Regulations 1995 to make sure that food is safe to eat. A method of food safety management and risk assessment is done by carrying out HACCP. This identifies critical control points where food safety may be at risk. The storage of chilled foods in chill cabinets and frozen food in freezers are critical control points. The temperature must be maintained within critical limits, e.g. chill cabinets −1 to 4°C; freezer cabinets below −28°C to prevent the growth of micro-organisms.

TUTORIALS

T1 *Low temperatures inhibit the growth of micro-organisms. Bacteria, yeasts and moulds are not destroyed but they will remain dormant, i.e. they are prevented from multiplying and contaminating the food. Food poisoning is an illness caused by eating contaminated food. Storing high-risk foods at room temperature is a common cause of food poisoning.*

T2 *Different methods can be used to record, monitor and control the temperature of chill cabinets or freezers.*

They include:
- *a temperature sensor or thermometer to record the temperature*
- *a thermostat to maintain the temperature at a set point or within a range*
- *a temperature probe to monitor temperature*
- *the continuous digital display of the temperature reading*
- *connection to a central computer system which activates an alarm system if the temperature moves out of the critical range*
- *regular checks by food handlers/workers of the temperature readings, e.g. every hour.*

A3 ANSWERS

Food	Preservation Method	Principle
Raspberries	● canned in sugar syrup ● jam ● freezing ● chilling	Canning at high temperatures High temperatures + sugar Low temperatures −18°C Refrigerate −1 to 4°C
Tomatoes	● canned in tomato juice ● sun dried tomatoes ● chutney ● bottled tomato sauce	Canning at high temperatures Drying High temperatures, vinegar, sugar + sterilisation. High temperatures
Fish	● canned in tomato sauce or brine/ oil ● smoked (kippers or haddock) ● freezing (fish or fish products) ● modified atmosphere packaging	Canning, high temperatures Smoking process Low temperatures −18°C Mixture of gases in sealed packaging

T3 TUTORIALS

Many methods are used to preserve large quantities of different foods. Some techniques use the principle of temperature to preserve or extend shelf life. High temperature methods include pasteurisation, sterilisation, ultra-heat treatment, canning, bottling, jamming. Low temperature methods include freezing and chilling. A combination of temperature and a high concentration of salt, sugar or vinegar is used for jam, chutney, canning in brine and pickling.

A4

- Solid fat, e.g. butter and margarine softens at room temperature and this makes it easy to spread on bread or to cream with sugar in cake mixtures.
- Solid fat, e.g. butter/margarine melts at high temperatures and can be mixed in as a liquid, e.g. melted cake/biscuit mixture.
- Solid fat, e.g. lard melts at very high temperatures. At the very high temperature of 220°C it is used for cooking chipped potatoes. If overheated the fat starts to break down, smoke and will eventually burst into flames.

T4

An increase in temperature causes changes to the physical state of food. The texture, colour or flavour may alter. These changes can be useful as they increase the working characteristics of foods and create more opportunities for variety in food product development.

A5

The process of irradiation helps to delay the ripening of some foods and also prevents food spoilage, e.g. it:
- stops vegetables sprouting
- delays fruit from ripening
- destroys insects and pests which may damage foods, e.g. rice, wheat
- destroys micro-organisms.

T5

Irradiation means that X-rays are used to preserve food, i.e. rays from radioactive or electron beams are passed through the food. The food has been treated with ionising radiation.

A6

Your answer could include:
- Chilling, i.e. storing food below 4°C is suitable for high-risk foods. It reduces the risk of food poisoning.
- Chilling is suitable for a wide range of foods. Some of these foods are not suitable for other methods of preservation such as freezing.
- Chilling foods does not change the flavour, colour, texture or shape of the foods and therefore allows their natural characteristics to be maintained.
- Prepared and cooked foods can be stored by chilling. They require little or no preparation so they are very convenient to use.

T6

Chilling is the storage of food at low temperatures which inhibit the growth of micro-organisms and enzyme activity. It is required by law that chilled foods are stored within the temperature range of −1°C to 4°C. Chilled foods must be sold from chill cabinets in shops and stored in a refrigerator at home.

SAMPLE STUDENT'S ANSWERS
AND EXAMINER'S COMMENTS

1 The safe storage of food is very important. Some food are classified as 'high risk'.

(a) Explain the term 'high-risk' food. (4 marks)

A high-risk food is one which is suitable for the growth of bacteria. These foods are usually moist and high in protein. High-risk foods need to be kept in a refrigerator.

4/4

(b) Give four different examples of 'high-risk' foods. (4 marks)

Cooked meat

Cream

Shellfish, e.g. prawns

Mayonnaise

4/4

2 Many 'high risk' foods can be purchased from chill cabinets.

Explain the 'cook-chill' system. (4 marks)

This is a system which uses the normal methods for the preparation and cooking of food but it is then followed by a very fast chilling process just above freezing point at 3 degrees C. If a product is to be reheated after purchase it should be reheated to a temperature of 70 degrees C.

4/4

This student has answered questions 1 and 2 very well which seems to be due to good revision. She would have scored full marks.

Questions to Answer

The answers to Questions 3 and 4 can be found on page 244.

3 (a) What is the purpose of chilling food? (2 marks)
(b) Why is it so popular? (2 marks)

4 Accurate time and temperature control are essential in the 'cook-chill' system.

(a) What are the critical time and temperature control points? (3 marks)

(b) Explain how you would make sure the temperature of a chill cabinet is kept within the correct temperature range. (5 marks)

CHAPTER 27

ADDITIVES

WHAT ARE ADDITIVES?

Additives are substances which are added to foods during manufacturing or processing to improve their keeping properties, flavour, colour, texture, appearance or stability. Additives are used in a huge range of food products today.

Additives may be:

- obtained from natural sources, e.g. a red colouring made from beetroot juice (E162) is used in making ice cream and liquorice
- **synthesised** in a laboratory to be *chemically* the same as certain natural materials, such as vanillin which is found naturally in vanilla pods
- **manufactured synthetic** compounds which do not occur in nature, such as saccharin (E954) a low-calorie intensive sweetener.

The use of over 300 additives is permitted in the UK. Flavourings are not included in this figure. In the UK over 3000 flavourings are used in many different combinations.

You will find that consumers prefer food products to contain additives obtained from natural sources. For this reason many manufacturers try to use fewer synthetic additives, e.g. a cake manufacturer may use additives from natural sources and will then advertise the range of cakes as 'Home Style Baking'. Artificial additives are still used extensively by the food manufacturing industry but the use of these additives is controlled by the following government departments:

- FAC (Food Advisory Committee)
- MAFF (Ministry of Agriculture, Fisheries and Food)
- COT (Committee of Toxicity of Chemicals in Food, Consumer Products and the Environment).

Specific regulations controlling the use of additives include:

- The Preservatives in Food Regulations 1974
- The Sweeteners in Food Regulations 1983
- The Bread and Flour Regulations 1984

Safety

- Food additives must be safe for consumers to eat.
- Consumer groups constantly pressurise food manufacturers to use fewer or no additives in their products.
- Some people have unpleasant reactions to certain additives, but this is less common now than in the past.

Figure 27.1 *Some additives cause allergic reactions*

BEWARE!	MAY BE FOUND IN
E101 Tartrazine can affect some chidren and asthmatics	soft drinks
E110 sunset yellow can cause a skin rash	biscuits and sweets

The long-term effects of additives are not known.
Research must be continually carried out on the safety of food additives.

Quantity

- Legally enforced regulations control the maximum amount of additives that can be safely used in foods.
- Additives should be used in minimum quantities.
- Using large quantities of additives can be expensive for the manufacturer and harmful to consumers' health.

Labelling

Additives must be shown on food labels in the list of ingredients. Additives must be listed in the descending order of the amount used (greatest amount first) and by name or 'E' number. (See Chapter 28 page 198.)

A COFFEE AND WALNUT CAKE FILLED WITH COFFEE FLAVOUR BUTTERCREAM TOPPED WITH COFFEE FUDGE AND NIBBED WALNUTS
(i) INGREDIENTS:
Sugar, Vegetable Margarine, (with Emulsifier: Mono- And Di-Glycerides of Fatty Acids, Flavouring), Wheat Flour, Egg, Glucose Syrup, Butter, Walnuts, Dextrose, Sweetened Condensed Milk, Soya Flour, Flavouring, Modified Starch, Whey Solids, Sorbital Syrup, Emulsifier (Mono- And Di- Glycerides of Fatty Acids), Instant Coffee, Dried Egg White, Salt, Preservative (Potassium Sorbate), Sodium Caseinate, Stabiliser (Xanthan Gum).
NOT SUITABLE FOR VEGETARIANS

UNSUITABLE FOR YOUNG CHILDREN WHO CAN CHOKE ON NUTS

Figure 27.2 *Additives are shown on food labels*

ADVANTAGES AND DISADVANTAGES OF USING ADDITIVES

Why does a food manufacturer use additives? There are several advantages and disadvantages!

Advantages

- to produce a wide range of food products to meet consumer needs, e.g. quick, easy, convenient meals, such as pot noodles, instant whipped desserts, instant potato mash, etc.
- to improve a specific characteristic of a food, e.g. vanilla-flavoured ice cream, orange-flavoured soft centres in chocolates, chocolate and coffee liqueur-flavoured hot chocolate drinks, etc.
- to produce expected qualities in foods, such as colour and flavour, e.g. soft-centred chocolates with pink colouring and strawberry flavouring or green colouring with mint flavouring
- to produce a product range by using different additives in the basic food, e.g. potato crisps flavoured with salt and vinegar, cheese and onion, smoky bacon, chicken, prawn cocktail, etc.
- to help maintain product consistency in large-scale production, e.g. the use of emulsifiers to stabilise salad cream, anti-foaming agents to reduce foaming in jam, etc.
- to restore original characteristics of a food after processing, e.g. adding colour to processed vegetables
- to prevent food spoilage, to preserve foods and give them a longer shelf life, e.g. bread.

Disadvantages

The disadvantages of using additives include:

- Additives could be used to disguise inferior ingredients.
- Some colours and flavourings may not really be necessary.
- Some people may have an allergy to additives. A problem here is that it is often difficult to find out which additive is causing the allergic reaction. Examples of allergies caused by food additives include asthma attacks, skin rashes, and hyperactivity in children.

All additives have to be approved by the Government Food Advisory Committee. Long, strict tests are carried out before approval is given. On approval each additive is given a number as a means of identification. If the additive is given an 'E' prefix to the number this means that it is accepted for use throughout the European Union.

TYPES OF FOOD ADDITIVES AND THEIR FUNCTIONS

COLOURS

Colours are added to make foods look attractive. During manufacture and processing colours:

- replace colour lost during heat treatment, e.g. in canned peas
- boost colours already in foods, e.g. strawberry yogurt
- maintain consistency between different batch productions as they are added in precise quantities, e.g. yellow colouring in tinned custard
- make foods that are normally colourless look attractive, e.g. carbonated drinks.

It is interesting to note that:

- caramel (E150) is the most popular colouring used in soft drinks
- some colours are artificial, e.g. titanium dioxide (E171) used in sweets
- some colours come from natural sources, e.g. beetroot red (E162) which is used in ice cream and liquorice
- no colours are allowed to be added to baby foods. However, three **micronutrients**, i.e. vitamins that are used in baby foods, do add colour to the food. These are riboflavin (E101), riboflavin-5'-phosphate (E101a) and beta-carotene (E160a).

Some consumers believe that the addition of colour additives is not necessary for foods to taste good. Should we therefore cut down on the quantity of food colouring added to food products?

Figure 27.3 *Food colouring is listed in the ingredients*

PRESERVATIVES

Preservatives help to keep food safe for longer than they would normally last. They are added to foods to:

- extend their shelf life, which is of benefit to consumers, e.g. preservatives in salad dressing, concentrated lemon juice, etc.

- prevent the growth of micro-organisms which can cause food spoilage and lead to food poisoning (see Chapter 24).

Preservatives are found in:

- many processed foods with a long shelf life
- cured meats, such as bacon, ham, corned beef
- dried fruit, such as sultanas, raisins, etc.

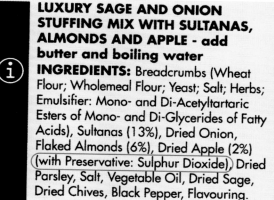

LUXURY SAGE AND ONION STUFFING MIX WITH SULTANAS, ALMONDS AND APPLE - add butter and boiling water
INGREDIENTS: Breadcrumbs (Wheat Flour; Wholemeal Flour; Yeast; Salt; Herbs; Emulsifier: Mono- and Di-Acetyltartaric Esters of Mono- and Di-Glycerides of Fatty Acids), Sultanas (13%), Dried Onion, Flaked Almonds (6%), Dried Apple (2%) (with Preservative: Sulphur Dioxide) Dried Parsley, Salt, Vegetable Oil, Dried Sage, Dried Chives, Black Pepper, Flavouring.

Figure 27.4 Preservatives are listed on food labels

SWEETENERS

There are two types of sweeteners: **intense sweeteners** and **bulk sweeteners**.

Intense sweeteners are:

- artificial sweeteners such as aspartame, acesulfame-k, thaumatin and saccharin
- approximately 300 times sweeter than sugar
- low in calories
- used in low-calorie drinks and reduced-sugar products, and are also available as sweetening tablets
- useful for people who want to eat less sugar in their diet.

However they:

- lack the bulk that is needed in recipes which normally use cane or beet sugar
- do not have the same characteristics as sugar for cooking
- may leave a bitter aftertaste.

Bulk sweeteners are:

- hydrogenated glucose syrup, sorbitol (E420) and mannitol
- similar to sugar in levels of sweetness
- used in similar amounts to sugar
- used in sugar-free confectionery and preserves for diabetics.

However, bulk sweeteners are not absorbed by the body's digestive system or used by it as efficiently as sugar.

INGREDIENTS
WATER, ORANGES, PINEAPPLE JUICE, CITRIC ACID, ACIDITY REGULATOR (TRISODIUM CITRATE), PRESERVATIVES (POTASSIUM SORBATE, SODIUM METABISULPHITE), SWEETENERS (ASPARTAME, SACCHARIN), STABILISER (E466), FLAVOURING, COLOUR (BETA-CAROTENE), CONTAINS A SOURCE OF PHENYLALANINE

DILUTE ONE PART CONCENTRATE WITH AT LEAST 4 PARTS WATER. IT IS IMPORTANT TO ADD EXTRA WATER IF GIVING TO TODDLERS

Figure 27.5 Intense sweeteners are listed on food labels

Figure 27.6 Bulk sweeteners are listed on the label

STUTE
DIABETIC
Morello Cherry Extra Jam with sweetener
STUTE is a genuine NO SUGAR ADDED DIABETIC jam with 45% less calories and higher fruit content than ordinary jam.
INGREDIENTS: Sweetener (Sorbitol), Morello Cherries, Gelling Agent (Citrus Pectin), Citric Acid.

INGREDIENTS:
Water, Soya Oil, Pasteurised Egg Yolk, Glucose Syrup, Modified Starch, Vinegar, Salt, Lactic Acid, Preservative (Potassium Sorbate), Stabiliser (Xanthan Gum) Flavourings.

INGREDIENTS:
Spirit Vinegar
Vegetable Oil
Water, Sugar
Mustard, Salt
Egg Yolks
Modified Cornflour
Stabilisers –
Xanthan Gum
and Guar Gum
Colour –
Riboflavin

Figure 27.7 Emulsifiers are listed on the packaging

EMULSIFIERS AND STABILISERS

These help to improve the consistency of food during processing and storage.

Emulsifiers and stabilisers are:

- used to help substances such as oil and water to mix together, form an emulsion and stay mixed. Normally, when shaken together, oil and water would separate
- found in eggs, e.g. lecithin is a natural emulsifier and is used to make mayonnaise, low-fat spreads, salad dressings, etc.
- important for giving foods a smooth creamy texture
- used to lengthen the shelf life of baked products
- also made from locust beans, e.g. xanthan gum which is used to thicken salad cream.

FLAVOURINGS AND FLAVOUR ENHANCERS

These are used to improve the taste of foods by:

- adding flavour to food, e.g. vanilla in vanilla-flavoured yogurt or ice cream
- restoring flavours lost in processing, e.g. acetaldehyde gives an apple flavour.

Flavourings and flavour enhancers must meet the requirements of the Food Safety Act 1990 and all other flavouring regulations. They can be classified into three groups:

- natural, e.g. herbs and spices
- natural identical, e.g. flavours extracted from natural substances
- artificial, e.g. substances which are not themselves natural flavours but have the ability to make other flavours stronger, e.g. monosodium glutamate (E621)

Monosodium glutamate (MSG):

- intensifies the flavours of other foods
- is used in Chinese recipes and savoury foods
- may cause allergies in some people, producing sickness and dizziness. (For this reason some foods are advertised as 'MSG free'.)

ANTIOXIDANTS

These are used to:

- prevent fat in foods combining with oxygen and becoming **rancid**. This process is called **oxidation**. Rancid foods have an unpleasant odour and flavour.
- slow down enzyme activity in fruit and vegetables which go brown when cut.

INGREDIENTS
Water, Mushrooms
Dried Skimmed Milk
Vegetable Oil
Modified Cornflour, Salt
Whey Protein
Flavour Enhancer -
Monosodium Glutamate
Flavouring
Yeast extract, Sugar
Stabiliser - Polyphosphates
and Sodim Phosphates
Spice Extract

Figure 27.8 Mushroom soup ingredients. Some people are allergic to monosodium glutamate

Ascorbic acid (vitamin C) is a natural antioxidant found in fruit. It helps to prevent other fruits going brown. For example, apple/pears/bananas for a fruit salad can be dipped in lemon juice first to prevent them from browning.

- Another natural antioxidant is tocopherol (vitamin E) which is used to increase the shelf life of food products. Sulphur dioxide is also an antioxidant.
- Antioxidants are used in dried soups, preserved meat and fish products, stock cubes, cheese spreads, etc.

ANTI-CAKING AGENTS

These are used to stop crystals and powders from sticking together and to keep them free flowing. They are found in dried milk, cocoa, salt, etc.

ANTI-FOAMING AGENTS

These are used to stop large amounts of foam and froth occurring during the making of jam, syrup and fruit juices.

ACIDS, BASES AND BUFFERS

These are used to control the **acidity** or **alkalinity** of food products. Acids used include: citric acid (E330); acetic acid (E260); tartaric acid (E334).

There are other categories of additives. Look up the following list and find out what they are used for:

firming agents	packaging gases	gelling agents	raising agents
glazing agents	propellants	humectants	sequesterants
modified starch	thickeners		

KEY WORDS

These are the key words. Tick them if you think you know what they mean. Otherwise check on them.

additives	**allergy**	**antioxidants**
artificial	**colours**	**emulsifiers**
'E' number	**flavouring**	**flavour enhancer**
natural	**permitted**	**preservatives**
stabiliser	**sweeteners**	

Check yourself

QUESTIONS

Q1 Some foods contain preservatives. What are the advantages to the consumer of these food products?

Q2 The following two pieces of information are printed on a tin of creamed rice pudding.

Figure 27.9

No Preservatives	✓
Gluten Free	✓
No Added Colours	✓

INGREDIENTS

Full Cream Milk, Skimmed Milk, Whey, Rice, Sugar

What does this information tell the consumer?

Q3 A chocolate bar has the following information printed on the label.

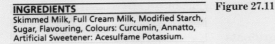

Figure 27.10

Milk Chocolate with Raisins and Almonds
Ingredients: milk chocolate (milk, sugar, cocoa mass, cocoa butter, vegetable fat, emulsifiers: E442 and E476, flavourings), raisins, almonds.

Why are emulsifiers used in the manufacture of chocolate products?

Q4 A tin of low-fat custard has the following information on the label.

Figure 27.11

INGREDIENTS
Skimmed Milk, Full Cream Milk, Modified Starch, Sugar, Flavouring, Colours: Curcumin, Annatto, Artificial Sweetener: Acesulfame Potassium.

No Artificial Colours ✓

What does this tell the consumer about the colour additives in the custard?

Q5 Dried packet soups contain flavourings and flavour enhancers (E621, E635). Why are these additives used in these food products?

CREAM OF CHICKEN & SWEETCORN SOUP WITH CROUTONS
INGREDIENTS as served (greatest first)
Water, Glucose Syrup, Cornflour, Hydrogenated Vegetable Oil, Sweetcorn, Croutons, Potato Starch, Salt, Chicken, Milk Proteins, Flavourings, Flavour Enhancers (E621, E635), Acidity Regulator (Potassium Phosphates), Emulsifier (E471), Herb and Spice Extracts including Celery, Sage, Black Pepper and Spices.

Figure 27.12

Q6 Mashed potato can be formed into shapes such as potato waffles which can be served individually grilled or baked. The ingredients of one brand of frozen potato waffles are:

INGREDIENTS
Potato, Vegetable Oil, Starch, Salt, Stabiliser (E464), Pepper, Vitamin C, Mustard.

Figure 27.13

The stabiliser E464 is included in this list of ingredients. Why has the manufacturer added a stabiliser to the potato waffles?

REMEMBER! Cover the answers if you want to.

ANSWERS

A1 Foods that contain preservatives have an extended shelf life, i.e. they keep for longer periods of time. They do not have to be used immediately. Consumers can shop less frequently which saves time by reducing the

TUTORIALS

T1 Preservatives prevent the growth of micro-organisms which can cause food spoilage and lead to food poisoning. Preservatives extend the shelf life of food products.

ANSWERS

number of shopping trips. Food is available out of season and this increases the choice of food products available on a regular basis. Manufacturers can safely transport such foods from other countries and can also transport processed food over long distances to retail outlets.

A2 The list of ingredients shows that the rice pudding does not contain any additives. The manufacturer is informing the consumer that the product is free from preservatives and that no colours have been added. Consumers who prefer to buy food products with no or few additives would be interested in this product. Some people may be allergic to additives. Sometimes they do not know which additives they are allergic to. It is better for them to be safe by choosing food products that do not contain any additives.

A3 Emulsifiers are additives which help to improve the texture and consistency of food. They will help to form an emulsion when the cocoa, milk, sugar, cocoa butter and vegetable fat are mixed together. Emulsifiers help to prevent ingredients separating. The emulsifiers help to give the chocolate a smooth creamy texture. They also help to lengthen the shelf life of the chocolate.

A4 Colours are added to the custard during processing to:
- make it look attractive
- produce the yellow colour that consumers expect
- make sure that the colour is the same between different batches.

The colours used are curcumin and annatto. These colours come from natural sources. The manufacturer has not added any artificial colours and tells the consumer this by printing this information on the label.

A5 Flavourings and flavour enhancers are used to add flavours to food products or to restore flavours lost in processing. Artificial flavour enhancers, such as monosodium glutamate (E621), have the ability to make other flavours stronger.

A6 An important feature of potato products is the shape. The stabiliser is used to maintain the shape and texture of the potato waffle during storage and during the cooking process. Stabilisers help to keep a product in the same condition as when it was produced.

TUTORIALS

T2 *Additives must be declared on the list of ingredients printed on a food label. This is a legal requirement. The ingredients must be listed in descending order of the amount used, and by name or 'E' number.*
Note the label also states that this rice pudding contains no gluten. It would therefore be a suitable product for people who require a special diet that is gluten free, i.e. people with coeliac disease.

T3 *Emulsifiers are used in many foods. Lecithin is a naturally occurring emulsifier found in eggs. It is used to form an emulsion of oil and water in mayonnaise and creamed cake mixtures.*
Other examples of emulsifiers used in food products include:
- *E471 in ice-cream*
- *E472e in bread mix.*

T4 *Colours often improve the aesthetic appearance of food products. They do not improve flavour or taste. Some consumers think that colour is not necessary and that it need not be added to foods.*

T5 *Flavourings and flavour enhancers have to meet the strict requirements of the Food Safety Act 1990 and all other flavouring regulations.*

T6 *Stabilisers are used in a variety of foods to improve and maintain the consistency of the food during processing, storage and cooking. Another example of a stabiliser is xanthan gum (X415) which is used to stabilise salad dressing, sweet pickle, coleslaw, etc.*

CHAPTER 28

PRODUCT LABELLING

LABELLING INFORMATION REQUIRED BY LAW

It is a legal requirement to inform customers about the food products they are buying. The Food Labelling Regulations 1996 state the type of information that must be displayed on a food product label. We can look in detail at each of these eight requirements.

1 FOOD PRODUCT NAME

Figure 28.1 *Products must be clearly named*

- The name of the product must clearly tell consumers what the product is, e.g. cornflakes, teabags, etc.
- Sometimes extra words are needed. For example, the word 'jam' would not let you know the type of jam. It would be necessary to use the name of the flavour, e.g strawberry jam.
- Processed foods must be identified by printing the process in the title, e.g. smoked salmon, roasted peanuts, etc.
- Differences between similar products must be indicated, e.g. fruit-flavoured yogurt and strawberry yoghurt.
- Well-known foods are allowed to keep traditional names as long as a subtitle is given naming the food product, e.g. 'Chicken Madras – marinated pieces of chicken breast in a spicy tomato sauce with fresh coriander'.
- Some foods are allowed to keep their names even though they are not accurate. For example swiss roll does not come from Switzerland.
- The pictures must not mislead the consumer. For example, raspberry-flavoured instant dessert must not have a picture of raspberries on the label.

2 LIST OF INGREDIENTS

INGREDIENTS
Suitable for vegetarians

Wheat Flour, Water, Currants, Sultanas, Sugar, Yeast, Vegetable Fat, Wheat Gluten, Salt, Emulsifiers E471, E472e, E481, Soya Flour, Preservative Calcium Propionate (added to inhibit mould growth), Dextrose, Flour Treatment Agents Ascorbic Acid (Vitamin C), 920.

Figure 28.2 *The list of ingredients for teacakes*

- All ingredients must be listed on the label.
- Ingredients are listed in descending order of weight, starting with the largest amount and finishing with the smallest.
- The amount of each ingredient does not have to be given.
- Food additives and water must be included. The name of the additive can be used or else the UK name or the 'E' number. The category name of the additive must be written before each additive or group of additives, e. g. preservatives or flavour enhancers.
- Some foods, e.g. unwrapped bread, do not have an ingredient list but information must be displayed at the point of sale if they contain such additives as preservatives and colourings, without giving individual names or 'E' numbers.

3 STORAGE CONDITIONS

The storage instructions give details of the best conditions in which to keep the food in order to prevent food spoilage.

Temperature guidelines are important. A temperature range or a symbol may also be given, e.g:

- keep refrigerated
- keep refrigerated max. 5°C
- store 0°C to +5°C.
- Should be −18°C or colder.
- Suitable for home freezing

Figure 28.3 *Advice on storing*

Figure 28.4 *The home freezing symbol*

4 SHELF LIFE

Date marking is used to indicate how long foods should be kept. The dates marked on food labels help to ensure the quality of the food and reduce the risk of food poisoning or food spoilage.

Two ways of date marking include:

- 'use by ' date
- 'best before' date.

'Use-by' Date

- A 'use-by' date is for high-risk foods such as raw and cooked meat, fish, pâté, etc. These highly perishable foods spoil quickly and the 'use-by' date is a clear instruction that the food is safe to eat until this time.
- After the 'use-by' date food may not look or taste different but it will be unsafe to eat.

'Best-before' Date

- A 'best-before' date is used for low-risk foods or foods which are processed and packaged to have a long shelf life, e.g. UHT milk.
- The date gives the day, month and year.
- After this date foods will start to deteriorate in terms of flavour, colour, texture or taste.
- The date on food products with a shelf life of three months or less must be shown as a day and month.

'Display-until' Date

Another date sometimes shown on food products is 'display until'. This is not a legal requirement.

- The 'display-until' date is usually a few days before the 'use-by' date so that the consumer has a number of days in which to use the product.
- It also informs the retailer when to remove the product from the shelves or chill/freezer cabinets.

DISPLAY UNTIL	USE BY
11 APR	**13 APR**
KEEP REFRIDGERATE · DO NOT FREEZE	

Figure 28.5 *Use by ...*

Figure 28.6 *Best before ....*

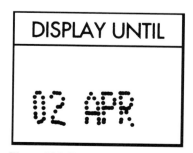

Figure 28.7 *Display until ...*

5 INSTRUCTIONS FOR USE

Instructions on how to prepare and cook the food are given, e.g:

- temperature and cooking time for conventional ovens
- preparation guidelines and times for cooking in microwave ovens
- guidelines for cooking from frozen in either conventional ovens or microwaves
- the defrosting times, cooking times and temperatures as tested by the manufacturer.

Figure 28.8 *Instructions on how to serve an instant cup a soup*

TO SERVE:

Empty a sachet into a cup or mug

Make up to 250ml (9 fl oz) with boiling water

Stir well, wait a few moments

Put your feet up and enjoy!

Figure 28.9 *The name and address of the manufacturer are given*

6 NAME AND ADDRESS OF THE MANUFACTURER

Consumers must be given the name and address of either:

- the manufacturer, e.g. Heinz, or
- the supplier/retailer, e.g. Tesco Stores Ltd.

This information is a point of contact for consumers who wish to know more about the product or to make a complaint.

7 PLACE OF ORIGIN

This shows the place the food has come from, e.g. 'product of Spain'

Figure 28.10 *Place of origin*

8 WEIGHT OR VOLUME

The Weights and Measures Act 1985 makes short weight an offence. Most pre-packed food is required to carry on the container an indication of the net weight or volume. When sold other than pre-packed, most food has to be sold either by quantity or number. The Act covers both the minimum and the average system of quantity control. The 'average' system of quantity control is mainly for pre-packed goods and is indicated next to the weight declaration on the pack by the symbol '℮'. The seller has to make the quantity known to the purchaser.

- The actual weight of the product must be given, i.e. within a few grams of the weight.
- Weights under 5 g do not have to be stated.
- Some foods are sold in standard amounts.
- A large ℮ placed alongside the amount shows that it is an average quantity.

| OVEN COOK, GRILL, FRY | 600 g ℮ | CONTAINS MINIMUM 4 FILLETS |

Figure 28.11 *Weight or volume*

OTHER LABELLING INFORMATION

Manufacturers may decide to give extra information. Look to see if you can find any of the following:

1 BAR CODES

- Bar codes appear on most food labels.
- An electronic scanner at the checkout reads the bar code.
- The price of the product is recorded and displayed.
- Details can be recorded for stocktaking.
- In the future more information will be stored on the bar code, e.g. production date.

Figure 28.12 *A bar code*

2 LOT OR BATCH MARK

- A lot or batch mark helps to identify each stage of the food product production process.
- It records details such as the date of production, the production line and the packaging system.
- Manufacturers must also be able to trace the making process of goods back to the raw ingredients and their origin.
- A unique code is used for each product and this is known in the food industry as **traceability**.

| DISPLAY UNTIL: | 03APR UOWUW |
| BEST BEFORE: | 05APR CLCK6 |

Figure 28.13 *A batch mark*

Figure 28.14
Suitable for vegetarians

3 SPECIAL INFORMATION

Symbols or word 'flashes' may be printed on the label to give information about:

- dietary group, e.g. 'suitable for vegetarians'
- storage, e.g. 'suitable for home freezing'
- ingredients, e.g:
  - 'This product contains traces of nuts.'
  - 'Made with 100% chicken breast.'
  - 'Although every care has been taken to remove bones some may remain.'
- cooking, e.g. 'suitable for microwave'
- special features, e.g. 'medium hot curry'.

Figure 28.15
Suitable for home freezing

Figure 28.16 Suitable for microwave

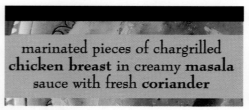

Figure 28.17 Ingredients with special features

Figure 28.18 Ingredients

4 OPENING INSTRUCTIONS

RESEALABLE PACK ➤ CUT OR TEAR

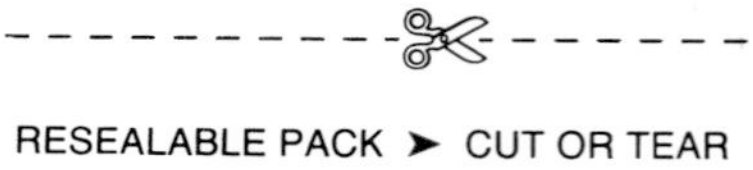

Figure 28.19 Opening instructions

These are often given to prevent spillage or leakage, e.g. 'Cut along dotted line.'

5 ENVIRONMENTAL ISSUES

Figure 28.20 Waste disposal

Symbols or statements are used to inform the customer about:

- types of plastics used in packaging
- any recycled materials or the origin of packaging materials
- disposal of packaging by recycling methods.

6 NUTRITIONAL INFORMATION

Many manufacturers put nutritional information on food product labels, although they are not required to do so by law unless a special claim is made about the product, e.g. 'high in fibre', 'low in fat'.

The advantages of stating nutritional information on the label include:

- Consumers know what nutrients are in the product.
- Comparisons of the nutrient content of one food can be made with another.
- Informed choices can be made.
- Foods which have a specific nutrient content can be selected, e.g. low in sugar.

Nutritional information that is stated on labels must comply with EU regulations and be given in one of the following formats.

Group 1	Energy Protein Carbohydrate Fat	Group 2	Energy Protein Carbohydrate Fat Sugars Saturates Fibre Sodium

NUTRITION INFORMATION

	As sold 100g provides:	Per 3 Dippers grilled provides:
Energy	1063kJ/255kcal	590kJ/140kcal (Calories)
Protein	12.7g	7.0g
Carbohydrate	14.8g	8.0g
(of which sugars)	0.3g	0.2g
Fat	16.1g	9.0g
(of which saturates)	5.8g	3.2g
Fibre	0.2g	0.1g
Sodium	0.6g	0.4g

Figure 28.21

NUTRITION

TYPICAL COMPOSITION	A 200G (7oz) serving provides	100g (3 1/2oz) provide
Energy	176kJ/42kcal	88kJ/21kcal
Protein	2.2g	1.1g
Carbohydrate	7.0g	3.5g
of which sugars	6.2g	3.1g
Fat	0.2g	0.1g
of which saturates	trace	trace
Fibre	1.6g	0.8g
Sodium	0g	0g
This can contains approx 2 servings.		

INFORMATION

Figure 28.22

Additional information about the amounts of polyunsaturates, monounsaturates, starch, cholesterol, vitamins and minerals can be given.

Calibration

The values of each nutrient must be given as follows:

- Average amounts present are given in 100 g or 100 ml so that comparisons between different products can be made.
- Energy values are given in kilojoules (kJ) and kilocalories (Kcal).
- Protein, fat and carbohydrate are given in grams (g).
- Fibre is given as non-starch polysaccharide (NSP).
- Sodium is given in grams (g).
- Vitamins and minerals must be shown as a percentage of the reference nutrient intake (RNI) in the product or recommended daily allowance (RDA).

KEY WORDS

These are the key words. Tick them if you think you know what they mean. Otherwise check on them.

barcode	'best before' date	calibration
'display until' date	ingredients list	legal requirements
lot or batch mark	nutritional information	shelf-life
storage instructions	traceability	'use by' date
volume	weight	

Check yourself

QUESTIONS

Q1 A tin of chopped tomatoes in rich tomato juice has the following instructions printed on the label. Give a reason for this.
Preparation guidelines
All appliances vary. The following are guidelines only.

To heat on the hob.
Empty contents of can into a saucepan.
Heat gently for 3-4 minutes, stirring occasionally.
DO NOT ALLOW TO BOIL.

Q2 A packet of crisps has a 'best before' date printed on the back of the packet:
06:Mar 99
Why does this product have a 'best before' date?

Q3 A jar of marmalade has this code printed on the lid. Give a reason for this.
Oct 2000
09:03 8331

Q4 A packet of digestive biscuits has these two pieces of information printed on the wrapping:
Ingredients
Wheat flour, vegetable oil and hydrogenated vegetable oil, sugar, wholemeal, cultured skimmed milk, partially inverted sugar, syrup, raising agents (sodium bicarbonate, tartaric acid), salt.
Suitable for vegetarians.
(i)   Does the manufacturer have to give both pieces of information?
(ii) Why would the manufacturer put both pieces of information on the label?

Q5 A packet of vacuum-packed Double Gloucester cheese has the following date stamps on the label:
Display until 21st January
Use by 28th January
Why does this product have a 'use by' date?

REMEMBER! Cover the answers if you want to.

ANSWERS

A1 It is a legal requirement to give instructions to the consumer about how to prepare and cook food products. The instructions may include:
- the method of cooking, e.g on the hob in a saucepan
- the time required to heat, e.g. 3-4 minutes
- any special instructions, e.g. 'Do not boil'.

A2 Crisps are low-risk foods and have a longer shelf life than a food like cheese. They are processed and sealed in a bag. A three-month shelf life is the expected time for safe storage.

A3 This is a lot or batch mark. It helps to identify each stage of the production process of the marmalade. It can be used to record details such as the date of production, the production line and the packaging system.

A4 (i)   No. The list of ingredients *is* a legal requirement.
The information or symbol showing that the biscuits are suitable for vegetarians is not required by law.

A5 Cheese is a high-risk food and will spoil quickly once the packet is open. The 'use by' date is a clear instruction that the food is safe to eat until this time.

TUTORIALS

T1 *This type of information helps the consumer to enjoy the product as the manufacturer intended it to be prepared and eaten.*

T2 *A 'best-before' date is another form of date marking. It is a legal requirement for manufacturers to indicate the shelf life of a product and this is used for low-risk foods.*

T3 *Manufacturers must be able to trace the product back to the raw ingredients. A unique code is used for each product and this is known as 'traceability'.*

T4 *The ingredients are listed in descending order of weight. The main ingredient is shown first.*
The information on nutrition and the symbols for specific food groups help the consumer to select food products to suit their specific nutritional requirements, e.g. vegetarians.

T5 *It is a legal requirement to inform the customer of the shelf life of a food product. Date marking is used to indicate how long high-risk food may be kept for.*

WHAT IS PACKAGING FOR?

Food packaging and the design of the packaging play an important part in food production. You will find that nearly all the foods we buy today come in some form of packaging. Over the years the materials and methods of packaging have changed as new technology has been introduced.

Figure 29.1 *A grocery shop in the 1940s*

Figure 29.2 *A modern supermarket*

Food packaging legislation states that food packaging must not:

- be hazardous to human health
- cause the food to deteriorate
- cause unacceptable changes in the substance or quality of the product.

Packaging has a number of important functions. It helps to identify, contain or protect food products or ingredients. You will need to be aware of these different functions.

Figure 29.3 *Food products can be packaged in all sorts of ways*

CONTAINING THE PRODUCT

Packaging holds the contents together and, when sealed, prevents spillage and loss. The packaged products can then be transported, stored and displayed easily and used conveniently.

The packaging can be a uniform shape and size, e.g. rectangular or square boxes for cakes, cake mixes and breakfast cereals. These can be further packaged into larger boxes or plastic shrink-wrap for transportation.

Sometimes the packaging has to hold difficult or irregular shapes which are not easy to fit, e.g. vegetables and fruit. These are often packed into nylon nets or plastic bags.

Crates, trays and pallets are used to load and hold packaged foods during transportation. These are often made from rigid plastic to prevent contamination from splinters or staples, which often occurs when wooden or cardboard containers are used.

Figure 29.4 *Food products being transported*

Figure 29.5 *Tamperproof seals*

PROTECTION

The food product must be protected from:

- physical damage which can be caused by vibration, collision or being crushed during storage, display or transportation. For example, fragile foods such as eggs are protected by rigid plastic/cardboard boxes. Cornflakes are protected by firm cardboard. Soft fruits are protected in glass jars or metal cans

- atmospheric conditions, such as the effect of changes in temperature, light, humidity or air controls. For example, warm temperatures may cause fruit to overripen, bright light may cause vegetables to lose colour, oxygen may cause cut foods to change colour and start to go brown

- contamination from chemicals, micro-organisms, insects or rodents. Foods that are contaminated by any of these are unsafe to use

- tampering which is a problem because products can become contaminated if they are opened by mistake and then reclosed. The design of the packaging can help to prevent food products from being tampered with. Tamperproof packaging techniques make it easy to see if the packaging has been opened. Examples include:
  - plastic collars on bottle lids, e.g. sauce bottles
  - film overwraps on cardboard boxes, e.g. on a box of teabags
  - paper strips across jar lids, e.g. on a jar of mayonnaise
  - plastic rings on the caps of screw-top bottles, e.g. lemonade
  - tin foil seals in pourable boxes, e.g. fruit juices.

IDENTIFICATION

Information about the product can be printed on the packaging. Labelling information is required by law to describe and inform consumers about products.

The presentation of the packaging at the point of sale helps to attract customers to buy the product.

The design of the packaging, which may include the shape, colour, size, etc., is used to identify a specific manufacturer and the product range.

MATERIALS

In past times natural materials such as wood and pottery were used to pack and store foods, e.g. apples in wooden crates and honey in stoneware jars. Today several types of material are used, including glass, paper, metal and plastic. These materials are constantly being adapted and improved to produce a wide variety of packaging which often includes a mixture of materials.

GLASS

Glass bottles are used to package milk, wine, sauces, salad dressings, etc. Glass jars are used to package herbs, jam, honey, fruit, cook-in sauces, etc.

Glass can be:

- brittle and will often break easily
- moulded into a variety of shapes
- transparent so the product can be seen
- coloured to enhance appearance
- resistant to high temperatures when contents are added
- tough and rigid to withstand crushing
- impermeable to substances which may contaminate the contents
- recycled
- cheap to produce
- heavy, giving additional weight to the product.

Figure 29.6 *Glass is a frequently used packaging material*

METALS

Two types of metal are used to make cans and a range of packaging parts, such as tops, screwcaps, bottle tops, trays, foil wrappings and laminates.

These two types are **tinplate** and **aluminium**. Tinplate and aluminium can be:

- strong, to retain shape and withstand crushing
- heat treated to high temperatures
- impermeable to substances which would contaminate the contents
- lightweight
- used in different thicknesses
- moulded into a variety of shapes.

Figure 29.7 *Metal trays and containers are used to package many foods*

PLASTICS

Several types of plastic are used for packaging food. Some are rigid and some are flexible. They include:

- polyethylene terephthalate, used for bottles to hold liquids
- polystyrene, used for trays and containers. The polystyrene is expanded and pressed into different shapes to hold liquid or solid foods. It a poor conductor of heat and is often used to make insulated containers for hot drinks and takeaway foods
- polythene, which can be of high density, withstanding high temperatures, e.g. boil in the bag foods, or of low density for use at room temperature or in the refrigerator or freezer. Polythene can also be used as a stretchable film, e.g. cling film. It can also be bonded to another material to act as a lining. This is called **lamination**
- cellulose film is available in a range of colours and is used for many different purposes.

Figure 29.8 *Plastics are used by many manufacturers*

Plastic can be:

- moulded into a variety of shapes
- very lightweight
- impermeable to substances which would contaminate the food contents
- difficult to dispose of
- biodegradable (these plastics are more expensive)
- sealed under pressure and heat treatment.

PAPER AND PAPERBOARD

Paper has been used for packaging for many years and it is still very popular. It can be used for all or parts of the packaging, e.g. as paper bags, labels, greaseproof paper, parchment and cartons.

Paper and paperboard can be:

- made in a variety of thicknesses
- used in sheets for flexible wrapping
- moulded into a variety of shapes, e.g. cartons
- recycled to reduce costs and save natural resources
- coated or laminated
- easy to print on
- lightweight.

Figure 29.9 *Paper and card packaging*

CHOOSING THE RIGHT TYPE OF FOOD PACKAGING

The characteristics of the food determine the type of packaging that is needed. You can check out the characteristics of food products by asking the following questions:

Is the food product:

- light or heavy in weight?
- sensitive to light, oxygen, temperature or moisture?
- cheap or expensive to produce?
- dry or wet?
- liquid or solid?
- brittle or rigid?
- stored at an ambient room temperature, or does it need chilled or frozen storage?
- capable of a short or long shelf life?

Food manufacturers need to ask these questions and must also consider a range of other factors when choosing the right type of packaging for their product. You should also ask yourself similar questions when taking a close look at packaging during your coursework project. For example:

- Will the packaging help to sell the product?

First, the manufacturer will define the characteristics of the food product, e.g:

- weight – light or heavy?
- volume – solid or aerated?
- firmness – fragile or robust?
- keeping quality – short or long shelf life?
- cost – cheap or expensive?
- sensitivity – to oxygen, light or moisture?
- risk factor – high-, medium-, or low-risk food?
- moisture content – wet or dry?
- storage temperature – frozen, chill, room temperature?
- density – solid or liquid?

What is the characteristic of the food product?

Second, what characteristics are required by the packaging:

- type of protection – rigid, firm, flexible, mouldable?
- size or quantity – large, small, single or double wrapped?
- compatibility – must be a material which will not react with the food
- resistance to temperature change – e.g plastics suitable for frozen foods or boil in the bag products
- cost of packaging material – cheap, expensive?
- suitable for storage and cooking – e.g. stored by chilling → cooked by microwave
- method of sealing – airtight, no leakages
- weight of packaging – heavy, e.g. glass, or lightweight, e.g. plastic film
- surface area – for printing information on
- shape and style – tray, bag, carton, jar, drum, tube, can, bottle, sachet
- opening mechanism – to prevent spillage, e.g. ring pull, screwtop, foil cap
- storage mechanism – stackable on shelves?

What is required of the packaging?

Third, the marketing aspect of the packaging must be considered. Packaging informs the customer about the product. Factors to consider include:

- information, e.g. pictures printed on the package
- the ability to view the product, e.g. through a cellophane window
- product identity, e.g. value or economy brand (simple yellow, blue and white stripes) or luxury brand (gold or silver)?
- computer graphics, e.g. on a cardboard box of breakfast cereals, the label of tinned foods, the cardboard sleeve around a cook chill product.

What is the marketing concept of the packaging?

	Product Characteristic	Packaging Requirement	Packaging Method
Novelty Birthday Cake Figure 29. 10 *A novelty birthday cake*	Squashable, expensive, limited shelf life. Moist, special features, e.g. decorations. Not easy to handle.	Moisture barrier. Impact protection, window feature, stable base for ease of serving.	Cardboard box with cellophane window. Covered foil cardboard base for serving.
Teabags Figure 29.11 *Teabags are packed to keep out moisture*	Light, moisture-sensitive, fragile, cheap, long shelf life at ambient temperatures.	Impact protection, moisture barrier. Cheap, prevent leakage of tea particles.	Thin cardboard box, cellophane outer wrapping with peel-back strip.
Jam or Marmalade Figure 29.12 *Jam is packed in airtight conditions*	Moist, sticky, runny, oxygen-sensitive. Fairly expensive, long life at ambient temperatures.	Moisture and oxygen barrier to prevent growth of yeasts and moulds. Impact protection. Firm structure to contain runny texture.	Glass jar can be heated to sterilisation temperature. Screw top lid with seal to provide airtight conditions.

Table 29.1 *Product characteristics*

PACKAGING AND THE ENVIRONMENT

Many people are concerned about the environment, i.e. **green issues**, and you may be too. Food packaging can cause a number of environmental problems because:

- It uses up natural resources, e.g. oil, trees, metal ore.
- It causes air, land or water pollution.
- It cannot always be recycled and is not biodegradable. It has to be disposed of in landfill sites.

Consumers can reduce waste by:

- buying re-usable containers, e.g. bags, jars, egg cartons
- re-using carrier bags, e.g. plastic or thick paper
- taking waste packaging to recycling centres, e.g. glass, cans, paper
- buying minimum packaging, e.g. single-wrapped rather than double-wrapped products
- selecting biodegradable materials wherever possible.

Manufacturers can reduce waste by:

- reducing the amount of packaging
- using paper or card which has come from sustainable forests
- avoiding harmful processes, such as bleaching wood pulp with chemicals
- using materials which the consumer can recycle
- printing symbols on the packaging which inform consumers, e.g. recycling logos, plastic identification symbols, anti-litter symbols
- providing information about the packaging materials.

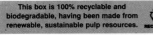

Figure 26.13 *Recyclable packaging*

PACKAGING FOR TAKEAWAY FOOD PRODUCTS

Many of us buy takeaway food products and it is particularly important that the packaging of such products can be disposed of easily.

This packaging often includes the use of paper sheets, plastic trays, pots and lids or cardboard boxes that aim to:

- protect the food during transportation
- prevent leakage or spillage
- keep the food hot.

Over the last few years there has been a huge increase in the range of takeaway food products, e.g. burgers, fish and chips, pizza, kebabs.

Manufacturers, retailers and consumers all need to be aware of the environmental issues involved in producing, using and disposing of such a large amount of packaging.

Have you noticed that some foods are packed in plastic bags or plastic trays with lids from which the air has been removed or changed to preserve the contents?

You need to be aware of these two packaging methods. They are called **vacuum packing** and **modified atmosphere packaging**.

VACUUM PACKAGING

- This has been used for several years now. All the air around the food is removed and the plastic package is sealed.
- The food is kept in **anaerobic** conditions, i.e. there is no oxygen around it.
- This sort of packaging is used for bacon, fish and coffee.

Figure 29.14 *Foods packed in vacuum packaging*

MODIFIED ATMOSPHERE PACKAGING (MAP)

This may also be referred to as **controlled atmosphere packaging (CAP)**.

MAP or CAP preserves food in sealed packs that contain a mixture of three gases:

- oxygen
- nitrogen
- carbon dioxide.

The process involves:

- packaging fresh foods in peak condition
- replacing the air by 'gas flashing' a combination of gases around the food
- sealing the plastic bag or plastic lid to a food tray by means of a **hermetic** sealing process.

Figure 29.15 *Foods packed in MAP packaging*

GASES USED IN FOOD PACKAGING

Carbon Dioxide

- retards the growth of bacteria
- can cause damage to the food if used in too great a quantity
- is absorbed by the foods, which can cause the packaging to collapse.

Oxygen

- helps to retain the colour of the food, e.g. meat stays red
- retards the action of some micro-organisms
- can cause oxidation of foods and make them deteriorate.

Nitrogen

- is used to replace some of the oxygen
- reduces the rate of oxidation.

The ratio of nitrogen, carbon dioxide and nitrogen varies according to the food being packaged.

The new technique of MAP allows:

- the consumer to see the food product through the clear pack
- a wide range of foods to be stored in this way, e.g. meat, fish, smoked fish, bacon, salads, fruit, fresh pasta, bread, poppadums
- an increase in shelf life by retarding microbial activity, e.g. meat up to seven days at chill temperature, bread up to three months at room temperature
- the colour of the food to stay the same until the pack is opened.

However, once the packaging is opened the food has a normal shelf life and must be stored accordingly.

KEY WORDS

These are the key words. Tick them if you think you know what they mean. Otherwise check on them.

ambient room temperature	atmospheric conditions	biodegradable
characteristics	contamination	containing
environmental	function	identification
modified atmosphere	physical properties	protection
recycle	tampering	transportation
vacuum		

Check yourself

QUESTIONS

Q1 Why is it important to package food products or ingredients?

Q2 Why do sandwiches have to be wrapped before being sold?

Q3 Give two reasons why a pizza is often packaged in a cardboard box before being frozen?

Q4 How would a cook-chill lasagne that is to be reheated in a microwave be packaged?

REMEMBER! Cover the answers if you want to.

ANSWERS

A1 The desired qualities of food products and ingredients must be preserved during transportation and storage.

A2 The main reason why sandwiches are wrapped is to prevent contamination, i.e. to keep the sandwich in hygienic conditions.

A3 The cardboard carton is rigid and will protect the pizza from being damaged or crushed. These cartons will also stack easily in the freezer. Information labels can be printed on the outside of the carton.

A4 There would probably be three pieces of packaging:
- a plastic moulded tray to store, cook and serve the lasagne in
- a plastic film cover to seal the tray
- a cardboard outer sleeve to protect the plastic tray and to print information on.

TUTORIAL

T1 Many people think that the function of food packaging is only to make a food product look attractive. The important functions of the packaging are to protect or contain the product or to provide information about the contents.

T2 Sandwiches can be wrapped in flexible, stretch-wrap plastic or in rigid plastic containers. The rigid plastic containers will stop the sandwich from being crushed during transportation or while on display.

T3 Other pieces of packaging may be used but this would increase the cost, e.g. the pizza may be put on a plastic-coated board and it may be overwrapped in a clear thin plastic film. These both protect the pizza and help to keep ingredients such as grated cheese on top of the pizza.

T4 The properties of the materials are:
(i) the plastic for the tray, moulded to shape:
- is resistant to moisture
- is non-toxic
- can be heated in a microwave
- is rigid yet lightweight
(ii) the plastic for the cover, very thin and lightweight:
- can be pierced to allow steam to escape
- will fuse to the tray to form a seal
- is suitable for use in a microwave.
(iii) the cardboard sleeve
- can be folded to fit the shape of the tray:
- is rigid to prevent crushing
- is easy to print on
- is sometimes made from renewable resources.

USING SENSORY ANALYSIS IN YOUR COURSEWORK

Sensory analysis is used to **evaluate** food products. When you use sensory analysis on the food products you design and make you will discover details about their qualities such as:

- flavour and taste
- texture
- appearance – colour, shape, size
- smell or aroma
- sound.

Sensory analysis will provide answers to questions about your food products in three main areas:

Description

- What does the product taste like?
- What are its sensory characteristics?
- How does a change in production, packaging or storage affect sensory characteristics?

Discrimination

- Is this product different to a similar product made by another manufacturer or competitor?
- Would people notice the difference?
- How great is the difference?

Preference or Hedonics

- How much do people like the food product?
- Which attributes are liked?
- Is this an improvement over another product?

USING SENSORY ANALYSIS IN THE FOOD INDUSTRY

Sensory analysis is used by the food industry at several stages of product formulation and development.

Figure 30.1 *Sensory analysis being carried out in the food industry*

By carrying out sensory analysis manufacturers are able to:

- compare a product with a competitor's product
- improve products by modifying or changing the ingredients
- make judgements about the sensory characteristics of a food product
- check during production that the specification is being met
- monitor quality control by checking regular samples from the production line against the specification
- detect differences between products from different production runs or batches
- profile the characteristics of a new product or a modified product
- describe specific characteristics, e.g sweetness
- test that the quality of a product is maintained throughout its shelf life
- check that a new product is acceptable to consumers
- demonstrate new products to a marketing or sales team
- promote new or reformulated products to consumers.

Sensory analysis is carried out by:

- trained testers in controlled conditions

or

- untrained testers – consumers in uncontrolled conditions, e.g. market place, shop or home environment.

To obtain reliable results the tests are set up in a controlled way to ensure fair testing. Arrangements could include:

- an environment controlled by lighting and temperature
- an atmosphere free from other smells
- individual booths to reduce influence from other testers
- food samples presented on or in identical sized and shaped plain containers
- a small number of samples presented at one time
- coded samples with random numbers
- correct serving temperature for the food samples
- drinking water or eating a plain cracker biscuit between samples to clear the mouth
- clear instructions for the tester
- straightforward response sheets to record the results.

Figure 30.2 *A sensory analysis testing booth*

WHICH SENSES ARE USED IN SENSORY ANALYSIS?

Your sensory organs collect information about the food you eat. Sensory organs are: eyes, nose, tongue, skin and ears. They detect the senses of:

- sight – appearance
- smell and taste – aroma and flavour
- touch, texture and mouthfeel
- sound – noise.

The characteristics of food that affect our organs of sense are known as **organoleptic** qualities.

SIGHT

The appearance of food is important because you see the food before you eat it. But what makes food look attractive? Colour, size, shape, age and texture can all make food look more or less appetising.

Colour

- Foods are expected to be specific colours, e.g. tomato soup is usually red, peas are usually green.
- Sometimes artificial colours are used to give improved colours or shades to some foods, e.g. tartrazine (E 102) in soft drinks.
- Some foods are processed to be sold white, e.g. salt, sugar, flour and rice.

Aesthetics

Food can be made to look appealing by attractive presentation, e.g. garnishes for savoury products, decorations on sweet products, placing products in or on appropriate containers, e.g. plates, dishes, glasses.

HEARING

Some food products make sounds. These make the food interesting during preparation, cooking, serving or eating, e.g. the crackle of popcorn, the sizzle of bacon, the crunch of crisps, the fizz of sparkling drinks, the crunch of raw carrot.

SMELL AND TASTE

These two senses work together to develop the flavour of food.

- Smell is sensed in the upper cavity of the nose. It detects freshness, ripeness and the individual scents of foods, e.g strawberries, cabbage.
- Your sense of smell is reduced when you have a cold or flu.

Taste

Taste buds on the tongue detect four groups of flavours: bitter, sweet, sour, salt

- The flavours develop when the food is chewed and mixed with saliva.
- The sensitivity of food is reduced when food is either very hot or very cold.
- Sensitivity is most distinct when the temperature range is between 22°C to 41°C.

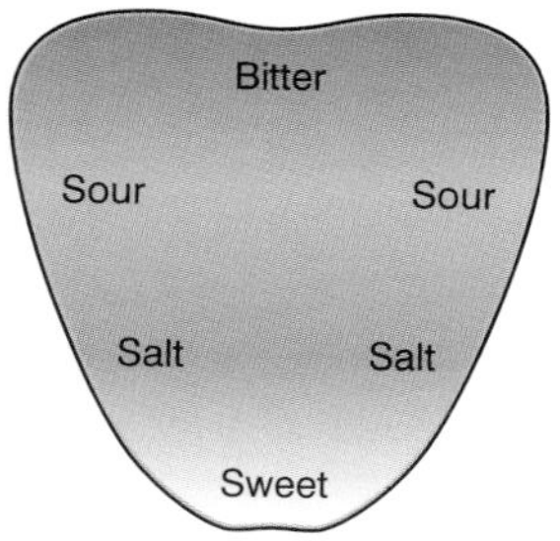

Figure 30.3 *Taste areas on the tongue*

TOUCH

If you touch or feel food with your fingers you will sense qualities such as softness, stickiness, hardness, etc. The surface of the tongue and other areas of sensitive skin in the mouth also detect different sensations, e.g moistness, dryness. These qualities are known as **mouthfeel**.

There are many textures, e.g gritty, brittle, mushy, crumbly.

SENSORY ANALYSIS TESTS

Sensory analysis tests can be used on food products to establish their most important characteristics. There are several types of sensory analysis test. These meet British Standard (BS5929).

PREFERENCE OR ACCEPTANCE TESTS

These tests would be used to evaluate 'product acceptability' by finding out the opinions, likes and dislikes of the consumer.

There are no right or wrong answers. The tests gather subjective information about what consumers prefer. To get a reliable result these tests often involve using large numbers of people in market place testing.

You may already know about two of these tests:

- paired preference test
- hedonic ranking test.

Paired Preference Test

- A 'tester' is presented with two samples and asked which sample they prefer.
- They may prefer one sample but could find both samples unacceptable.

Hedonic Ranking Test

- Hedonic ranking indicates consumer preferences. This test does not evaluate the quality of specific product attributes.
- This test finds out the degree of liking for a product from 'extreme like' to 'extreme dislike'.
- A 'tester' is presented with one or more food samples and asked to mark on a five to nine-point scale the point that represents their preference or degree of liking for the product.
- Comments may also be recorded.
- Numerical scales can contain five, seven or nine ranks:

1 like extremely
2 like very much
3 like slightly
4 like moderately
5 neither like nor dislike
6 dislike moderately
7 dislike slightly
8 dislike very much
9 dislike extremely

The choice of test depends on the age of the tester or the type of product being evaluated.

DIFFERENCE TESTS

You would use these tests to find out if there is a perceptible difference between two or more products. They are **objective** tests. They use comparative judgements to determine:

- differences in particular sensory characteristics
- small differences between products.

Food manufacturers use these sensory analysis tests in product development, e.g:

- reducing the fat content in a 'healthy option' product range
- reducing the fruit content in an economy range of biscuits.

You will find several types of difference tests:

- paired comparison tests
- triangle tests
- duo-trio tests
- taste threshold tests
- two out of five tests.

PAIRED COMPARISON TEST

- A pair of coded samples is presented for the comparison of a specific characteristic, e.g. sweetness.
- This involves fewer samples and less tasting than the triangle test.
- A minimum of 20 tastes will give a useful result.

Triangle Test

- Three coded samples are presented to the tester at the same time.
- Two of the samples are identical, one is different.
- The tester is asked to identify the 'odd one out'.
- Further questions about the samples may be asked.
- A minimum of five 'testers' are required.
- It is a useful test to detect very small differences between a small number of samples.

Triangle tests are often used during:

- product development, to see if consumers can tell the difference between the same product made by different manufacturers, e.g. different brands of crisps, cola drinks, biscuits or cheese
- manufacture, to ensure quality control to make sure that the products from each batch or production run are the same.

Duo-trio Test

You will find that this test is often used in place of the triangle test when less tasting is required. It is particularly useful when strong flavours are involved, e.g. curry, chilli, spicy sausages, etc.

- A control sample is presented to the tester.
- Two further samples are presented together for evaluation.
- One of these samples is the same as the control, the other is different.
- The tester has to select the sample they feel is different from the control sample.

Two Out of Five Test

This test is used to see if differences can be detected between two products.

- Each 'tester' is presented with coded sets of five samples.
- Three of the samples are the same, and two are different.
- The 'tester' must select which two are different.
- The results from each 'tester' are recorded and evaluated to decide if there is a noticeable difference.

Taste Threshold Test

This test is occasionally used to find out the lowest or minimum quantity of an ingredient or substance which can be added to a product before a noticeable change occurs, e.g. in flavour, colour, etc.

GRADING TEST

These test for the degree of intensity of a specific sensory property, e.g. sweetness. The food samples are ranked in order to reflect this or to show consumer preference. You would use these tests to:

- sort a large number of samples so that a smaller number could be selected from them for a more precise test
- find out consumer preferences as part of market research
- obtain rapid results as less skill is required than in other tests.

You could use three grading tests: **ranking**, **rating** and **profiling**.

Ranking

- A set of coded samples, arranged in a random order, is presented to the tester.
- The tester has to rank the samples in order of either:
  - a **specified** attribute, e.g. sweetness, saltiness, or
  - a **preference** on a hedonic scale or ranking.
- A minimum of 10 untrained assessors are needed.
- This test is rapid, allowing several samples to be tested at once.

  When testing the sweetness of yogurt, for example, the descriptor for 5–8 would be sweet and the descriptor for 1–4 would be sour.

8	Extremely	sweet	4	Slightly	sour
7	Very	sweet	3	Moderately	sour
6	Moderately	sweet	2	Very	sour
5	Slightly	sweet	1	Extremely	sour

This is an example of a **bi-polar scale**. The statements are two different or opposite characteristics, e.g. dry/juicy; thick/thin; fine/coarse; hard/soft; tough/tender; weak/strong.

  (ii) Extremely sweet _____ least sweet.

  (iii) Codes or symbols. These are used as there is no traditional way of ranking them, whereas testers tend to arrange numbers or letters in automatic order.

Rating

- A tester is presented with a set of coded food products and asked to rate a particular characteristic or preference.
- A minimum of 20 assessors are needed.
- They are asked to rate the products according to a particular scale, e.g. this five-point scale could be used when tasting yogurt:

  1 dislike a lot
  2 dislike a little
  3 neither like nor dislike
  4 like a little
  5 like a lot

or this scale could be used when testing tomato ketchup:

1. much too salty
2. too salty
3. just right
4. too little salt
5. far too little salt

This is an example of a unipolar scale because all the statements relate to the same characteristic, i.e. salt.

- Rating tests are more informative than ranking tests because the *extent* of the sensory attribute or preference is assessed rather than just putting them in order.

Profiling Tests

This is also called **sensory profiling**. Sensory profiling is used to obtain a detailed, descriptive evaluation of the differences between products and to find out how much of each difference there is.

A sensory profile of each product is developed which may include the characteristics of: texture, flavour, aroma, appearance, mouthfeel and sound. These may be assessed separately or together.

For sensory profiling tests you need:

- Trained assessors as the tests are more complex than other tests
- Six or more trained assessors who are presented with a set of coded samples.
- Each assessor has to rate the intensity on a scale of one to six. (One is lowest; six is highest.)
- The results from each assessor are added up and the average rating for each descriptor is worked out.
- The results are plotted on a spider diagram or star diagram, to provide a visual product profile.

KEY WORDS

These are the key words. Tick them if you think you know what they mean. Otherwise check on them.

aesthetic	**attributes**	**blind tasting**
controlled conditions	**hedonic**	**hedonic scale**
mouthfeel	**organoleptic**	**preference**
ranking	**rating**	**sensory**
descriptors	**sensory profiling**	**bi-polar**
senses: sight, smell and taste, hearing, touch		

Check yourself

QUESTIONS

Q1 Give three reasons why food manufacturers use sensory analysis during the development of a new bread product?

Q2 Why do trained testers carry out sensory analysis?

Q3 Your sensory organs collect information about the foods you eat. The senses they detect are listed below. Give two sensory descriptors that describe the characteristics associated with each of the senses.
- sight/appearance
- sound
- smell
- taste
- touch/mouthfeel.

Q4 Explain why a research and development team of food technologists would use a hedonic ranking test to evaluate a new chocolate cake product.

Q5 During a production run why would a food manufacturer use the triangle test for sensory analysis of custard cream biscuits?

Q6 Profiling is a method of showing test results from rating tests. Explain why a food manufacture would use sensory profiling.

REMEMBER! Cover the answers if you want to.

ANSWERS

A1 The food manufacturer could use sensory analysis to:
- evaluate existing breads made by other manufacturers
- make judgements about the sensory characteristics of a bread product
- improve the prototype bread product during the development stage by modifying or changing ingredients.

A2 Testers can be trained to:
- detect very small differences between products
  or
- make an assessment of specific attributes of a food product.

TUTORIALS

T1 *Remember that sensory analysis is used to evaluate food products because it enables the food manufacturer to measure and define sensory qualities. Sensory analysis can be used at several stages of product formulation, development or manufacture.*

T2 *Trained testers regularly carry out sensory analysis in controlled conditions. They contribute to the production of reliable, accurate and unbiased test results. Untrained testers are often invited to test products in less controlled conditions. They are asked to give general information about the products that they prefer. A balance of consumers may be required, i.e. people of different age, sex or ethnicity. On other occasions a similar group of consumers may be targeted, e.g. teenagers or students.*

ANSWERS

A3 Your answer could include two of the following descriptors:

Table 30.1

Sense	Descriptor
Sight/appearance	glossy, dark red, golden brown, dull
Sound	sizzling, crackling, bubbling, crunchy
Smell	spicy, fruity, musty,
Taste	sour, sweet, salty, bitter, hot, strong
Touch/mouthfeel	soft, greasy, sticky, hard, gritty, mushy, brittle, crumbly

A4 A hedonic ranking test finds out how much consumers like the new chocolate cake product. It does not evaluate the quality or specific attributes of the chocolate cake but shows only if the consumer prefers or likes the product.

A5 A triangle test is used to detect any differences between the same product. During manufacture it would be used in quality control to make sure that each batch of custard creams is the same or to check that the standard of production is the same at all times.

A6 Sensory profiling gives a detailed descriptive evaluation about a product. The results for each sample are plotted onto a star diagram or spider diagram. The profile may include characteristics of texture, flavour, aroma, appearance, mouthfeel and sound.
The results can be compared to see what consumers think about the product. The profile can detail a small number of characteristics or more complex descriptions, using up to 15 characteristics for very detailed analysis.

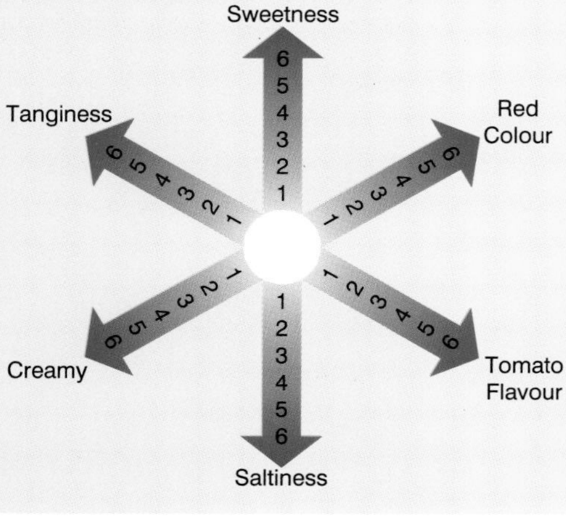

TUTORIALS

T3 *The characteristics of food that affect the organs of sense are known as organoleptic qualities. These are measured to gather information about the qualities of a food product. The descriptors are used by the trained testers when they record their answers to sensory analysis tests.*

T4 *For a hedonic ranking test the tester is presented with one or more samples (in this case chocolate cake). They are asked to mark on a five-nine-point scale the point which represents their preference or degree of liking for the product. The scale would range from extremely like to extremely dislike.*
This test could be carried out by untrained testers, e.g. shoppers in a supermarket.

T5 *Triangle testing is one of the 'difference tests'. These tests are used to see if there are any differences between two or more products. They may also be used to tell the difference between the same product made by different manufacturers.*
Other difference tests include paired comparison tests, duo-trio tests, two out of five tests, threshold tests.

T6 *Profiling is a grading test which tests for the degree of intensity of a specific sensory characteristic. For example, a manufacturer may wish to evaluate three different brands of tomato soup. For each sample assessors are asked to rate, on a scale of one to six, the sensory descriptors of sweetness, red colour, tomato flavour, saltiness, creamy, tanginess.*
The results are plotted onto a star diagram to provide a visual product profile for each brand of tomato soup. These can be compared and evaluated by the manufacturer. Modifications could then be made to improve their own brand of tomato soup.

Figure 30.4 *A star diagram which evaluates tomato soup*

SAMPLE STUDENT'S ANSWERS AND EXAMINER'S COMMENTS

EXAMINER'S COMMENTS

The student gains full marks for this question. She has shown that she understands the legal requirements of labelling.

1 This is part of a label from a chilled lemon mousse.

Chilled Lemon Mousse
Low Fat Whipped Lemon Dessert
Ingredients Reconstituted Skimmed Milk, Lemon Juice, Sugar, Skimmed Milk, Vegetable Extract, Cocoa Butter, Lemon Zest, Pork Gelatine, Emulsifier E472b, Modified Maize Starch, Colour E161b, Stabilisers E415, E410, E412

Why are the ingredients on the label listed in this order? (2 marks)

Because, by law, the ingredients list must go in order from the heaviest to the lightest. Therefore these products are listed in descending order of weight starting with the greatest and ending with the least.   2/2

EXAMINER'S COMMENTS

The student gets two marks out of three for this answer. She has named an additive correctly and has given a correct reason for including it. However, she has omitted the scientific understanding of an emulsifier. To get full marks she needed to say that an emulsifier holds tiny drops of oil suspended in water and this is how separation is prevented.

Other additives, e.g. modified maize starch, colour, stabilisers, could have been given and explained instead of E472b These would have gained equal marks providing an explanation of their use was given. However, naming more than one additive would not have gained any additional marks. There needed to be a named additive and an explanation of its function.

2 From the label, name one ingredient which is an additive and explain fully why it has been used. (3 marks)

One additive which is used in the lemon mousse is emulsifier E472b. This is used to prevent the ingredients separating out because an emulsifier stops ingredients like oil and water from separating and keeps them mixed together.   2/3

Questions to Answer

The answers to Questions 3, 4, 5 and 6 can be found on pages 244 and 245.

3 Why is it important that the product label lists all the additives used?

(2 marks)

4 In addition to the ingredient information other points of information are equally important on the label.

What are theses and how do they help the consumer? (8 marks)

5 Packaging is necessary for a lemon cheesecake which is to be sold from a chill cabinet.

BOX

COVER/LID
AND CONTAINER

Explain the function of the packaging for a cheesecake. (5 marks)

6 Complete the table below.

(a) Name three materials used for packaging a cheesecake product.

(b) State two properties for each packaging material you have suggested which make it suitable for the product. (9 marks)

Part of packaging	Material	Properties of material chosen
Container	Material 1	1 . . . .
	. . . .	2 . . . .
Cover/lid	Material 2	1 . . . .
	. . . .	2 . . . .
Box	Material 3	1 . . . .
	. . . .	2 . . . .

7 Give two environmental problems which result from the use of packaged food.

(2 marks)

225

DESIGN AND TECHNOLOGY: FOOD TECHNOLOGY TIER H (HIGHER)

SAMPLE STUDENT'S ANSWERS

The examiner's comments explain why some answers did not gain full marks and show what the student should have written.

1 A food manufacturer wants to develop a new range of sweet baked products.

Products already on the market.

During research the design team evaluate similar existing products already on the market. Give five questions the design team might ask about an existing product from looking at the packaging label. (5 marks)

1   Does it look appealing to the consumer?
2   Does it contain additives?
3   Does the product look like any picture shown?
4   What kind of sweet baked product is it?
5   How much does it cost?

3/5

EXAMINER'S COMMENTS

The student only scored three marks out of a possible five because some of the answers are vague e.g. 'Does the product look like any picture shown?'

The student has omitted very important points of information about the development of a new product. There is no mention about the type of ingredients which could be used, the nutritional profile which the product needs to meet, the cooking and storage methods which could be considered and any special dietary needs at which the product might be aimed, all of which could be gained from examining the existing products.

2 Nutritional profiles were gathered from products already on the market.

Table to show nutritional information.

Food products per 100 grams	KJ	Carbo-hydrate (g)	Starch (g)	Sugar (g)	Dietary fibre (g)	Protein (g)	Fat (g)	Saturated fat (g)	Sodium (g)
Chocolate biscuits	2,197	67.6	24.2	43.4	3.1	5.7	27.6	17.4	1.6
Sandwich biscuits	2,151	69.3	39.1	30.2	1.2	5.1	25.9	14.8	2.2
Shortbread	2,115	65.5	48.3	17.2	2.1	6.2	26.1	13.6	1.4
Fruit cake	1,490	57.9	14.8	43.1	2.8	5.1	12.9	6.1	2.5
Jam sponge	1,280	64.2	16.5	47.7	1.2	4.2	4.9	2.1	4.2
Jam tart	1,616	62.8	25.3	37.5	1.7	3.5	14.9	n/a	2.3
Nutri-Grain Bars	1,550	69.1	39.9	29.2	3.5	4.1	8.1	1.5	0.3

(a) Sweet baked products are not generally 'healthy options'.

With reference to the table explain this statement.

(8 marks)

The statement that they are not generally 'healthy options' is taken from the figures of certain amounts of things in the products. It would appear from this table that sweet baked products contain quite a lot of fat, maybe even high amounts — going up to 27.6 g of fat in a chocolate digestive, although also going down to 8.1 g in Nutri-Grain bars though this could really be considered high amounts just for a snack. They also have quite high amounts of sugar in them, the lowest being shortbread at 17.2 g to jam sponge 47.7 g. These, again, are high amounts for just a snack. Neither large amounts of sugar or fat are considered good for you — rotting teeth and excess body fat are known to result from overdoses of recommended daily amounts. So this is probably why the statement considers them not 'healthy options'. Also perhaps they do not really contain any other valuable mineral or anything not able to be gained from healthier foods. Also we should notice that the fat in the table shows large amounts of it being saturated which is known as not being good for us.

(b) How are manufacturers adapting their existing cake and biscuit products to meet consumer requirements for a 'healthy' option?

(5 marks)

Manufacturers tend to advertise products with less fat — 'virtually fat free', 'half the fat' and '95% fat free'. So this would suggest that they are cutting down on sugars used and perhaps using additives to gain some flavours these could give. They also add things people see as giving the product healthier components and more nutrition, such as nuts. They could be adding additives to do the job of things like fat and sugar. They are also experimenting to find how much they can take out of the recipe without compromising taste and texture.

EXAMINER'S COMMENTS

The student has lost marks because her knowledge about fat and sugar is inaccurate. Also no reference has been made to the specific ingredients which would make the product a healthy option. There needed to be some reference to reduced salt or increased starch and dietary fibre, protein or the overall energy value.

3 In the test kitchen when designing a new cake product components must be combined in the correct proportions if the finished product is to be successful.

(a) Complete the table below:

(i) fill in the correct quantities in grams of fat and sugar;
(ii) give **one** different example of a food product made by each method.

(12 marks)

Method	Ratio	Flour	Fat	Egg	Sugar	Example
Creaming/all in one	Equal	100 g	100 g	2	100 g	Victoria Sandwich
Rubbing in	8:4:2:3	200 g	100 g	2	90 g	Fruit cake
Whisking	1:2:1	50 g	0 g	2	50 g	Sponge cake/Swiss roll
Melting	8:6:2:8	200 g	150 g	2	200 g	Gingerbread

11/12

EXAMINER'S COMMENTS

(a) *The student has given the wrong answer for the weight of the sugar in the rubbed in mixture. The answer should have been 75 grams not 90 grams*

3 (b) The main ingredients in cakes are fat, sugar, eggs, flour, a raising agent and sometimes a liquid. Each ingredient performs an important function.

Explain the function of each of the ingredients listed.

(12 marks)

Name of ingredient	Use of ingredient in preparation and cooking
FAT	Gives the cake flavour and texture. Gives the cake soft tender crumb and richness. Is also a shortening agent. Gives colour — waterproof flour stops it becoming glutenous and stretchy like bread dough.
SUGAR	Gives volume as air particles stick to the sugar crystals. Gives taste and flavour as well as colour — due to Millard reaction.
EGGS	Stabilises the mixture both in the mixing process and in baking. Also acts as a coagulating agent helping to set the cake — correct use doesn't alter flavour.
RAISING AGENT	Gives the cake volume from a chemical reaction causing air in mixture, steam rising giving a nicely shaped cake — Correct use doesn't
FLOUR	Forms the foam structure of the cake. Gives a soft and tender crumb to the cake.
LIQUID	Gives the cake its moisture, as well as acting alongside the raising agent to give volume as it turns to steam and rises.

10/12

228

See examiner's comments on page 240.

4 A food manufacturer decides to develop a range of cake and biscuit products which will be sold from a **vending machine**.

(a) The design team works to a general **design** specification.

Complete the **five** point specification for a cake or biscuit product for a vending machine. Do not include packaging material.

(4 marks)

The **first** point has been done for you.

1 long shelf life.
2 Suitable for falling or being dropped without breaking.
3 Look good and appetising.
4 Taste good and not be too unhealthy.
5 Be cheap and fairly easy to make.

(4/4)

(b) A range of cakes and biscuits are needed for the vending machine.

With the aid of a labelled sketch give **two** different product ideas.

(6 marks)

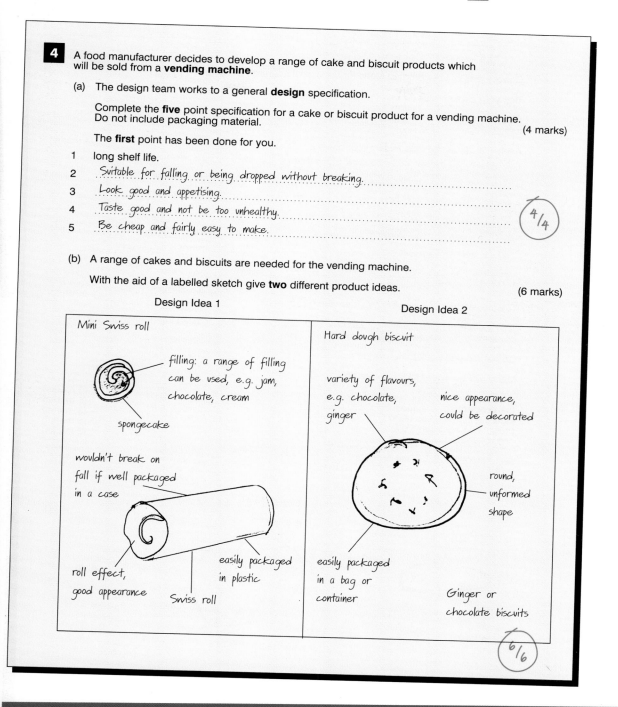

Design Idea 1

Mini Swiss roll

filling: a range of filling can be used, e.g. jam, chocolate, cream

spongecake

wouldn't break on fall if well packaged in a case

roll effect, good appearance

Swiss roll

easily packaged in plastic

Design Idea 2

Hard dough biscuit

variety of flavours, e.g. chocolate, ginger

nice appearance, could be decorated

round, unformed shape

easily packaged in a bag or container

Ginger or chocolate biscuits

(6/6)

EXAMINER'S COMMENTS

The student has scored high marks for this question for the following reasons:

- The question shows a general understanding of food product development.
- Good vocabulary used in the design specification.
- Detailed labelled sketches are provided Two completely different product ideas are used not a variation of the same.
- The annotated sketch of the final product is clear. A firm proposal with a clear and appropriate solution has been given. It considers all the necessary factors. The detail of the products can be easily seen.

- The product specification is very detailed and this is where the student shows real understanding.
- One mark was lost on the ingredient information as only the base mixture had been considered.
- A very good production schedule, clearly set out with control points, clear instructions and use of appropriate terminology, processes, timings and health and safety requirements. All these contributed to this very good answer.

(c) Choose **one** of your product ideas for the manufacturer to develop.

Tick your chosen idea

Idea 1
Idea 2 ✓

Explain in detail the reasons for your choice. (4 marks)

A variety of things could be done to a biscuit like this — such things as having chocolate toppings makes the appearance look good. Or interesting flavours such as ginger. Also they can be easily packaged to withstand a drop and not break. They are also of good size, shape and weight to be contained in a small space without jamming the vending machine. Lots of people like biscuits — they won't break and nothing will squish out of them if they fall. Biscuits are considered healthier as there is less fat in a hard biscuit design.

4/4

(d) The test kitchen will develop this idea into a prototype.

With the aid of notes, sketches and charts as appropriate, give detailed information for the development, manufacture and production of your idea.

Do **not** include packaging detail.

Marks will be awarded for details of:

an annotated sketch of your final product	(5 marks)
the **product** specification	(5 marks)
ingredients/materials used	(3 marks)
production schedules/plan	(5 marks)
control checks	(2 marks)

Annotated sketch of final product.

Side view

size to fit in
machine – bitesize

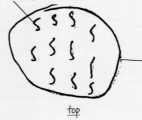

lines on biscuit cracked appearance of biscuit
looks good — from cooling of biscuit

round shape all to
be exact same
size plus shape

top

underneath

a dark even colour formed from
Millard reaction and caramelisation
and also ginger in the biscuits

5/5

Product specification

Each biscuit must:

Be 3 cm in diameter.

Be 0.5 cm in thickness.

Be of a golden brown colour — no darker or lighter.

Contain 10 g flour.

Contain 5 g fat.

Contain 2 g ginger powder.

Have no more than 4 cracks on surface — each no more than 2 mm wide.

Cost no more than 1p to produce.

Look good and appealing.

Be made of highest quality ingredients and manufacture.

Each product:

Will contain 15 biscuits

Cost between 30p and 50p in a vending machine.

5/5

Ingredients/materials used

Ingredients in the biscuit are: flour, small amounts of fat, ginger for flavour and appearance of biscuits, water, some sugar. Also some stabilisers to increase shelf life so the biscuit will not go off in the machine quickly. Some sugar for flavour but not too much to be considered unhealthy.

3/3

Average recipe — making 15 biscuits

100 g flour

50 g fat

40 g ginger powder

water — binds ingredients

40 g sugar

Scaled up for factory — makes approx. 4000

40 kg flour

20 kg fat

18 kg ginger powder

water

18 kg sugar

stabilisers

Would be made in factory on large scale — stabilisers needed when lots of ingredients are used in order to ensure mixture is stable, also to keep it stable.

Production schedules/plan/control checks

Made in factory — with a mixture of an assembly line, continuous flow, containing machines and humans. Undergoing computer checks as well as visual checks — checking for things such as bacteria, correct cooling temperatures and lengths, size and shape of biscuits.

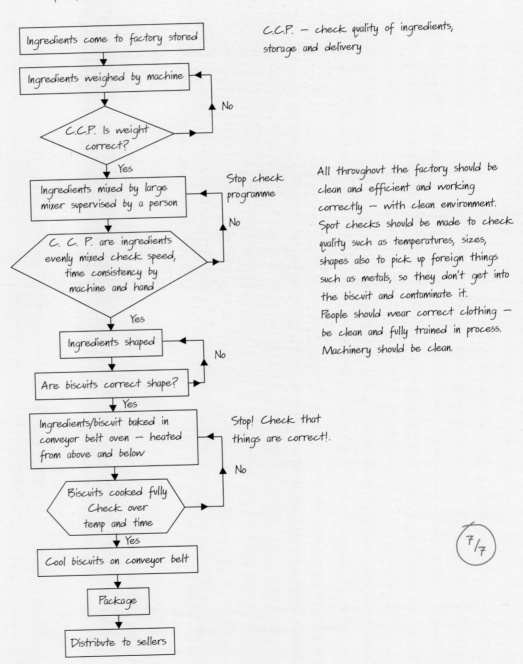

C.C.P. — check quality of ingredients, storage and delivery

All throughout the factory should be clean and efficient and working correctly — with clean environment. Spot checks should be made to check quality such as temperatures, sizes, shapes also to pick up foreign things such as metals, so they don't get into the biscuit and contaminate it. People should wear correct clothing — be clean and fully trained in process. Machinery should be clean.

232

5 In the test kitchen a prototype cake is made.

For mass production other ingredients may be added.

(a) Choose two of the following ingredients and explain their function. (4 marks)

Glycerine, Salt, Water, Preservatives, Emulsifiers.

Preservatives — these increase the shelf life of the product allowing it to be sold for longer and still of high quality with no effect on taste or appearance. Stops the product going off.

Emulsifiers — hold the mixture together and keep large quantities of ingredients, such as are used in mass production, stable so that the mixture is correct and the end result is still all right and correct even though on large scale.

2/4

(b) Manufacturers often use sugar substitutes. Give reasons why sugar substitutes are not always suitable for use in cake production. (3 marks)

Due to the fact the sugar gives the cake extra volume, as when mixing and baking the mixture, air sticks to the fine sugar granules, adding air and giving good volume. Without the sugar air would not be as present and the cake wouldn't have as much volume. Also the taste may be affected as no sugar leaves a strange taste, poor texture, and colour and the cake would be much denser.

3/3

EXAMINER'S COMMENTS

The student lost marks for the following reasons:

Preservative
There was repetition in the answer and the student omitted to say that a preservative slows down decay.

Emulsifier
The most important fact about an emulsifier is that it keeps fats and oils mixed in water. The student did not show that she understood this in the answer given and consequently lost marks. There was also some confusion over the difference between emulsifiers and stabilisers in the answer given.

6 (a) Explain why a cake manufacturer uses free standing electrical equipment for the production of large quantities of cake mixture. (6 marks)

Drawing of a free standing electric mixer.

Using things such as a mixer make making the cake a lot easier when large quantities are included. As the process becomes quicker and more efficient, it can evenly mix the ingredients in much less time then a person. Air can be added as needed and control from the different speed settings will get the mixing correct. Having it free standing means it can be controlled by people for as long as necessary and at the speed necessary. — also could be programmed.

2/4

(b) What health and safety precautions would need to be followed by people using this equipment?

Protective eye goggles to prevent things going in their eyes. They should be wearing rubber gloves, only to be worn once to prevent them contaminating ingredients. Also they shouldn't wear outside clothes or shoes that could bring in bacteria. They should be wearing some kind of clean white coat and also have hair tied back under a hat to prevent contamination — maybe wear a mask on their face to stop breathing on and contaminating food. They should be trained in safety rules when using the equipment and on how to use it so not to spoil food, injure themselves or others or to damage the machine. They would also need to ensure the machine is kept clean and bacteria free.

5/6

EXAMINER'S COMMENTS

(a) The student only gained two marks out of four for this question because of the very general nature of the answer. The student needed to comment on how a consistent product could be made with the use of electrical equipment, e.g. how the equipment can be used to ensure consistency of volume, aeration, mixing time, mixing speed etc.

(b) The student did not give specific details about the safety requirements of operating the equipment which was needed in order to obtain full marks. For example, some reference should have been made to the use of 'Stop' buttons, regular servicing, safety guards etc.

7 Most food products are packaged for sale.

(a) Explain the functions of food packaging.

(5 marks)

To protect food by covering it and preventing tampering or contamination of the product. To keep the food product safe from breaking. Stop foreign bodies getting in. Help to prolong shelf life by keeping oxygen out and prevent food from going stale. Labels can go on the packaging which inform the customer of what it is, the ingredients contained, and perhaps show pictures of the product. Packaging should draw the consumer's eye to the product so that they will buy it. – advertise the product and inform the customer.

5/5

(b) Name a suitable material for each part of the packaging of jam tarts.

Material for jam tart container ... Foil tin .... (1 mark) 1/1

Reason for choice Easily shaped to required shape, will hold the jam tart (2 marks) 1/2
easily in place and shape and it is clean and won't pass on bacteria.

Material for inner packaging ... Plastic .... (1 mark) 1/1

Reason for choice Cheap and easily shaped to desired shape – hygienic (2 marks) 2/2
and will help prevent contamination. Stop the tarts from moving and breaking.

Material for box ... Cardboard .... (1 mark) 1/1

Reason for choice Cheap and easily shaped – can be printed on so that (2 marks) 2/2
information such as name and label and picture can be on it.

EXAMINER'S COMMENTS

(b) Although this was a good answer, in order to have gained full marks the student needed to give additional information when giving the reasons for choosing various materials for packaging the tarts.

Materials for Tart Container
The statement 'won't pass on bacteria is vague'. A more definite reason is needed, e.g. Foil is light, Tarts can be baked or re-heated in this type of case.

Material for Box
The student should have qualified the term cardboard by stating that it needed to be paperboard or thin card. An additional reason, e.g. can be coated, folded or cheap would have gained full marks.

235

The student mixed up the answers on 7c and 7d.
Nutritional information and bar-code are consumer advice.
Cooking instructions and special claims are required by law.
Additional legal requirements which the student could have given are:

- Special Claims
- Weight or volume.

The examples of Consumer Advice could have included:

- Nutritional Information
- Serving suggestions/portion size
- Guarantees
- Environmental considerations
- Bar-code if related to 'self scan'.

- CAD – computer aided design
- CAM – computer aided manufacture

(c) Strict legal regulations apply to food labelling.

List the information that must be on the label by law. (7 marks)

1 The product's name and explanation
2 Ingredients list
3 Manufacturer's name and address
4 Nutritional information
5 Storage instructions/cooking instructions
6 Best before/sell by date
7 Barcode

6/7

(d) Give **three** items of consumer advice that may also be on the packaging. (3 marks)

1 If a product may contain nuts warnings may be printed clearly for people with allergies.
2 If needed, how the product should be cooked, with time and temperatures.
3 The recommended price — any special offers that are on and what the customer should do if they win, or how to win.

1/3

8 (a) (i) What do the initials CAD stand for? (1 mark)
Computer analysed data

0/1

(ii) What do the initials CAM stand for? (1 mark)
Computer analysed mechanism

0/1

(b) With examples describe ways in which computer technology can help in development and production of a food product. (5 marks)

Computers can help in the development and production of a food product at stages such as quality control. By keeping records and recording information such as temperatures and sizes – like in a biscuit factory – the computer could then give warnings if the oven was becoming too warm or too cold. The computer could also keep track of the quality of the biscuit thickness, size, weight and density to make sure the whole process is correct. It can store these records in little space compared with hand written data and do so for a while. The computer could keep track of a design team's progress – what they've tried – and give print outs of graphs of people's opinions. – what things they've done, like how much ingredients used. The computer could also keep track of orders of ingredients and the delivery and quality of them by on arrival. Also of stock in the warehouse and its rotation. And also perhaps of sales of the product.

5/5

9 Sensory testing takes place during the development of a product.

(a) Explain **four** reasons why sensory testing takes place.

(8 marks)

1 To ensure that people actually like the product and think it tastes good and to find out how it could be changed and improved.

2 To check which product people like the most and for what reasons and to see if this is the majority opinion. Paired comparison of two products tested.

3 To check that an assembly line, batch production is producing identical and uniformed products with no variation in taste or appearance that the consumer can see.

4 Check if improvements can be noticed and see if these are liked and to check a product against its specification. If you've added extra nuts can the consumer tell or not, so does it matter and do they still like it?

8/8

(b) Product profiling was carried out on a final product by trained testers.

The specification stated that the biscuit should be crisp, sweet, nutty, with a soft, toffee filling and a smooth outer coating.

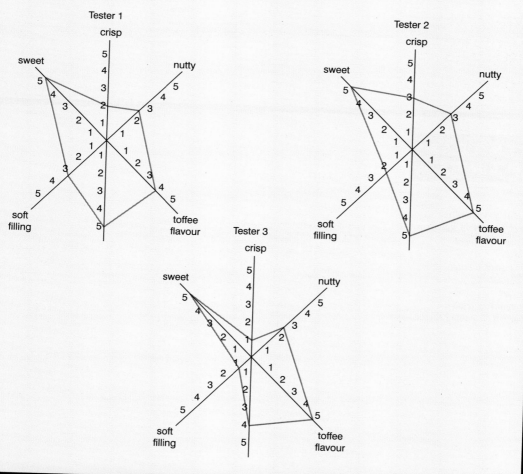

Using the information given on the taster profiles complete the table below.

(i)   Identify three characteristics which require improvement.   (3 marks)

(ii) Give **two** improvements for each.   (6 marks)

Characteristic requiring improvement	Improvements
Crisp	1 Removing some fat makes the dough harder, biscuit crisper 2 Bake for longer to make harder and crisper — more dry
Nutty	1 Add more nuts to the ingredients ensure evenly mixed in 2 Add different varieties of nuts to give more nuttier flavours
Soft filling	1 Add more toffee to make a softer filling 2 Try a new filling as well to improve softness

3/3   3/6

EXAMINER'S COMMENTS

Improvements
Biscuit   Bake at higher temperature
          Cool completely before storing
          Add a 'crisp' ingredient
          Add a glaze
          Make the biscuit thinner
Filling   Change ingredients
          Add more fat
          Weigh more accurately
          Increase or reduce boiling time

10 Labelling must inform the consumer of any additive. Food manufacturers are allowed to add safe substances to foods if they are needed.

(a) List **five** reasons for using additives.

(5 marks)

1 To preserve food for longer
2 Add extra colours
3 Add extra flavours
4 To stabilise the ingredients – hold it all together
5 Emulsifying agent to the ingredients

5/5

(b) What does the 'E' in front of a number mean?

(2 marks)

That it is an additive, an emulsifying agent – or an extra ingredient – the number is the designated one given to that product

0/2

(c) Discuss why there are an increasing number of food manufacturers and retailers selling foods with fewer or no additives in them and the consequences of this action.

(10 marks)

Manufacturers and retailers are adding less additives to foods probably due to consumer demand. Some children are allergic to some additives which make them hyperactive so children can't eat them but parents want the children to be able to have these foods — a consequence of this could mean more of the products are sold as they can now be bought by more people.

Also consumers demand foods without additives in them as they want to know exactly what they are eating and people often feel that additives contain products that are unsafe even though the government has approved them. They don't want to be eating weird things — so they won't buy things if they feel eating them is unsafe. The manufacturer taking them out means the consumers will buy more of the product again and people will trust them again. But it could also result in a distrust of people in the food industry as it is like admitting the additives were harmful in the first place.

Additives may also be taken out due to government policies finding them unnecessary in the food product or even dangerous. Again this could lead to distrust of food manufacturers making unsafe food or adding unneeded things. However removing unneeded things could result in changes in colour or flavour, which may result in a drop of sales. It's like the situation of the European Union wanting us to take green colouring out of peas — it is needed but people could be allergic to it as well. But lack of colour could make the peas less appealing to look at and sales may drop — the same is relevant with all foods.

Taking additives out could result in change in sales for the good or maybe for the worse if under bad circumstances. But it could also shorten the life of some of the food so we would have to eat things quicker but people don't mind if the food doesn't contain things they don't know they're eating. — and it could also change appearance and colour.

10/10

E X A M I N E R ' S   C O M M E N T S

Recognised by the European Union on the permitted 'safe' list.

EXAMINER'S COMMENTS

The student has scored highly on this paper.

STRENGTHS

Good revision carried out.

Good application of knowledge and understanding when given a situation or problem.

Questions read carefully.

Mark allocation was used to generate specific numbers of points for answers.

In the design question (number 4) the student has ensured that all the areas are covered as detailed in the mark allocation.

Good annotation of drawings and sketches showing thoughts and ideas.

WEAKNESSES

Where questions ask for explanation, discussion, description or where there is a need for extended writing, i.e. more than one or two sentences, the student is repetitive and the answers 'ramble on'. The student could have gained just as many marks by writing much less. Some planning of the answer before beginning to write would have helped.

AREAS FOR IMPROVEMENT

Question 3 (b)

The student has lost marks for the following reasons:
- A raising agent produces carbon dioxide not air.
- The carbon dioxide expands on heating making the mixture rise.
- Flour forms the structure of the cake not the foam structure

Any of the following functions of ingredients could have been accepted.

FAT
- Holds tiny air bubbles which create texture and volume
- Adds colour and flavour, particularly butter and margarine
- Helps increase shelf life
- Produces a cake with a short crumb or rich texture

SUGAR
- With fat helps to hold air in the mixture
- Increases the volume of the cake
- Sweetens the mixture and adds flavour
- Holds the fat in emulsion

EGGS
- Contain the protein albumin which, when beaten, traps air to form a foam adding air to the mixture
- Hold the fat in emulsion once the mixture has been beaten
- Contain lecithin in the egg yolk which helps keep the emulsion stable
- Increase the volume and help to hold air in the mixture
- Add colour and flavour
- Can be a glaze to add shine and colour to the top of the cake
- Help to set the cake due to the coagulation of the protein

RAISING AGENT
- Alters texture
- Produces gas which expands on heating
- Makes cake light and airy
- Makes cake rise
- Might alter taste and colour, e.g. bicarbonate of soda in gingerbread

FLOUR
- Forms the main structure of most cakes
- Soft flour has low gluten content and gives a soft crumb
- Some flours improve texture and colour, e.g. wholemeal
- Is usually the main ingredient and gives the bulk to the cake
- Absorbs fat and liquid during gelatinisation

LIQUID
- Produces steam to help the mixture rise during baking
- Combines with the protein in the flour to develop gluten
- Necessary for gelatinisation of starch to prevent cake having raw taste

EXAM PRACTICE 1

4 a)   i) Margarine, lard, solid white vegetable fat, e.g. white fat or compound fat, e.g. Trex or a mixture.   1/1

ii) Reason — firm, hard fat to rub into the flour to coat the flour. Margarine adds colour.   2/2

iii) Fat coats the flour grains with fat to stop gluten forming when water is added. This makes sure the pastry has a short crumbly texture.   3/3

iv) Eggs are a protein food. They set when heated. Eggs can set a liquid. The two eggs in the recipe will set the milk.   3/3

Examiner's Comments

All the answers are factually correct. The student has a good understanding of the function of ingredients and what happens when they are combined with other ingredients. In question 4 (a) (iv) the term 'coagulate' would help to explain the reason required. Try to use the correct terminology in your answers. It shows depth of understanding and it helps you to be concise with your answers.

4 b)   Vegetarian Option

Broccoli and Blue Cheese Flan

150 g broccoli

2 eggs

250 ml milk

100 g blue cheese, e.g. stilton

25 g parmesan cheese

salt and pepper

Value for Money Option

Bacon, Cheese and Vegetable Flan

250 ml milk

2 eggs

50 g cheddar cheese

4 rashers streaky bacon

1 small onion

1 small leek

25 g margarine

salt and pepper

Reasons for Choice

No meat included. Strong flavours from the vegetable and the blue cheese. Good contrast of colour. Unusual combination

Reasons for Choice

Economy priced ingredients often sold with cheaper alternatives, i.e. own brand. Vegetables strong flavours, can be boiled or fried before adding. Bacon adds colour and crisp texture.   12/12

Examiner's Comments

In this type of question you can apply knowledge gained through practical sessions. This student has given correct answers. The basic recipe has been modified in two different ways. For the vegetarian option a meat alternative such as tofu could have been included. The examiner will be looking for a mixture of interesting colours, flavours and textures, combined in a palatable and appetising way.

4 c) i) Carrot (grated)

Carrot has a firm, crunchy texture and it gives colour to the coleslaw.

ii) Courgette

It can be sliced or cut in strips. The skin can be left on to give colour.

iii) Sun dried tomatoes

These are strong flavoured and dark coloured. They are a bit unusual and would be crunchy in the bread.

Examiner's Comments

The student has chosen appropriate vegetables and given good reasons to justify their choice. This type of question gives plenty of scope for the student to select from the wide range of vegetables available. The reason must reflect the characteristics of the vegetable chosen. Marks will be lost if the two do not link together. Again try to explain your answer in sentence form.

EXAM PRACTICE 2

4 a) i) Melting method

ii) There is a high proportion of sugar, sticky syrup and fat in this recipe. These ingredients are melted in a pan so that they can be easily mixed with the flour and spices.

Examiner's Comments

This is a basic cake method used in recipes with a high proportion of sugar and fat. You will need to know the four basic methods for making cakes, i.e. creamed, rubbed-in, melted, whisked.

4 b) The bicarbonate of soda is a chemical raising agent. When heated in the cake mixture it produces steam and carbon dioxide which makes the mixture rise.

Examiner's Comments

Bicarbonate of soda is the simplest type of raising agent. It does, however, produce sodium carbonate as well as the steam and carbon dioxide. This leaves a dark yellow colour and a sharp taste. Bicarbonate of soda is used mainly in recipes that have strong-flavoured ingredients to disguise it, e.g. ground ginger and golden syrup in this recipe.

4 c) The manufacture should use a cutter, which is shaped so that it will fit closely to each biscuit. Turning the cutter so that it dovetails together will avoid waste. Planning the cutting pattern will also help. Avoid using irregular shapes that create a lot of wasted space on the rolled out biscuit mixture.

Examiner's Comments

There are some good points made in this answer. A manufacturer must avoid wastage. It would also cost time and effort to roll out the biscuit mixture a second time. Very often the mixture becomes firmer or drier when it is rolled again so the aim is to cut out as many biscuits as possible first time. Sketches might have helped the student communicate their ideas about the layout of the cutter on the biscuit mixture.

4 d i) (This answer would contain diagrams of biscuit shapes to reflect the Olympic games.)

ii) ● Ready made icing in tube ready to pipe. This comes in different colours and is very useful for drawing thin lines or for filling in blocks of colours.
● Coloured sweets — can be bought in the quantity required in the correct size and colour.
● Ready made marzipan — guaranteed consistency of marzipan mixture used to make individual shaped pieces. It can also be coloured.

Examiner's Comments

The content of the answer offers good reasons for the selection of standard components. The student has written in note form and should really have given a well reasoned answer in sentence form.

EXAM PRACTICE 3

3 a) i) Hazard Analysis Critical Control Points   2/2

ii) It is used for planning how to identify where possible problems would occur in the production of a food product and how these could be prevented. The problems are identified as possible hazards, the effects of the hazards are known as risks and the ways they are stopped are controls.

Examiner's Comments

i) The student gained full marks for the meaning of HACCP. If part of it had been wrong the student could still have gained one mark.
ii) Despite giving a lot of points the student cannot gain more than the maximum mark of 2.

4

Stages in the production of a frozen chicken pie	Possible Hazards	Controls Used	Quality Control Checks
Collect raw ingredients	Cross contamination Temperature control	Separate storage areas for dry and perishable goods	Reputed supplier, visits to supplier, quality standards
Weigh ingredients	Cross contamination	Separate scales	Different storage and preparation areas
Mix ingredients for pastry	Bacteria present	Correct storage	Stock rotation
Cook chicken	Food poisoning	Cook to 72°C	Food probe
Make white sauce for chicken filling	Raw flavour	Cook to 100°C	Temperature
Combine sauce with chicken and cool	Cross contamination	Cool and store rapidly	Temperature and time
Roll out pastry		Accurate measurement	Computer controlled rollers
Add filling		Portion control	Accurate measurement
Bake	Food Poisoning	Temperature	Food probe
Freeze	Bacterial growth	Time and temperature	Cooling tunnel, quick freezing
Store	Cross contamination Metal detection	Temperature	Thermometers/computer control

8/10

Examiner's Comments

Although there are gaps in this answer the student has shown understanding of the question and has attempted to give possible hazards and controls for most of the process. The mark allocation for this would have been 8 marks out of 10 for giving a nearly complete answer with some detail.

EXAM PRACTICE 4

3 a) Chilling is a short-term preservation method which prolongs the storage life of a food product and slows down bacterial growth. $^2/_2$

b) It is very popular because it does not change the look, appearance or taste of food which other methods of preservation do. $^2/_2$

4 a) Food should be chilled within 30 minutes of it being made. The food must reach its cold temperature within 90 minutes of it being chilled. The critical temperature is between 1 and 3 degrees C.

b) It is very important that the temperature of a chill cabinet is kept correct. This can be done by using a thermometer in the chill cabinet which can be checked at regular intervals. Also a food probe could be used to check certain products at certain times. If a food probe is used on one of the products the product would then have to be thrown away. Some chill cabinets are fitted with alarms which will sound if the temperature becomes too low or too high. $^3/_3$

Staff are used to check temperatures of chill cabinets and to record these over the day. Sometimes there are small computer-controlled devices in a chill cabinet which record and print the temperature each hour. This means that a careful check can be kept on variations and patterns. $^5/_5$

Examiner's Comments

The answers to all parts of the question are clear and concise. The answer to question 4 (b) on checking the temperature of the chill cabinet has been done particularly well. Overall the student would have scored full marks for all parts of the question.

EXAM PRACTICE 5

3 By law all of the additives must be listed to ensure that the consumer knows exactly what the product contains. The additives are often hidden factors that cannot initially be seen in the product but some people may be allergic to them and if they are not stated then if the consumer was allergic to them they would be liable to sue the company.

$^2/_2$

Examiner's Comments

The student gets full marks for this answer as he has mentioned that by law the additives must be named and the reasons for this from a consumer's point of view. Nothing has been omitted.

4 The product packaging must be bright and colourful and attract the consumer because the packaging will basically act as the salesperson. The labelling must have a title and sub heading to tell the customer immediately what the product is. The label must display any special flashes, i.e. fat free, to show the consumer what the product is. If special flashes are present then there must be proof on the label that the special claims are true. This enables the consumer to believe them. The address of the manufacturer must be on the labelling so that if the consumer would like to make any comments or complaints then they can do so.

A bar code is normally present, however that is for the convenience of the shopkeeper for stock keeping and pricing goods. The volume or weight of the food must be given to show the consumer how much they can expect in the product. A nutritional table is also required which is essential for the consumer especially if they are on a diet or have special dietary requirements. The cost is often given. Storage instructions are essential on labelling to ensure no bacteria contaminate the food. Also if the product needs to be cooked or prepared these instructions must be stated to ensure the food is cooked properly by the consumer to prevent food poisoning.

Examiner's Comments

The student gains 7 marks out of 8 for this answer. Many different points of information given on a label are discussed, however the student fails to identify specifically what are legal requirements and what are there for consumer advice, despite referring to these and giving reasons for each piece of information.

5 Packaging is used to protect the cheesecake from being squashed, to prevent people from tampering with it and to protect it from exposure to the air and bacteria. The packaging is also able to give information which is useful to the consumer. It also enables the cheesecake to be stored and stacked in the chill cabinet without being crushed.

Examiner's Comments

This is a good answer and covers the main functions of packaging. The student would have gained full marks for this answer. Other points which could have been added or used instead would have been:
- preserves/reduces food spoilage
- helps people to choose
- guarantees safety and hygiene
- promotes and advertises the product.

6 (a and b)

Part of Packaging	Material	Properties of material chosen
Container	Material 1 Rigid foil	1 Non Crushable 2 Moisture proof
Cover/lid	Material 2 Transparent plastic film	1 Dust proof 2 Stops liquids leaking out
Box	Material 3 Thin cardboard	1 Protects the cheesecake from being crushed 2 Information can be printed on it

9/9

Examiner's Comments

This answer would have gained full marks. The student has used the mark allocation in the margin and ensured that sufficient points have been made to gain the marks needed.

7 i) The packaging needs to be recyclable to conserve the natural resources of the world.

ii) It can be expensive if it is not able to be recycled.

Examiner's Comments

Both these points are relevant and would gain a mark each.

ACKNOWLEDGEMENTS

Published by Collins Educational
An *imprint of* HarperCollins*Publishers* Ltd
77–85 Fulham Palace Road
London W6 8JB

The HarperCollins website address is: www.**fire**and**water**.com

© HarperCollins*Publishers* Ltd 2000

First published 2000

ISBN 0 00 323539 4

Jenny Hotson and Jill Robinson assert the moral right to be identified as the authors of this book.

British Library Cataloguing in Publication Data
A catalogue record for this publication is available from the British Library

Edited by Lesley Young
Production by Kathryn Botterill
Picture research by Tamsin Miller
Cover design by BCG Communications
Book design by Rupert Purcell and produced by Gecko Limited
Index compiled by Marie Lorimer
Printed and bound by Scotprint

Acknowledgements
The Authors and Publishers are grateful to the following for permission to reproduce copyright material:

HMSO Figures 24.8 and 24.9; Northern Examinations and Assessment Board: p.163, qu.1 (full course, foundation, 1998 qu.7); p.163 qu.2 (short course, higher, 1997 qu.6a-b); p.164 qu.3 (short course, foundation, 1997 qu.7a-b); p.189 qu.1 and qu.2 (short course, higher, 1997 qu.11a-c); p.189 qu.3 and qu.4 (short course, higher, 1997 qu.11c-d); p.225 qu.5 and qu.6 (short course, higher, 1997 qu.9a-c); pp.226-239 (full course, higher, 1999).

Photographs
The Publishers wish to thank the following for permission to reproduce photographs:
Anthony Blake Photographic Library 8.3 top and bottom, 11.6 (Milk Marque), 11.7 (Andy Knight), 11.8, 13.5, 13.7, 13.9, 13.10 (Heather Brown), 13.11 (Heather Brown), 13.13, 13.14 (Heather Brown), 13.20 (Charlie Stebbings), 15.1 (Timothy Ball), 15.2 (Maximilian Stock), 15.4 (top Gerrit Buntrock, bottom Paola Zucchi), 15.5 (Scott Morrison), 15.6 (top Robert Lawson, bottom Philip Wilkins), 15.7 (Graham Kirk), 17.1 (top Maximilian Stock, bottom Anthony Blake), 17.2 (Milk Marque), 17.7, 17.8 (Milk Marque), 17.9, 17.10 (Milk Marque), 17.11 (Timm Hill), 17.12 (Gerrit Buntrock), 17.13 (Milk Marque), 17.14 (Joff Lee), 17.15 (Milk Marque), 17.16 (Maximilian Stock), 17.17 (Maximilian Stock); Beamish Museum 24.5; (Sue Atkinson) 29.1; British Sugar 11.4, 11.5; Food Future 12.10; Jane Asher 16.2; Marks & Spencer 20.1; Meat & Livestock Commission 8.2, 30.1, 30.2; Science Photo Library 11.3, 17.3, 17.4, 19.1, 24.1, 24.2, 24.3, 24.10, 24.11, 29.8; Strathaird Ltd 25.10; Tesco 22.1, 24.12

Extra photographs were taken on behalf of Collins Educational by Martin Sookias and Trevor Clifford.

Illustrations
Gecko Ltd, Dave Mostyn, Geoff Ward.

The Authors and Publishers wish to thank all NEAB Food Technology Centres who have supplied examples of work for this book, including The Broxbourne School, Easingwold School, Northallerton College, Richmond School and Biddick School.

Every effort has been made to contact the holders of copyright material, but if any have been inadvertently overlooked, the Publishers will be pleased to make the necessary arrangements at the first opportunity.